MINNESOTA
PEDAGOGY: ELEMENTARY (K-6)

By: Sharon Wynne, M.S.

XAMonline, INC.
Boston

To obtain permission(s) to use the material from this work for any purpose including workshops or seminars, please submit a written request to:

XAMonline, Inc.
25 First Street, Suite 106
Cambridge, MA 02141
Toll Free 1-800-509-4128
Email: info@xamonline.com
Web: www.xamonline.com
Fax: 1-617-583-5552

Library of Congress Cataloging-in-Publication Data

Wynne, Sharon A.
    Minnesota Pedagogy: Elementary (K-6) / Sharon A. Wynne. 1st ed
    ISBN 978-1-60787-074-6
    1. Pedagogy: Elementary (K-6)
    2. Study Guides
    3. Minnesota
    4. Teachers' Certification & Licensure
    5. Careers

Disclaimer:
The opinions expressed in this publication are the sole works of XAMonline and were created independently from the National Education Association, Educational Testing Service, or any State Department of Education, National Evaluation Systems or other testing affiliates.

Between the time of publication and printing, state specific standards as well as testing formats and Web site information may change and therefore would not be included in part or in whole within this product. Sample test questions are developed by XAMonline and reflect content similar to that on real tests; however, they are not former test questions. XAMonline assembles content that aligns with state standards but makes no claims nor guarantees teacher candidates a passing score. Numerical scores are determined by testing companies such as NES or ETS and then are compared with individual state standards. A passing score varies from state to state.

Printed in the United States of America   œ-1

Minnesota Pedagogy: Elementary (K-6)
ISBN: 978-1-60787-074-6

Table of Contents

DOMAIN I
STUDENT DEVELOPMENT AND LEARNING 1

COMPETENCY 1
UNDERSTAND DEVELOPMENT DURING THE ELEMENTARY YEARS AND HOW TO PROVIDE LEARNING OPPORTUNITIES THAT SUPPORT STUDENTS' PHYSICAL, SOCIAL, EMOTIONAL, MORAL, AND COGNITIVE DEVELOPMENT 5

Skill 1.1: Demonstrating knowledge of developmental characteristics, processes, and progressions in the physical, social, emotional, moral, and cognitive domains 5

Skill 1.2: Demonstrating knowledge of developmental variation among elementary students in the physical, social, emotional, moral, and cognitive domains and instructional practices that are responsive to this variation 8

Skill 1.3: Applying knowledge of how a student's development in any one domain may affect development and performance in other domains 11

Skill 1.4: Applying knowledge of how students' physical, social, emotional, moral, and cognitive development influences learning and how to address these factors when making instructional decisions 11

Skill 1.5: Identifying developmentally appropriate instruction that meets student needs and supports student growth in the cognitive, social, emotional, moral, and physical domains 11

Skill 1.6: Recognizing how individual factors *(e.g., prior learning, talents, language and cultural background)* **and factors in the home, school, and community** *(e.g., peer interactions; use of tobacco, alcohol, and drugs)* **may affect elementary students' development and readiness to learn** 13

COMPETENCY 2
UNDERSTAND LEARNING PROCESSES AND HOW TO PROVIDE INSTRUCTIONAL OPPORTUNITIES THAT PROMOTE STUDENT LEARNING AND ACHIEVEMENT 14

Skill 2.1: Demonstrating knowledge of how students learn, internalize knowledge, and develop performance and thinking skills and how to use various instructional strategies to promote achievement of these goals 14

Skill 2.2: Applying knowledge of the concept of readiness in various learning contexts and strategies for using student strengths as a basis for promoting learning and student errors as opportunities for learning 19

Skill 2.3: Demonstrating knowledge of strategies for helping students build meaning *(e.g., linking new ideas to familiar ideas; making connections to student experiences; providing opportunities for active engagement, manipulation, and testing of ideas and materials)* 20

Skill 2.4: Demonstrating knowledge of factors that influence student learning *(e.g., prior knowledge and experience, developmental readiness, health, economic conditions, teachers' classroom practices, family circumstances, community environment)* **and how to provide learning experiences that are responsive to students' varied experiences, characteristics, and needs** 24

Skill 2.5: Identifying strategies for encouraging students to assume responsibility for shaping their learning tasks and outcomes 31

Skill 2.6: Demonstrating knowledge of how particular instructional methods and procedures, including the use of technology, can be expected to influence learning processes and outcomes 32

COMPETENCY 3

UNDERSTAND STUDENT DIVERSITY AND HOW TO PROVIDE INSTRUCTIONAL
OPPORTUNITIES THAT MEET THE NEEDS OF STUDENTS WITH DIVERSE BACKGROUNDS
AND EXCEPTIONALITIES AND PROMOTE ALL STUDENTS' LEARNING AND ACHIEVEMENT 33

Skill 3.1: Demonstrating knowledge of differences in approaches to learning and performance *(e.g., variation in learning styles and preferred performance modes, multiple intelligences)* and how to design instruction that is responsive to student needs and that uses student strengths to promote learning 33

Skill 3.2: Applying knowledge of areas of exceptionality *(e.g., learning disabilities, perceptual difficulties, special physical or mental challenges, gifts, talents)* and strategies for promoting learning for students with exceptionalities, including knowing when and how to access appropriate services and resources to meet student needs 33

Skill 3.3: Demonstrating knowledge of the process of second-language acquisition and strategies for supporting learning for students whose first language is not English, including knowing when and how to access appropriate services and resources to meet student needs 42

Skill 3.4: Demonstrating knowledge of how to use technological resources to facilitate learning for students with diverse backgrounds, characteristics, needs, and abilities 45

Skill 3.5: Demonstrating knowledge of the contributions, characteristics, and lifestyles of various groups in U.S. society; the government, history, language, and culture of Minnesota-based American Indian groups; and ways to provide learning experiences that reflect and are responsive to students' diverse social, cultural, and family backgrounds 45

Skill 3.6: Demonstrating knowledge of cultural and community diversity and norms; how to learn about and incorporate students' experiences, cultures, and community resources into instruction; and how to bring multiple perspectives to content-area instruction 46

Skill 3.7: Demonstrating knowledge of how to recognize and respond to negative attitudes regarding diversity, including but not limited to bias, discrimination, prejudice, and institutional or personal racism and sexism, and how to create a learning community in which differences among groups and individuals are valued and respected 47

Skill 3.8: Recognizing the importance for teachers of a belief in all students' ability to learn at the highest levels and a commitment to persist in helping all students achieve success as learners 48

DOMAIN II
LEARNING ENVIRONMENT 51

COMPETENCY 4

UNDERSTAND HOW TO ESTABLISH A SAFE, INCLUSIVE, AND POSITIVE LEARNING
ENVIRONMENT THAT ENCOURAGES POSITIVE SOCIAL INTERACTION, ACTIVE
ENGAGEMENT IN LEARNING, AND SELF-MOTIVATION 55

Skill 4.1: Demonstrating knowledge of how to establish a positive classroom climate and create a learning environment that promotes self-esteem, active engagement, and positive interpersonal relationships for all students 55

Skill 4.2: Demonstrating knowledge of how to help students work productively and cooperatively with each other in various contexts and how to establish peer relationships that promote learning 56

Skill 4.3: Demonstrating knowledge of expectations for student interactions, academic discussions, and individual and group responsibility that create a positive classroom climate of openness, mutual respect, support, inquiry, and learning 57

Skill 4.4: Applying knowledge of human motivation, behavior, and social groups, including principles of psychology, anthropology, and sociology, to identify effective strategies for promoting student learning and for organizing and supporting individual and group work 57

Skill 4.5: Demonstrating knowledge of factors and situations that are likely to promote or diminish intrinsic motivation and strategies for helping students become self-motivated *(e.g., relating lessons to students' personal interests, allowing students to have choices in their learning, leading students to ask questions and pursue problems that are meaningful to them)* 57

Skill 4.6: Recognizing how intrinsic motivation promotes students' lifelong learning and how the use of various motivational strategies can encourage continuous student development of skills and abilities 59

Skill 4.7: Demonstrating knowledge of how to analyze the classroom environment and make decisions and adjustments to enhance social relationships and increase student motivation and engagement 61

COMPETENCY 5
UNDERSTAND HOW TO CREATE AN ORGANIZED AND PRODUCTIVE LEARNING ENVIRONMENT THAT PROMOTES ALL STUDENTS' PARTICIPATION AND LEARNING 61

Skill 5.1: Demonstrating knowledge of effective, developmentally appropriate classroom routines and procedures that promote an organized and productive learning environment and encourage purposeful learning and the full participation of all students in independent and group work 61

Skill 5.2: Applying knowledge of strategies for managing the instructional environment to maximize class time spent in learning *(e.g., creating expectations for communication and behavior, managing transitions, managing materials, implementing appropriate schedules)* 62

Skill 5.3: Demonstrating knowledge of strategies for organizing the physical environment of the classroom to facilitate student learning and achieve defined goals 64

Skill 5.4: Demonstrating knowledge of how to organize, allocate, and manage resources *(e.g., time, space, attention)* to promote students' learning and active engagement in productive tasks 67

Skill 5.5: Applying knowledge of how to design and manage learning communities in which students assume responsibility for themselves and one another, exhibit commitment, participate in decision making, work both collaboratively and independently, and engage in purposeful learning activities 67

Skill 5.6: Applying knowledge of effective classroom management, including methods for encouraging students to monitor their own behavior and for promoting students' cooperation and sense of responsibility and accountability in the classroom 69

Skill 5.7: Demonstrating knowledge of how to analyze the classroom environment and make decisions and adjustments to enhance productivity and participation 74

COMPETENCY 6
UNDERSTAND HOW TO USE EFFECTIVE VERBAL, NONVERBAL, AND MEDIA COMMUNICATION TECHNIQUES TO PROMOTE ACTIVE INQUIRY, LEARNING, COLLABORATION, AND SUPPORTIVE INTERACTION IN THE CLASSROOM 75

Skill 6.1: Applying knowledge of communication theory, language development, the role of language in learning, and the use of language for various purposes *(e.g., to promote self-expression, identity development, learning)* 75

Skill 6.2: Demonstrating knowledge of how various student characteristics *(e.g., age, gender, cultural background, linguistic background, exceptionality)* may affect communication in the classroom and how to communicate effectively with all students *(e.g., using active listening skills, appropriate vocabulary, nonverbal indicators)* 76

Skill 6.3: Demonstrating knowledge of effective verbal, nonverbal, and media communication techniques for conveying ideas and information and for achieving specified goals *(e.g., providing feedback, building student self-esteem)* 78

Skill 6.4: Identifying strategies for supporting and expanding elementary students' expression in speaking, writing, and other media and for fostering sensitive communication by and among all students 79

Skill 6.5: Demonstrating knowledge of how to use a variety of media and educational technologies to enrich learning opportunities 79

Skill 6.6: Applying knowledge of strategies for adjusting communication to enhance student understanding and engagement 82

Skill 6.7: Demonstrating knowledge of different purposes for questioning *(e.g., stimulating discussion, probing for student understanding, helping students articulate their ideas and thinking processes, promoting productive risk taking and problem solving, facilitating recall, encouraging convergent and divergent thinking, stimulating curiosity)* and techniques for effective questioning in various learning contexts 83

DOMAIN III
INSTRUCTION AND ASSESSMENT 85

COMPETENCY 7
UNDERSTAND VARIOUS TYPES OF ASSESSMENT; RELATIONSHIPS AMONG ASSESSMENT, INSTRUCTION, AND LEARNING; AND THE USE OF ASSESSMENT TO ENSURE STUDENTS' CONTINUOUS DEVELOPMENT AND ACHIEVEMENT OF DEFINED STANDARDS AND GOALS 89

Skill 7.1: Demonstrating knowledge of the characteristics, uses, advantages, and limitations of different types of formal and informal assessment *(e.g., criterion-referenced test, norm-referenced test, teacher-made test, performance-based assessment, portfolio, teacher observation, peer assessment, student self-assessment)* 89

Skill 7.2: Demonstrating knowledge of measurement theory, central concepts in assessment *(e.g., validity, reliability, bias)*, differences between assessment and evaluation, and the role of assessment in teaching and learning 94

Skill 7.3: Demonstrating knowledge of the purposes of assessment *(e.g., monitoring, comparing, screening, diagnosing)* and how to select, construct, and use assessment strategies, instruments, and technologies for different purposes and needs, including assessing student progress in achieving state standards 96

Skill 7.4: Applying knowledge of strategies for integrating assessment and instruction and for using assessment to identify student strengths and needs, monitor student progress, evaluate and modify instruction, and promote student growth and access to effective learning opportunities 97

Skill 7.5: Demonstrating knowledge of how to promote elementary students' use of self-assessment to identify their own strengths and needs and set personal goals for learning 100

Skill 7.6: Recognizing the importance of using multiple assessments and strategies for modifying classroom assessments for students with various characteristics and needs *(e.g., English language learners, students with exceptionalities)* 101

Skill 7.7: Demonstrating knowledge of how to establish and maintain records of student performance, use technological resources to collect and analyze data and interpret results, and communicate responsibly and effectively with students, parents/guardians, and colleagues about performance and progress 102

COMPETENCY 8
UNDERSTAND INSTRUCTIONAL PLANNING PROCEDURES AND HOW TO USE EFFECTIVE PLANNING TO DESIGN INSTRUCTION THAT PROMOTES LEARNING AND ACHIEVEMENT FOR ALL STUDENTS 102

Skill 8.1: Demonstrating knowledge of key factors to consider in planning instruction *(e.g., state standards; curriculum goals; nature of the subject matter; learning theory; students' development, characteristics, thinking, and prior experiences; students' current knowledge and skills; available time and resources)* 102

Skill 8.2: Applying knowledge of how to use different types of information and sources of data during planning to define learning goals, select appropriate instructional approaches and materials, and accommodate varied student learning styles, needs, and experiences 103

Skill 8.3: Demonstrating knowledge of how to plan and implement learning experiences that are appropriate for curriculum goals, relevant to students, and based on principles of effective instruction *(e.g., activating students' prior knowledge, anticipating preconceptions, encouraging exploration and problem solving, building new skills on those previously acquired)* 106

Skill 8.4: Demonstrating knowledge of how to design lessons and activities that are differentiated to meet students' varied developmental and individual needs and to help all students progress 107

Skill 8.5: Applying knowledge of how to create short-range and long-range plans that are linked to student needs and performance, evaluate plans in relation to short-range and long-range goals, and adjust plans to meet student needs and enhance learning 110

Skill 8.6: Demonstrating knowledge of skills and strategies for engaging in effective planning in specified situations *(e.g., collaborating with colleagues to plan instruction, integrating curricula and creating interdisciplinary units of study, managing technological resources during learning activities, managing student learning in a technology-integrated environment)* 110

COMPETENCY 9
UNDERSTAND HOW TO USE A VARIETY OF INSTRUCTIONAL STRATEGIES TO PROVIDE EFFECTIVE AND APPROPRIATE LEARNING EXPERIENCES THAT PROMOTE ALL STUDENTS' ACHIEVEMENT AND FOSTER DEVELOPMENT OF CRITICAL-THINKING, PROBLEM-SOLVING, AND PERFORMANCE SKILLS

.... 112

Skill 9.1: Demonstrating knowledge of various instructional strategies *(e.g., cooperative learning, interdisciplinary instruction, hands-on activities, technology-based learning, guided discovery, guided practice, modeling)*; **their characteristics, advantages, and limitations; and their use in promoting student learning and achievement of state standards**.........112

Skill 9.2: Identifying cognitive processes associated with various kinds of learning and instructional strategies that stimulate these processes and nurture the development of students' critical-thinking, independent problem-solving, and performance capabilities 112

Skill 9.3: Demonstrating knowledge of how to develop, implement, and evaluate lesson plans that use various strategies, methods, and materials, including technological resources, to enhance student learning 113

Skill 9.4: Demonstrating knowledge of the importance of continuously monitoring instructional effectiveness and responding flexibly to student understanding, ideas, needs, engagement, and feedback *(e.g., by changing the pace of a lesson, using a different instructional approach, taking advantage of an unanticipated learning opportunity)* 115

Skill 9.5: Applying knowledge of how to design teaching strategies that achieve different instructional purposes and meet varied student needs *(e.g., using various grouping strategies; differentiating instruction; using multiple strategies for teaching the same content; using effective resources and materials, including computers and other technological resources)*..118

Skill 9.6: Demonstrating knowledge of how to use multiple approaches to promote student engagement and learning and how to vary the instructional process to achieve given purposes and respond to student needs 121

Skill 9.7: Demonstrating knowledge of how to develop clear, accurate presentations and representations of concepts, use alternative explanations to promote student understanding, and present varied perspectives to encourage critical thinking 122

Skill 9.8: Applying knowledge of how to use educational technology to deliver effective instruction to students working at different levels and paces, stimulate advanced levels of learning, and broaden students' knowledge about technology and its uses 122

DOMAIN IV
PROFESSIONAL ROLES AND RESPONSIBILITIES 125

COMPETENCY 10
UNDERSTAND HOW TO COMMUNICATE AND INTERACT EFFECTIVELY WITH FAMILIES, COLLEAGUES, AND THE COMMUNITY TO SUPPORT AND ENHANCE STUDENT LEARNING AND WELL-BEING................. 129

Skill 10.1: Applying knowledge of skills and strategies for establishing productive relationships with parents/guardians to support student learning and well-being and for addressing parents'/guardians' concerns in given situations 129

Skill 10.2: Demonstrating knowledge of the importance of communicating with families on a regular basis and strategies for initiating and maintaining effective communication with families 131

Skill 10.3: Applying knowledge of skills and strategies for collaborating effectively with other professionals in the school *(e.g., teachers in other classrooms, special education teachers, media specialists, arts teachers, paraprofessionals)* to improve student achievement and enhance the overall learning environment 132

Skill 10.4: Demonstrating knowledge of skills and strategies for consulting with parents/guardians, counselors, other teachers, and professionals in community agencies to link student environments and promote student development and learning...133

Skill 10.5: Demonstrating knowledge of resources in the community *(e.g., cultural institutions, businesses, individuals, social service agencies)* and strategies for using these resources to meet student needs and promote student development and learning...134

COMPETENCY 11
UNDERSTAND PROFESSIONAL DEVELOPMENT OPPORTUNITIES AND RESOURCES AND HOW TO BE A REFLECTIVE PRACTITIONER WHO CONTINUALLY EVALUATES THE EFFECTS OF CHOICES AND ACTIONS ON OTHERS, INCLUDING STUDENTS, PARENTS/GUARDIANS, AND COLLEAGUES, AND WHO ACTIVELY SEEKS OUT OPPORTUNITIES FOR PROFESSIONAL GROWTH..... 136

Skill 11.1: Demonstrating knowledge of the role of reflection and self-assessment in continuous professional growth and of effective strategies for using reflection, self-assessment, critical thinking, problem solving, and self-directed learning to improve teaching practice and achieve professional goals...136

Skill 11.2: Demonstrating knowledge of how to use classroom observation, information about students, and various types of research as sources for evaluating the outcomes of teaching and learning and as a basis for reflecting on and modifying teaching practice 137

Skill 11.3: Demonstrating knowledge of various professional development opportunities and resources *(e.g., professional journals, educational research, online resources, workshops)* and how to use them to promote reflection, solve problems, and support professional growth, including continuous development of technology skills relevant to education 140

Skill 11.4: Demonstrating knowledge of the roles and responsibilities of various members of the school community and methods for working effectively with others in the school community *(e.g., colleagues, mentors, principals, supervisors)* to strengthen teaching knowledge, skills, and effectiveness 142

COMPETENCY 12
UNDERSTAND THE HISTORICAL AND PHILOSOPHICAL FOUNDATIONS OF EDUCATION; THE RIGHTS AND RESPONSIBILITIES OF STUDENTS, PARENTS/GUARDIANS, AND EDUCATORS IN VARIOUS EDUCATIONAL CONTEXTS; AND LEGAL AND ETHICAL GUIDELINES FOR EDUCATORS IN MINNESOTA 143

Skill 12.1: Demonstrating knowledge of the historical and philosophical foundations of education, the purposes of educational organizations, and the operation of schools and school systems as organizations within the community.....................143

Skill 12.2: Demonstrating knowledge of teachers' roles as public employees and their rights and responsibilities as professionals *(e.g., obtaining and maintaining licensure, engaging in appropriate professional practices, addressing the needs of the whole learner, maintaining confidentiality, providing an appropriate education for students with disabilities, reporting cases of known or suspected abuse or neglect, using appropriate practices related to information and technology)* 146

Skill 12.3: Demonstrating knowledge of the standards of professional conduct in the Code of Ethics for Minnesota Teachers 149

Skill 12.4: Demonstrating knowledge of student rights in various contexts *(e.g., in relation to due process, discipline, privacy, free speech, equal educational opportunity)* 150

SAMPLE TEST

Sample Test 155

Answer Key 173

Rigor Table 174

Sample Test with Rationales..175

MINNESOTA
PEDAGOGY: ELEMENTARY (K-6)

SECTION 1

ABOUT XAMONLINE

XAMonline—A Specialty Teacher Certification Company

Created in 1996, XAMonline was the first company to publish study guides for state-specific teacher certification examinations. Founder Sharon Wynne found it frustrating that materials were not available for teacher certification preparation and decided to create the first single, state-specific guide. XAMonline has grown into a company of over 1,800 contributors and writers and offers over 300 titles for the entire PRAXIS series and every state examination. No matter what state you plan on teaching in, XAMonline has a unique teacher certification study guide just for you.

XAMonline—Value and Innovation

We are committed to providing value and innovation. Our print-on-demand technology allows us to be the first in the market to reflect changes in test standards and user feedback as they occur. Our guides are written by experienced teachers who are experts in their fields. And our content reflects the highest standards of quality. Comprehensive practice tests with varied levels of rigor means that your study experience will closely match the actual in-test experience.

To date, XAMonline has helped nearly 600,000 teachers pass their certification or licensing exams. Our commitment to preparation exceeds simply providing the proper material for study—it extends to helping teachers **gain mastery** of the subject matter, giving them the **tools** to become the most effective classroom leaders possible, and ushering today's students toward a **successful future**.

SECTION 2

ABOUT THIS STUDY GUIDE

Purpose of This Guide

Is there a little voice inside of you saying, "Am I ready?" Our goal is to replace that little voice and remove all doubt with a new voice that says, "I AM READY. **Bring it on!**" by offering the highest quality of teacher certification study guides.

Organization of Content

You will see that while every test may start with overlapping general topics, each is very unique in the skills they wish to test. Only XAMonline presents custom content that analyzes deeper than a title, a subarea, or an objective. Only XAMonline presents content and sample test assessments along with **focus statements**, the deepest-level rationale and interpretation of the skills that are unique to the exam.

Title and field number of test

→Each exam has its own name and number. XAMonline's guides are written to give you the content you need to know for the specific exam you are taking. You can be confident when you buy our guide that it contains the information you need to study for the specific test you are taking.

Subareas

→These are the major content categories found on the exam. XAMonline's guides are written to cover all of the subareas found in the test frameworks developed for the exam.

Objectives

→These are standards that are unique to the exam and represent the main subcategories of the subareas/content categories. XAMonline's guides are written to address every specific objective required to pass the exam.

Focus statements

→These are examples and interpretations of the objectives. You find them in parenthesis directly following the objective. They provide detailed examples of the range, type, and level of content that appear on the test questions. **Only XAMonline's guides drill down to this level.**

How Do We Compare with Our Competitors?

XAMonline—drills down to the focus statement level.
CliffsNotes and REA—organized at the objective level
Kaplan—provides only links to content
MoMedia—content not specific to the state test

Each subarea is divided into manageable sections that cover the specific skill areas. Explanations are easy to understand and thorough. You'll find that every test answer contains a rejoinder so if you need a refresher or further review after taking the test, you'll know exactly to which section you must return.

How to Use This Book

Our informal polls show that most people begin studying up to eight weeks prior to the test date, so start early. Then ask yourself some questions: How much do you really know? Are you coming to the test straight from your teacher-education program or are you having to review subjects you haven't considered in ten years? Either way, take a **diagnostic or assessment test** first. Also, spend time on sample tests so that you become accustomed to the way the actual test will appear.

This guide comes with an online diagnostic test of 30 questions found online at *www.XAMonline.com*. It is a little boot camp to get you up for the task and reveal things about your compendium of knowledge in general. Although this guide is structured to follow the order of the test, you are not required to study in that order. By finding a time-management and study plan that fits your life you will be more effective. The results of your diagnostic or self-assessment test can be a guide for how to manage your time and point you toward an area that needs more attention.

After taking the diagnostic exam, fill out the **Personalized Study Plan** page at the beginning of each chapter. Review the competencies and skills covered in that chapter and check the boxes that apply to your study needs. If there are sections you already know you can skip, check the "skip it" box. Taking this step will give you a study plan for each chapter.

Week	Activity
8 weeks prior to test	Take a diagnostic test found at www.XAMonline.com
7 weeks prior to test	Build your Personalized Study Plan for each chapter. Check the "skip it" box for sections you feel you are already strong in. ✗ SKIP IT ☐
6-3 weeks prior to test	For each of these four weeks, choose a content area to study. You don't have to go in the order of the book. It may be that you start with the content that needs the most review. Alternately, you may want to ease yourself into plan by starting with the most familiar material.
2 weeks prior to test	Take the sample test, score it, and create a review plan for the final week before the test.
1 week prior to test	Following your plan (which will likely be aligned with the areas that need the most review) go back and study the sections that align with the questions you may have gotten wrong. Then go back and study the sections related to the questions you answered correctly. If need be, create flashcards and drill yourself on any area that you makes you anxious.

SECTION 3

ABOUT THE MINNESOTA PEDAGOGY: ELEMENTARY (K-6) EXAM

What is the Minnesota Pedagogy: Elementary (K-6) Exam?

The Minnesota Pedagogy: Elementary (K-6) exam is meant to assess mastery of the principles of pedagogy required to teach elementary students in Minnesota public schools. All candidates for initial licensure are required to take a pedagogy test that corresponds to the grade level/s they wish to teach at.

Often **your own state's requirements** determine whether or not you should take any particular test. The most reliable source of information regarding this is your state's Department of Education. This resource should have a complete list of testing centers and dates. Test dates vary by subject area and not all test dates necessarily include your particular test, so be sure to check carefully.

If you are in a teacher-education program, check with the Education Department or the Certification Officer for specific information for testing and testing time-lines. The Certification Office should have most of the information you need.

If you choose an alternative route to certification you can either rely on our website at *www.XAMonline.com* or on the resources provided by an alternative certification program. Many states now have specific agencies devoted to alternative certification and there are some national organizations as well, for example:
National Association for Alternative Certification
http://www.alt-teachercert.org/index.asp

Interpreting Test Results

Contrary to what you may have heard, the results of the Minnesota Pedagogy: Elementary (K-6) test are not based on time. More accurately, your score will be based on the raw number of points you earn in each section, the proportion of that section to the entire subtest, and the scaling of the raw score. Raw scores are converted to a scale of 100 to 300. It is likely to your benefit to complete as many questions in the time allotted, but it will not necessarily work to your advantage if you hurry through the test.

Scores are available by email if you request this when you register. Score reports are available 21days after the testing window and posted to your account for 45 days as PDFs. Scores will also be sent to your chosen institution(s).

What's on the Test?

The Minnesota Pedagogy: Elementary (K-6) exam is a computer-based test and consists of two subtests, each lasting one hour. You can take one or both subtests at one testing appointment. The breakdown of the questions is as follows:

Category	Approximate Number of Questions	Approximate Percentage of the Test
SUBTEST 1	50	
I: Student Development and Learning		50%
II: Learning Environment		50%
SUBTEST 2	50	
I: Instruction and Assessment		50%
II: Professional Roles and Responsibilities		50%

Question Types

You're probably thinking, enough already, I want to study! Indulge us a little longer while we explain that there is actually more than one type of multiple-choice question. You can thank us later after you realize how well prepared you are for your exam.

1. Complete the Statement. The name says it all. In this question type you'll be asked to choose the correct completion of a given statement. For example:

> **The Dolch Basic Sight Words consist of a relatively short list of words that children should be able to:**
>
> A. Sound out
>
> B. Know the meaning of
>
> C. Recognize on sight
>
> D. Use in a sentence

The correct answer is C. In order to check your answer, test out the statement by adding the choices to the end of it.

2. **Which of the Following.** One way to test your answer choice for this type of question is to replace the phrase "which of the following" with your selection. Use this example:

> **Which of the following words is one of the twelve most frequently used in children's reading texts:**
>
> A. There
>
> B. This
>
> C. The
>
> D. An

Don't look! Test your answer. _____ is one of the twelve most frequently used in children's reading texts. Did you guess C? Then you guessed correctly.

3. **Roman Numeral Choices.** This question type is used when there is more than one possible correct answer. For example:

> **Which of the following two arguments accurately supports the use of cooperative learning as an effective method of instruction?**
>
> I. Cooperative learning groups facilitate healthy competition between individuals in the group.
>
> II. Cooperative learning groups allow academic achievers to carry or cover for academic underachievers.
>
> III. Cooperative learning groups make each student in the group accountable for the success of the group.
>
> IV. Cooperative learning groups make it possible for students to reward other group members for achieving.
>
> A. I and II
>
> B. II and III
>
> C. I and III
>
> D. III and IV

Notice that the question states there are **two** possible answers. It's best to read all the possibilities first before looking at the answer choices. In this case, the correct answer is D.

4. Negative Questions. This type of question contains words such as "not," "least," and "except." Each correct answer will be the statement that does **not** fit the situation described in the question. Such as:

> **Multicultural education is not**
>
> A. An idea or concept
>
> B. A "tack-on" to the school curriculum
>
> C. An educational reform movement
>
> D. A process

Think to yourself that the statement could be anything but the correct answer. This question form is more open to interpretation than other types, so read carefully and don't forget that you're answering a negative statement.

5. Questions that Include Graphs, Tables, or Reading Passages. As always, read the question carefully. It likely asks for a very specific answer and not a broad interpretation of the visual. Here is a simple (though not statistically accurate) example of a graph question:

> **In the following graph in how many years did more men take the NYSTCE exam than women?**
>
>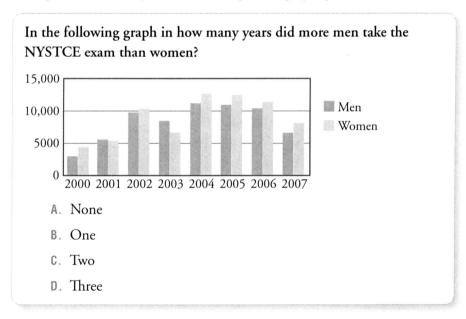
>
> A. None
>
> B. One
>
> C. Two
>
> D. Three

It may help you to simply circle the two years that answer the question. Make sure you've read the question thoroughly and once you've made your determination, double check your work. The correct answer is C.

SECTION 4
HELPFUL HINTS

Study Tips

1. You are what you eat. Certain foods aid the learning process by releasing natural memory enhancers called CCKs (cholecystokinin) composed of tryptophan, choline, and phenylalanine. All of these chemicals enhance the neurotransmitters associated with memory and certain foods release memory enhancing chemicals. A light meal or snacks of one of the following foods fall into this category:

   - Milk
   - Rice
   - Eggs
   - Fish
   - Nuts and seeds
   - Oats
   - Turkey

   The better the connections, the more you comprehend!

2. See the forest for the trees. In other words, get the concept before you look at the details. One way to do this is to take notes as you read, paraphrasing or summarizing in your own words. Putting the concept in terms that are comfortable and familiar may increase retention.

3. Question authority. Ask why, why, why? Pull apart written material paragraph by paragraph and don't forget the captions under the illustrations. For example, if a heading reads *Stream Erosion* put it in the form of a question (Why do streams erode? What is stream erosion?) then find the answer within the material. If you train your mind to think in this manner you will learn more and prepare yourself for answering test questions.

4. Play mind games. Using your brain for reading or puzzles keeps it flexible. Even with a limited amount of time your brain can take in data (much like a computer) and store it for later use. In ten minutes you can: read two paragraphs (at least), quiz yourself with flash cards, or review notes. Even if you don't fully understand something on the first pass, your mind stores it for recall, which is why frequent reading or review increases chances of retention and comprehension.

5. Get pointed in the right direction. Use arrows to point to important passages or pieces of information. It's easier to read than a page full of yellow highlights. Highlighting can be used sparingly, but add an arrow to the margin to call attention to it.

6. **The pen is mightier than the sword.** Learn to take great notes. A by-product of our modern culture is that we have grown accustomed to getting our information in short doses. We've subconsciously trained ourselves to assimilate information into neat little packages. Messy notes fragment the flow of information. Your notes can be much clearer with proper formatting. ***The Cornell Method*** is one such format. This method was popularized in *How to Study in College*, Ninth Edition, by Walter Pauk. You can benefit from the method without purchasing an additional book by simply looking up the method online. Below is a sample of how *The Cornell Method* can be adapted for use with this guide.

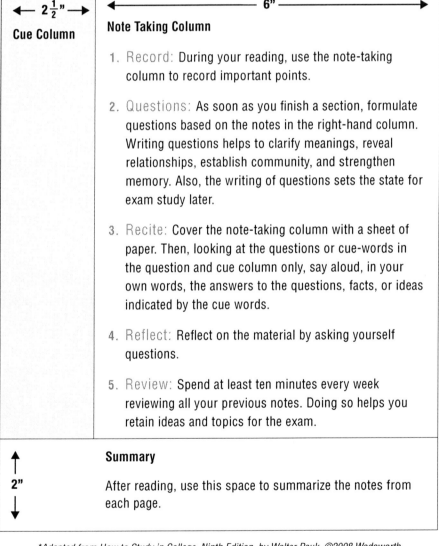

← $2\frac{1}{2}$" →	←————————— 6" —————————→
Cue Column	**Note Taking Column**
	1. Record: During your reading, use the note-taking column to record important points.
	2. Questions: As soon as you finish a section, formulate questions based on the notes in the right-hand column. Writing questions helps to clarify meanings, reveal relationships, establish community, and strengthen memory. Also, the writing of questions sets the state for exam study later.
	3. Recite: Cover the note-taking column with a sheet of paper. Then, looking at the questions or cue-words in the question and cue column only, say aloud, in your own words, the answers to the questions, facts, or ideas indicated by the cue words.
	4. Reflect: Reflect on the material by asking yourself questions.
	5. Review: Spend at least ten minutes every week reviewing all your previous notes. Doing so helps you retain ideas and topics for the exam.
↑ 2" ↓	**Summary** After reading, use this space to summarize the notes from each page.

Adapted from How to Study in College, Ninth Edition, by Walter Pauk, ©2008 Wadsworth

The proctor will write the start time where it can be seen and then, later, provide the time remaining, typically fifteen minutes before the end of the test.

7. Place yourself in exile and set the mood. Set aside a particular place and time to study that best suits your personal needs and biorhythms. If you're a night person, burn the midnight oil. If you're a morning person set yourself up with some coffee and get to it. Make your study time and place as free from distraction as possible and surround yourself with what you need, be it silence or music. Studies have shown that music can aid in concentration, absorption, and retrieval of information. Not all music, though. Classical music is said to work best

8. Check your budget. You should at least review all the content material before your test, but allocate the most amount of time to the areas that need the most refreshing. It sounds obvious, but it's easy to forget. You can use the study rubric above to balance your study budget.

Testing Tips

1. Get smart, play dumb. Sometimes a question is just a question. No one is out to trick you, so don't assume that the test writer is looking for something other than what was asked. Stick to the question as written and don't overanalyze.

2. Do a double take. Read test questions and answer choices at least twice because it's easy to miss something, to transpose a word or some letters. If you have no idea what the correct answer is, skip it and come back later if there's time. If you're still clueless, it's okay to guess. Remember, you're scored on the number of questions you answer correctly and you're not penalized for wrong answers. The worst case scenario is that you miss a point from a good guess.

3. Turn it on its ear. The syntax of a question can often provide a clue, so make things interesting and turn the question into a statement to see if it changes the meaning or relates better (or worse) to the answer choices.

4. Get out your magnifying glass. Look for hidden clues in the questions because it's difficult to write a multiple-choice question without giving away part of the answer in the options presented. In most questions you can readily eliminate one or two potential answers, increasing your chances of answering correctly to 50/50, which will help out if you've skipped a question and gone back to it (see tip #2).

5. Call it intuition. Often your first instinct is correct. If you've been studying the content you've likely absorbed something and have subconsciously retained the knowledge. On questions you're not sure about trust your instincts because a first impression is usually correct.

6. Graffiti. Sometimes it's a good idea to mark your answers directly on the test booklet and go back to fill in the optical scan sheet later. You don't get extra points for perfectly blackened ovals. If you choose to manage your test this way, be sure not to mismark your answers when you transcribe to the scan sheet.

7. Become a clock-watcher. You have a set amount of time to answer the questions. Don't get bogged down laboring over a question you're not sure about when there are ten others you could answer more readily. If you choose to follow the advice of tip #6, be sure you leave time near the end to go back and fill in the scan sheet.

Do the Drill

No matter how prepared you feel it's sometimes a good idea to apply Murphy's Law. So the following tips might seem silly, mundane, or obvious, but we're including them anyway.

1. Remember, you are what you eat, so bring a snack. Choose from the list of energizing foods that appear earlier in the introduction.

2. You're not too sexy for your test. Wear comfortable clothes. You'll be distracted if your belt is too tight or if you're too cold or too hot.

3. Lie to yourself. Even if you think you're a prompt person, pretend you're not and leave plenty of time to get to the testing center. Map it out ahead of time and do a dry run if you have to. There's no need to add road rage to your list of anxieties.

4. Bring sharp number 2 pencils. It may seem impossible to forget this need from your school days, but you might. And make sure the erasers are intact, too.

5. No ticket, no test. Bring your admission ticket as well as **two** forms of identification, including one with a picture and signature. You will not be admitted to the test without these things.

6. You can't take it with you. Leave any study aids, dictionaries, notebooks, computers, and the like at home. Certain tests **do** allow a scientific or four-function calculator, so check ahead of time to see if your test does.

7. Prepare for the desert. Any time spent on a bathroom break **cannot** be made up later, so use your judgment on the amount you eat or drink.

8. **Quiet, Please!** Keeping your own time is a good idea, but not with a timepiece that has a loud ticker. If you use a watch, take it off and place it nearby but not so that it distracts you. And **silence your cell phone**.

To the best of our ability, we have compiled the content you need to know in this book and in the accompanying online resources. The rest is up to you. You can use the study and testing tips or you can follow your own methods. Either way, you can be confident that there aren't any missing pieces of information and there shouldn't be any surprises in the content on the test.

If you have questions about test fees, registration, electronic testing, or other content verification issues please visit *www.mtle.nesinc.com*.

Good luck!

Sharon Wynne
Founder, XAMonline

DOMAIN I
STUDENT DEVELOPMENT AND LEARNING

PERSONALIZED STUDY PLAN

KNOWN MATERIAL/ SKIP IT

PAGE	COMPETENCY AND SKILL	
5	**1: Understand development during the elementary years and how to provide learning opportunities that support students' physical, social, emotional, moral, and cognitive development**	☐
	1.1: Demonstrating knowledge of developmental characteristics, processes, and progressions in the physical, social, emotional, moral, and cognitive domains	☐
	1.2: Demonstrating knowledge of developmental variation in the physical, social, emotional, moral, and cognitive domains	☐
	1.3: Applying knowledge of how a student's development in any one domain may affect development and performance in other domains	☐
	1.4: Applying knowledge of how students' physical, social, emotional, moral, and cognitive development influences learning	☐
	1.5: Identifying developmentally appropriate instruction that supports the cognitive, social, emotional, moral, and physical domains	☐
	1.6: Recognizing how many factors may affect elementary students' development and readiness to learn	☐
14	**2: Understand learning processes and how to provide instructional opportunities that promote student learning and achievement**	☐
	2.1: Demonstrating knowledge of how students learn, internalize knowledge, and develop performance and thinking skills	☐
	2.2: Applying knowledge of the concept of readiness in various learning contexts and strategies	☐
	2.3: Demonstrating knowledge of strategies for helping students build meaning	☐
	2.4: Demonstrating knowledge of factors that influence student learning	☐
	2.5: Identifying strategies for encouraging students to assume responsibility for shaping their learning tasks and outcomes	☐
	2.6: Demonstrating knowledge of how particular instructional methods and procedures can be expected to influence learning processes and outcomes	☐

PERSONALIZED STUDY PLAN

KNOWN MATERIAL/ SKIP IT

PAGE	COMPETENCY AND SKILL	
33	**3: Understand student diversity and how to provide instructional opportunities that meet the needs of students with diverse backgrounds and exceptionalities and promote all students' learning and achievement**	☐
	3.1: Demonstrating knowledge of differences in approaches to learning and performance	☐
	3.2: Applying knowledge of areas of exceptionality and strategies for promoting learning for students with exceptionalities	☐
	3.3: Demonstrating knowledge of the process of second-language acquisition and strategies for supporting learning for students whose first language is not English	☐
	3.4: Demonstrating knowledge of technological resources to facilitate learning for students with diverse backgrounds, characteristics, needs, and abilities	☐
	3.5: Demonstrating knowledge of the contributions, characteristics, and lifestyles of various groups in U.S. society	☐
	3.6: Demonstrating knowledge of cultural and community diversity and norms	☐
	3.7: Demonstrating knowledge of how to recognize and respond to negative attitudes regarding diversity	☐
	3.8: Recognizing the importance of belief in all students' ability to learn at the highest levels	☐

COMPETENCY 1

UNDERSTAND DEVELOPMENT DURING THE ELEMENTARY YEARS AND HOW TO PROVIDE LEARNING OPPORTUNITIES THAT SUPPORT STUDENTS' PHYSICAL, SOCIAL, EMOTIONAL, MORAL, AND COGNITIVE DEVELOPMENT

SKILL 1.1 **Demonstrating knowledge of developmental characteristics, processes, and progressions in the physical, social, emotional, moral, and cognitive domains**

Today, teachers are immediately faced with the challenge of deciding whether they believe that the classroom should be teacher-centered or student-centered. Usually, an appropriate combination of both is preferred; thus, most teachers must negotiate which areas of their instruction should be teacher-centered and which areas should be student-centered.

Classroom Styles

TEACHER-CENTERED CLASSROOMS generally focus on the concept that knowledge is objective and that students must learn new information through the transmission of that knowledge from the teacher. STUDENT-CENTERED CLASSROOMS are considered to be constructivist, in that students are given opportunities to construct their own meanings onto new pieces of knowledge. Doing so may require that students are more actively involved in the learning process. Indeed, constructivism is a strong force in teaching today, but it is often misinterpreted. Good constructivist teachers do NOT just let their students explore anything they want in any way they choose; rather, they give students opportunities to learn things in more natural ways, such as through experiments, hands-on projects, discussions, etc.

Constructivist theory

The most current theory of constructivist learning allows students to construct learning opportunities. For constructivist teachers, the belief is that students create their own reality of knowledge and how to process and observe the world around them. Students are constantly constructing new ideas, which serve as frameworks

TEACHER-CENTERED CLASSROOMS: classrooms that focus on the concept that knowledge is objective and that students must learn new information through the transmission of that knowledge from the teacher

STUDENT-CENTERED CLASSROOMS: classrooms in which students are given opportunities to construct their own meanings onto new pieces of knowledge; these classrooms are considered constructivist

for learning and teaching. Researchers have shown that the constructivist model is composed of four components:

CONSTRUCTIVIST LEARNING
Learner creates knowledge
Learner constructs and makes meaningful new knowledge to existing knowledge
Learner shapes and constructs knowledge by life experiences and social interactions
In constructivist learning communities, the student, teacher and classmates establish knowledge cooperatively on a daily basis

According to Kelly (1969), "human beings construct knowledge systems based on their observations." This statement parallels Jean Piaget's theory that knowledge is constructed as individuals work with others who have similar background and thought processes. Constructivist learning for students is dynamic and ongoing. For constructivist teachers, the classroom becomes a place where students are supported and encouraged to interact with the instructional process by asking questions and applying new ideas to old theories.

Learning Theories

A classic learning theorist, Piaget believed children passed through a series of stages to develop from the most basic forms of concrete thinking to sophisticated levels of abstract thinking. His developmental theory consists of four learning stages, which can be remembered with the following mnemonic, Stages Precious Children Follow (SPCF):

1. Sensory motor stage (from birth to age two)

2. Preoperation stage (ages two to seven or early elementary)

3. Concrete operational (ages seven to eleven or upper elementary)

4. Formal operational (ages seven to fifteen or late elementary/high school)

Additional prominent learning theories in education today include brain-based learning and the Multiple Intelligence Theory. Supported by recent brain research, brain-based learning suggests that knowledge about the way the brain retains information enables educators to design the most effective learning environments. As a result, researchers have developed twelve principles that relate knowledge about the brain to teaching practices.

The twelve principles of brain-based learning:

• *The brain is a complex adaptive system*
• *The brain is social*
• *The search for meaning is innate*
• *We use patterns to learn more effectively*
• *Emotions are crucial to developing patterns*
• *Each brain perceives and creates parts and whole simultaneously*
• *Learning involves focused and peripheral attention*
• *Learning involves conscious and unconscious processes*
• *We have at least two ways of organizing memory*
• *Learning is developmental*
• *Complex learning is enhanced by challenge (and inhibited by threat)*
• *Every brain is unique*

Caine & Caine, 1994, Mind/Brain Learning Principles

← KEEP these in mind when working in a classroom.

To maximize student learning, educators can use these principles to help design methods and environments in their classrooms.

To be successful, a teacher must have a broad knowledge and thorough understanding of the development that typically occurs during the students' current period of life. More importantly, the teacher understands how children learn best during each period of development. The most important premise of child development is that all domains of development (physical, social, and academic) are integrated. Development in each dimension is influenced by the other dimensions. Moreover, today's educator must also have knowledge of exceptionalities and how these exceptionalities affect all domains of a child's development.

Physical Development

It is important for the teacher to be aware of the physical stage of development and how the child's physical growth and development affect the child's cognitive learning. Factors determined by the physical stage of development include: ability to sit and attend, the need for activity, the relationship between physical skills and self-esteem, and the degree to which physical involvement in an activity (as opposed to being able to understand an abstract concept) affects learning.

understanding when children need to move around.

Cognitive (Academic) Development

Children go through patterns of learning, beginning with preoperational thought processes, and they move to concrete operational thoughts. Eventually they begin to acquire the mental ability to think about and solve problems in their head

The content needs to be relevant and meaningful

because they can manipulate objects symbolically. Children of most ages can use symbols such as words and numbers to represent objects and relations, but they need concrete reference points. To facilitate cognitive development, it is essential that children be encouraged to use and develop the thinking skills that they possess in solving problems that interest them. The content of the curriculum must be relevant, engaging, and meaningful to the students.

Social Development

Children progress through a variety of social stages. First, they begin with an awareness of their peers but have a lack of concern for the presence of these other children. Young children engage in "parallel" activities playing alongside their peers without directly interacting with one another. Next, during the primary years, children develop an intense interest in peers. They establish productive, positive social and working relationships with one another. This stage of social growth continues throughout the child's formative period including the primary, middle, and high school years. It is necessary for teachers to recognize the importance of developing positive peer-group relationships and to provide opportunities and support for cooperative small group projects that not only develop cognitive ability but also promote peer interaction. The ability to work and relate effectively with peers is of major importance and contributes greatly to the child's sense of competence. In order to develop this sense of competence, children need to be successful in acquiring the knowledge and skills recognized by their culture as important; in the United States, among the most important are those skills that promote academic achievement.

> **SKILL 1.2** **Demonstrating knowledge of developmental variation among elementary students in the physical, social, emotional, moral, and cognitive domains and instructional practices that are responsive to this variation**

Developmental Orientation

DEVELOPMENTALLY ORIENTED TEACHERS: teachers who approach classroom groups and individual students with a respect for their emerging capabilities

Knowledge of age-appropriate expectations is fundamental to both the teacher's positive relationship with students and his or her ability to develop effective instructional strategies. Equally important is the knowledge of what is appropriate for individual children in a classroom. DEVELOPMENTALLY ORIENTED TEACHERS approach classroom groups and individual students with a respect for their emerging capabilities. Developmentalists recognize that kids grow in common patterns but at different rates, which usually cannot be accelerated by adult pressure or input. These teachers also know that variations in the school performance of different children often results from differences in their general growth. Most school districts use inclusion to ensure that all children receive a free and appropriate education. Therefore, it is vital for teachers to know the characteristics of students' exceptionalities and their implications for learning.

Selection of Learning Activities

The effective teacher is cognizant of students' individual learning styles, human growth, and development theories, and how to apply these principles in the selection and implementation of appropriate instructional activities. Learning activities selected for early childhood (below age eight) should occur in short time frames in highly simplified form. The nature of the activity and the context in which the activity is presented affects the approach that the students will take in processing the information. During early childhood, children tend to process information at a slower rate than when they are older (age eight and beyond).

> The effective teacher is cognizant of students' individual learning styles, human growth, and development theories, and how to apply these principles in the selection and implementation of appropriate instructional activities.

Selecting activities

When selecting and implementing learning activities for older children, teachers should focus on more complex instructional activities for which these children are developmentally prepared. Moreover, effective teachers maintain a clear understanding of the developmental appropriateness of activities selected. They also present these activities in a manner consistent with the level of readiness of their students.

* teachers need to choose activities appropriate for the child's age.

Different Learning Theories

For quite some time, a movement called "multiple intelligences" has been popular in many classrooms. The MULTIPLE INTELLIGENCE THEORY, developed by Howard Gardner, suggests that students learn in (at least) seven different ways. It also proposes that verbal/linguistic and quantitative intelligences, the two types that are most often associated with intellect, should be reconsidered to be as (not more) important compared to the other forms of intelligence. Other intelligences included kinesthetic, interpersonal, musical, intrapersonal, and spatial. This theory has helped teachers understand that while some students may not excel in one style of learning, it is entirely possible that they are incredibly gifted in another.

> **MULTIPLE INTELLIGENCE THEORY:** a theory that states that students learn in at least seven different ways, including verbal/linguistic, quantitative, interpersonal, musical, intrapersonal, and spatial

Academic subject areas have also added to the philosophical debate on teaching. For example, reading teachers have long debated whether phonics or whole language was more appropriate as an instructional method. Language Arts teachers have debated the importance of a prescribed canon (famous works of literature) versus teaching literature simply to teach thinking skills and an appreciation of good literature. Math teachers have debated the extent to which application is necessary in math instruction; while some feel that it is more important to teach structure and process, others suggest that it is only relevant if math skills are taught in context.

Cognitive theory

THE THEORY OF METACOGNITION: the study of how to help the learner gain understanding about how knowledge is constructed

COGNITIVE APPROACH: an approach to learning that first helps the learner gain understanding about how knowledge is constructed, and second, arms that learner with the conscious tools for constructing that knowledge

Researchers Joyce and Weil (1996) described THE THEORY OF METACOGNITION as first the study of how to help the learner gain understanding about how knowledge is constructed; and second arming that learner with the conscious tools for constructing that knowledge. The COGNITIVE APPROACH to learning emphasizes that the teacher must understand that the greatest learning and retention opportunities in the classroom come from teaching the student to process his or her own learning to master the skill being taught. Students are taught to develop concepts and teach themselves skills in problem solving and critical thinking. The student becomes the active participant in the learning process and the teacher becomes the facilitator of that conceptual and cognitive learning process.

Social and behavioral theories

Social and behavioral theories look at how students' social interactions instruct or impact learning opportunities in the classroom. Both theories are subject to individual variables that are learned and applied either positively or negatively in the classroom. Innumerable stimuli in the classroom can promote learning or evoke behavior that is counterproductive for both students and teachers. As human beings, students are social and normally gravitate to action in the classroom; therefore, to maximize learning opportunities, teachers must be deliberate in planning classroom environments that provide both focus and engagement

* keeping the child focused and engaged is important

Designing a classroom

Designing classrooms that provide optimal academic and behavioral support for diverse students can be daunting for teachers. The ultimate goal is creating a safe learning environment where students can construct knowledge in an engaging and positive climate.

No one of these theories will work for every classroom, and a good approach is to incorporate a range of learning theories in a classroom. Still, under the guidance of any theory, good educators will differentiate their instructional practices to meet the needs of individual students' abilities and interests using various instructional practices.

SKILL 1.3 Applying knowledge of how a student's development in any one domain may affect development and performance in other domains

Elementary-age children face many changes during their early school years, and these changes will impact how learning occurs in either a positive or negative manner. Some cognitive developments (i.e., learning to read) may broaden their areas of interest as students realize the amount of information (i.e., novels, magazines, nonfiction books) that is available. On the other hand, a young student's limited comprehension may inhibit some of their confidence (emotional) or conflict with values taught at home (moral). Joke telling (linguistic) becomes popular with children aged six or seven, and children may use this newly discovered "talent" to gain friends or social "stature" in their class (social). Learning within one domain often spills over into other areas for young students.

*[handwritten margin note: * Changes are positive or negative ↓ Can effect students positively and/or negatively]*

SKILL 1.4 Applying knowledge of how students' physical, social, emotional, moral, and cognitive development influences learning and how to address these factors when making instructional decisions

Selecting Activities Based on Learning Objectives

The effective teacher selects learning activities based on specific learning objectives. Ideally, teachers should not plan activities that fail to augment the specific objectives of the lesson. Learning activities should be planned with a learning objective in mind. Objective-driven learning activities serve as a tool to reinforce the teacher's lesson presentation. Additionally, teacher-selected learning objectives should be aligned with state and district educational goals. State and district goals should focus on National Educational Goals (Goals 2000), and the specific strengths and weaknesses of individual students in the teacher's class.

Also see Skill 1.2

*[handwritten margin note: * activities need to help the student succeed and they need to go with the district]*

SKILL 1.5 Identifying developmentally appropriate instruction that meets student needs and supports student growth in the cognitive, social, emotional, moral, and physical domains

No two students are alike. It follows, then, that no students learn alike. To apply a one-dimensional instructional approach and have strict tunnel vision is to impose learning limits on students. All students have the right to an education, but there

*[handwritten margin note: * No students learn the same - switch it up.]*

A teacher must acknowledge the variety of learning styles and abilities among students within a class (and, indeed, the varieties from class to class) and apply multiple instructional and assessment processes to ensure that every child has appropriate opportunities to master the subject matter, demonstrate such mastery, and improve and enhance learning skills with each lesson.

DIFFERENTIATED INSTRUCTION (DI): the concept that because students have different ways of learning, teachers must utilize different methods of teaching

cannot be a singular path to that education. A teacher must acknowledge the variety of learning styles and abilities among students within a class (and, indeed, from class to class) and apply multiple instructional and assessment processes to ensure that every child has appropriate opportunities to master the subject matter, demonstrate such mastery, and improve and enhance learning skills with each lesson.

Differentiated Instruction

It is difficult to define intelligence, but teachers know and recognize the differences in the intelligence of their students. This complicates the development of DIFFERENTIATED INSTRUCTION (DI). Some of the children from homes where reading, books, and learning are not a high priority will, nevertheless, rank high on the intelligence scale, as will some where parents seem indifferent to their children's progress. Some will be very low on this scale regardless of background. It is very challenging to develop teaching approaches and methods that will make certain none of the children are left behind. Should a teacher choose the lowest common denominator and ignore the likelihood that many of the students in the class could grasp highly abstract ideas and concepts, or is it better to aim for the middle and hope for the best? * hard to plan activities so children don't fall behind.

Accepting students' differences

A committed educator not only accepts students' differences but also acts on them by differentiating his or her instructional practices. This means that differentiating instruction is not something done on Fridays; it is what effective teachers do every day in the classroom so that every student's learning needs are met. According to well-respected DI proponent Carol Ann Tomlinson, differentiation "occurs as teachers become increasingly proficient in understanding their students as individuals, increasingly comfortable with the meaning and structure of the disciplines they teach, and increasingly expert at teaching flexibly in order to match instruction to student need with the goal of maximizing the potential of each learner in a given area."

Understanding students

Teachers who differentiate their instruction begin by developing a broad and thorough understanding of their students. Gathering this data about students and using it to purposefully implement differentiated practices can be time consuming and cumbersome, especially as greater demands and expectations squeeze into teachers' already tight schedules. However, by promoting the focused and deliberate integration of technology, these challenging and sometimes difficult tasks can become both practical and increasingly more manageable in the differentiated classroom.

Implementing DI in the classroom

The effective teacher will seek to connect all students to the subject matter through multiple techniques, with the goal that each student, through his or her own abilities, will relate to one or more techniques and excel in the learning process. Differentiated instruction encompasses several areas:

- Content: What is the teacher going to teach? Or, perhaps better put, what does the teacher want the students to learn? Differentiating content means that students will have access to content that piques their interest about a topic, with a complexity that provides an appropriate challenge for their intellectual development.

- Process: This is a classroom management technique where instructional organization and delivery is maximized for the diverse student group. These techniques should include dynamic, flexible grouping activities, where instruction and learning occurs as whole-class units, teacher-led activities, and peer learning and teaching (while teacher observes and coaches) within small groups or pairs.

- Product: There are expectations and requirements placed on students to demonstrate their knowledge or understanding. The type of product expected from each student should reflect each student's own capabilities.

See Skill 1.4 for a discussion on selecting developmentally appropriate learning activities

> The effective teacher will seek to connect all students to the subject matter through multiple techniques, with the goal that each student, through his or her own abilities, will relate to one or more techniques and excel in the learning process.

SKILL 1.6 **Recognizing how individual factors** *(e.g., prior learning, talents, language and cultural background)* **and factors in the home, school, and community** *(e.g., peer interactions; use of tobacco, alcohol, and drugs)* **may affect elementary students' development and readiness to learn**

What city doesn't have restaurants that represent countries around the world—Italian, Chinese, Japanese, Mexican, Jamaican, etc.? The same is true of America's classrooms. Even in small towns, school classrooms tend to showcase the melting pot that makes up twenty-first century American culture. The challenge of our schools is to educate all students with equality, fairness, and success.

Diversity can be further defined as:

- Differences among learners, classroom settings, and academic outcomes

- Biological, sociological, ethnic, socioeconomic, psychological, and learning preferences and styles among learners

Diversity Cont... [handwritten]

{
- Differences in classroom settings that promote learning opportunities such as collaborative, participatory, and individualized learning groups

- Expected learning outcomes that are theoretical, affective, and cognitive for students

Addressing Diversity in the Classroom

Effective teaching and learning for students begins with teachers who can demonstrate an appreciation for diversity in relationships and within school communities. It is an old-fashioned notion, but true nonetheless: teachers are models, whether or not they choose to be. Students will imitate the teacher who leads with honesty. If the teacher is only pretending to like students, the children will know it. If that teacher is sensitive and caring, many of the challenges presented by a diverse classroom will be well-managed.

> *Effective teaching and learning for students begins with teachers who can demonstrate an appreciation for diversity in relationships and within school communities.*

At the same time, teachers must be in charge. They must be firm classroom leaders who are serious about their roles in preparing their young charges for the challenges they will face as they grow. Effective teachers use instructional techniques that enable students to enjoy learning and feel comfortable in the educational environment.

Also see Skill 2.4

Children know when the teacher is faking EVERYTHING! [handwritten]

Be geniune [handwritten]

COMPETENCY 2

UNDERSTAND LEARNING PROCESSES AND HOW TO PROVIDE INSTRUCTIONAL OPPORTUNITIES THAT PROMOTE STUDENT LEARNING AND ACHIEVEMENT

SKILL 2.1 Demonstrating knowledge of how students learn, internalize knowledge, and develop performance and thinking skills and how to use various instructional strategies to promote achievement of these goals

Teachers should have a toolkit of instructional strategies, materials, and technologies to teach and encourage students to problem solve and think critically about subject content. When districts choose a curriculum, it is expected that students will master established benchmarks and standards of learning. Research of national and state standards indicates that there are additional benchmarks and learning objectives measured in all state assessments. These apply to most subjects including science, foreign language, English/language arts, history, art, health, civics, economics, geography, physical education, mathematics, and social studies (Marzano & Kendall, 1996).

* encourage students to think critically and problem solve

Critical Thinking

It is important that students develop critical thinking skills. When a student learns to think critically, he or she learns how to apply knowledge to a specific subject area; but more importantly, the student knows how to apply that information in other subject areas. For example, in algebra, students are taught the order of numerical expressions. To foster critical thinking, the teacher would teach the concept and then provide a math word problem for students to compute the amount of material needed to build a fence around an eight-by-twelve-foot backyard. To solve the problem, students must think critically and group the fencing measurements into an algebraic word problem and perform minor addition, subtraction, and multiplication to determine the amount of material needed. Their new skill could be applied to geography, science, woodworking, sewing, baking, and many tasks that are outside of the mathematics classroom.

Classroom examples of critical thinking

As another example, students use basic reading skills to read passages, math word problems, or project directions. To fully comprehend the material read, however, students must apply additional thinking skills. These higher-order, critical thinking skills operate as students "think about thinking." Teachers are instrumental in helping students use these skills in everyday activities such as:

- Analyzing bills for overcharges

- Comparing shopping ads or catalogue deals

- Finding the main idea from readings

- Applying what's been learned to new situations

- Gathering information/data from multiple sources to plan a project

- Following a sequence of directions

- Looking for cause and effect relationships

- Comparing and contrasting information in synthesizing information

*technology varies between school districts.

Creative and Higher-Ordered Thinking

To create the ultimate environment for creative thinking and continuous learning, teachers should use diversity in instructional strategies, engaging and challenging curricula, and the latest technologies. When teachers are innovative and creative, they model and foster creative thinking in their students. Encouraging students to maintain portfolios from projects and assignments will allow them to make conscious choices to include diverse, creative endeavors that can be treasured throughout their educational journies.

INDIVIDUALIZED PORTFOLIOS are performance-based assessments that allow teachers to chart students' academic and emotional growth. Teachers can also use semester portfolios to gauge progress. This is particularly important for older students who are constantly changing their self-images and worldviews. Through a teacher's guidance, students can master a concept and create a bridge connecting knowledge to application. When this happens, the teacher can share an enjoyable moment of higher-level learning with the student.

> **INDIVIDUALIZED PORT-FOLIOS:** performance-based assessments that allow teachers to chart students' academic and emotional growth

Ways to encourage higher-ordered thinking

Art can be incorporated into most subjects including reading, math, and science. Mental mind mapping, graphic organizers, and concept web guides are all instructional strategies that teachers can use to guide students into deeper subject matter inquiry. Imagine fostering creativity in students that mimics that of German chemist Fredrich August Kekule; he looked into a fire one night and solved the molecular structure of benzene!

Other important, life-long educational processes include developing effective note-taking skills, welcoming diverse perspectives, and appreciating the greatest computer on record, the human mind. In addition, teachers should train students to use math manipulatives, a technique for visual processing. Next, the process of journaling can help students understand their own learning. Lastly, when students present information to the class using posters and PowerPoint presentations; these can be powerful, creative methods of teaching and learning.

> **DEDUCTIVE REASON-ING:** general concepts or principles supported by specific examples

Inductive and Deductive Thinking

In DEDUCTIVE REASONING or learning, a teacher presents general concepts or principles and provides specific examples supporting the generalizations. INDUCTIVE REASONING occurs in the reverse: a teacher presents information or data and encourages students to hypothesize, identify patterns, draw conclusions, and then finally produce generalizations. This tends to involve students more deeply in the learning process. A teacher should choose the method based on the goals of instruction and the needs of the students.

> **INDUCTIVE REASON-ING:** drawing conclusions from information or data

Examples of inductive and deductive thinking

For example, when a parent is working in the kitchen, children conclude that a meal is coming soon; when parents put coats on their kids, they believe that they are going outdoors. These conclusions are drawn not from one observation but from repeated ones. This is inductive thinking: observing particular occurrences and drawing conclusions. Deduction is the opposite. One begins with a conclusion, for example, "all men are mortal," and support the statement with particulars: "Socrates died, Plato died, all the men we have ever known have died; therefore, all men are mortal."

Challenges of inductive and deductive thinking

Sometimes wrong conclusions are drawn on the basis of particulars. There are many legal cases where particular pieces of evidence have been used to find a person guilty in a court of law. However, a significant bit of evidence that comes later, such as the person's DNA, proves that the conclusion of guilt was wrong. Drawing incorrect conclusions are also common when students use inductive and deductive reasoning; therefore, teachers must closely monitor this process for it to be a useful tool in helping students become critical thinkers.

* teachers must be on the look out for critical thinking problems

Memorization and Recall

Understanding students' learning styles allows a teacher to share and target specific memorization techniques. These then help students absorb the large quantities of material they are expected to recall and master. For example, MNEMONICS incorporate rhymes and acronyms and are effective for visual learners. Mnemonics rely not only on repetition to remember facts but also on associations between easy-to-remember constructs and lists of data. It is based on the principle that the human mind can more easily recall insignificant data when it is attached (in a logical way) to spatial, personal, or otherwise meaningful information. Kinesthetic learners use their imaginations to create mind-pictures of events and actions. In contrast, auditory learners rely on note taking, review, and recitation to facilitate memorization and recall.

It was once considered a mark of extraordinary intelligence and learning to be able to recite long poems or long selections from books, particularly the Bible. However, simple memorization no longer has the place in education that it once did. Now students are expected to apply their knowledge in new and challenging tasks. Even so, the ability to memorize and recall principles and ideas (even text) is an important attribute of the learned person. Thus, the classroom teacher has an obligation to promote and develop these skills.

Understanding students' learning styles allows a teacher to share and target specific memorization techniques. These then help students absorb the large quantities of material they are expected to recall and master.

MNEMONICS: memorization techniques that rely on associations between easy-to-remember constructs and lists of data

Social Reasoning

SOCIAL THEORY: the use of theoretical frameworks to explain and analyze social patterns and large-scale social structures

SOCIAL THEORY refers to the use of theoretical frameworks to explain and analyze social patterns and large-scale social structures. The goal of social reasoning is to see an issue from different perspectives, to understand social and ethical concerns surrounding an issue, and to be able to step back and view the issue as an historian would. A teacher can use questioning on a given issue to strengthen students' social reasoning abilities (e.g., what is the history of this issue and has it changed over time? How do diverse communities view this issue? What are some ethical questions surrounding this issue? Who benefits or is harmed by this issue? What can I [the student] do about this issue?).

Though many researchers consider social theory a branch of sociology, it is inherently interdisciplinary because it uses and contributes to a plethora of disciplines such as anthropology, economics, theology, history, and many others. Social theory attempts to answer the question "What is?" not "What should be?" One should therefore not confuse it with philosophy or with belief.

Representation of Ideas

A visual representation of an idea or concept is a powerful instructional and learning tool. Through these aides, a teacher can provide strong connections and foundations for student understanding. In turn, by producing a visual representation, a student demonstrates his/her understanding of the idea or concept. This ability is often critical in problem analysis and solving, as well as in creative pursuits where hard facts are absent and conceptualization is subjective.

Using visual representations

In society, many people often think of ideas as being represented in words; however, this thinking needs to be expanded. There are so many other means and devices that are available to the teacher. For example, the old adage, "a picture is worth a thousand words" is, in fact, a truism. Students incorporate ideas much better if they have an opportunity to absorb them through more than one sense. For example, when learning a unit on drama or even literature, nothing substitutes for seeing one of Shakespeare's plays performed. Graphs, charts, photographs, paintings, drawings, and videos all represent an idea (or set of ideas).

> **SKILL 2.2** Applying knowledge of the concept of readiness in various learning contexts and strategies for using student strengths as a basis for promoting learning and student errors as opportunities for learning

Readiness and Screening

A student's readiness for a specific subject is not an absolute concept, but, rather is determined by the relationship between the subject matter/topic and the student's prior knowledge, interest, motivation, attitude, experience, and other factors.

Thus, the student's readiness to learn about the water cycle depends on whether the student already knows related concepts such as evaporation, condensation, and filtration. Readiness, then, implies that no gap exists between what the student knows and the prerequisite knowledge base for learning.

Pretesting

A pretest designed to assess significant and related prerequisite skills and abilities is the most common method of identifying the students' readiness. This assessment should focus not on the content to be introduced but on prior knowledge judged to be necessary for understanding the new content. A pretest that focuses on the new content may identify students who do not need the new instruction (who have already mastered the material), but it will not identify students with readiness gaps.

Basic skill readiness

The most common areas of readiness concerns are in the basic academic skill areas. Mastery of the basic skill areas is a prerequisite for almost all subject area learning. Arithmetic skills and some higher-level mathematic skills are generally necessary for science learning or for understanding history and related time concepts.

Reading skills are necessary throughout the school years and beyond. A student with poor reading skills is at a disadvantage when asked to read a textbook chapter independently. Writing skills, especially handwriting, spelling, punctuation, and mechanics, are directly related to success in any writing-based activity. A weakness in any of these basic skill areas may at first glance appear to be a difficulty in understanding the subject area.

A teacher who attempts to help the student master the subject matter through additional emphasis on the content will be misusing instructional time and frustrating the student. An awareness of readiness issues helps the teacher to focus on treating the underlying deficiency instead of focusing on the overt symptoms.

> A student's readiness for a specific subject is not an absolute concept but is determined by the relationship between the subject matter/topic and the student's prior knowledge, interest, motivation, attitude, experience, and other similar factors.

> The most common areas of readiness concerns are in the basic academic skill areas.

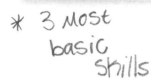

* 3 most basic skills

*handwritten: * Choosing Activities of the readiness gap*

Addressing readiness gaps

Once a readiness gap has been identified, the teacher can provide activities designed to close the gap. Specific activities may be of almost any form. Since most learning builds upon previous learning, a few activities or segments of learning can be viewed solely as readiness or nonreadiness activities. Very few types of learning can be identified solely as readiness activities without legitimacy in their own right.

While growth and maturation rates vary greatly from individual to individual, some generalizations can be made concerning development characteristics of children. Most children appear to go through identifiable, sequential stages of growth and maturation, although not at the same rate.

Curriculum and readiness

For the curriculum developers, it is often necessary to make some generalizations about the development level of the students of a particular age group or grade level.

For the curriculum developers, it is often necessary to make some generalizations about the development level of the students of a particular age group or grade level. These generalizations, then, provide a framework for establishing the expectations of the children's performance. Textbooks, scope and sequence charts, school curriculum planners, and more, translate these generalizations into plans and expectations for the students. The curriculum plan that emerges identifies general goals and expectations for the average student.

One of the teacher's responsibilities in this situation is to determine an initial rough estimate of what is appropriate for a given group of students. The teacher should expect to modify and adjust the instructional program based on the needs and abilities of the students. A teacher may do this by:

handwritten: adjust as seen fit.

- Grouping students for alternative instruction
- Adjusting or varying the materials (textbooks)
- Varying the teaching methods
- Varying the learning tasks

> SKILL **Demonstrating knowledge of strategies for helping students build**
> 2.3 **meaning** *(e.g., linking new ideas to familiar ideas; making connections to student experiences; providing opportunities for active engagement, manipulation, and testing of ideas and materials)*

Direct Instruction

Siegfried Engelmann and Dr. Wesley Becker are among the researchers who proposed DIRECT INSTRUCTION, a teaching method that emphasizes well-developed and carefully planned lessons with small learning increments. It assumes that learning outcomes are improved through clear instruction that eliminates misinterpretations. Their approach is currently used by thousands of schools. It recommends that teacher creativity and autonomy be replaced by a willingness to follow certain carefully prescribed instructional practices. At the same time, it encourages hard work, dedication, and commitment to students. It demands that teachers adopt and internalize the belief that all students, if properly taught, can learn.

DIRECT INSTRUCTION: a teaching method that emphasizes well-developed and carefully planned lessons with small learning increments

Discovery Learning

Beginning at birth, DISCOVERY LEARNING is a normal part of growing-up, and this naturally occurring phenomenon can be used to improve classroom outcomes. Discovery learning is based upon inquiry and has been a factor in most human advances. For example, Rousseau constantly questioned his world, particularly the philosophies and theories that were commonly accepted. Dewey, himself a great discoverer, wrote, "There is an intimate and necessary relation between the processes of actual experience and education." Piaget, Bruner, and Papert have all recommended this teaching method.

In discovery learning, students solve problems by using their own experience and prior knowledge to determine what truths can be learned. Bruner wrote "Emphasis on discovery in learning has precisely the effect on the learner of leading him to a constructionist, to organize what he is encountering in a manner not only designed to discover regularity and relatedness, but also to avoid the kind of information drift that fails to keep account of the uses to which information might have to be put."

DISCOVERY LEARNING: a learning technique that involves students solving problems by using their own experience and prior knowledge to determine what truths can be learned

Whole Group Discussion

Whole group discussion can be used in a variety of settings, but the most common is in the discussion of an assignment. With this strategy, learning is peer-based; thus, students gain a different perspective on the topic, while also learning to respect the ideas of others. One obstacle to this teaching method is that the same students tend to participate or not participate each time. However, with proper teacher guidance during this activity, whole group discussions are highly valuable.

Case Method Learning

Disseminating and integrating knowledge can be achieved effectively by providing opportunities for students to apply what they learn in the classroom to real-life experiences. The CASE METHOD is an instructional strategy that engages students in active discussion about issues and problems of practical application. It can highlight fundamental dilemmas or critical issues and provide a format for

CASE METHOD: an instructional strategy that engages students in active discussion about issues and problems of practical application

role-playing of ambiguous or controversial scenarios. A successful class discussion involves planning on the part of the instructor and preparation on the part of the students. Instructors should communicate this commitment to the students on the first day of class by clearly articulating course expectations. Just as the instructor carefully plans the learning experience, the students must comprehend the assigned reading and show up for class on time, ready to learn.

Concept Mapping

Concept mapping is a common tool used by teachers in various disciplines, and many kinds of maps have been developed for this purpose. They are useful devices, but each teacher must determine which is appropriate for use in his or her own classroom. Following is a common map that is used in writing courses:

Concept Mapping

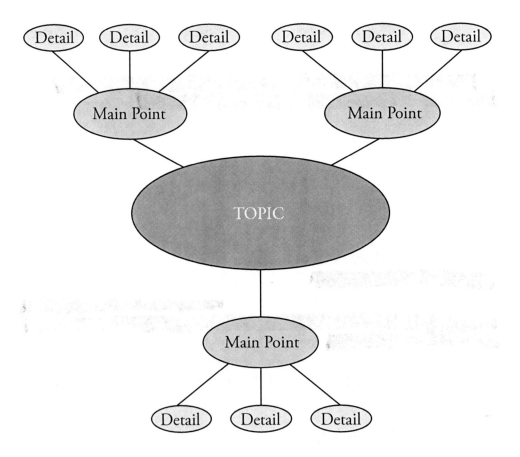

Inquiry

All learning begins with the student. What children know and what they want to learn are not just constraints on what can be taught; they are the very foundations for learning.

DEWEY'S PRIMARY INTERESTS OF THE CHILD
The child's instinctive desire to discover things
In conversation, the propensity children have to communicate
In construction, their delight in making things
Their gifts of artistic expression

Questioning

Questioning is a teaching strategy as old as Socrates. In fact, the Socratic method is a well-known form of questioning. It is important for the teacher to deliberately and carefully plan in order to lead students in critical thinking.

Play

There are so many educational games available that the most difficult task is choosing which will fit into a classroom. Some are electronic, some are board games, and some are designed to be played individually. Even in those cases, a review of the results by the entire classroom can be a useful learning experience.

Learning Centers

LEARNING CENTERS are extremely important in flexible classrooms. In this setup, students have some time during which they can choose their own activity. Under a teacher's guidance, learners can even take out-of-class time for creating the centers, collecting the necessary items, and then setting up the area.

LEARNING CENTERS: an instructional method where students have time during which they can choose their own activity

Small Group Work

Today's classrooms are usually diverse, and small group work is vital. Children can be grouped according to their developmental level. If the small groups themselves are diverse, this gives students who are struggling an opportunity to learn from students who are already proficient. The better-prepared student will learn from becoming a resource for the weaker student. In turn, the weaker student may sometimes be more likely to accept help from another student. This frees the teacher to perform other tasks.

Revisiting

Revisiting should occur during and at the end of a unit and at the end of a semester. This gives students more than one opportunity to grasp principles and skills and to integrate them.

Reflection

Teaching can move along so rapidly that students may fail to incorporate what they've learned. They may also lack the time to think about what they can bring to the topic. Providing time for reflection and guiding students in developing these tools is a wise teaching method.

Projects

Seeing a unit as a project is also very useful. It opens the door to approaching learning as multitasking. For example, in a unit on birds, not only will students learn about birds, they will have an opportunity to observe them, they can try their hands at drawing them, and they can learn to differentiate one from the other. It's easy to see how a lifetime interest in birdwatching can take root from such a project. This is more effective than simply reading and talking about the topic.

SKILL 2.4 **Demonstrating knowledge of factors that influence student learning** *(e.g., prior knowledge and experience, developmental readiness, health, economic conditions, teachers' classroom practices, family circumstances, community environment)* **and how to provide learning experiences that are responsive to students' varied experiences, characteristics, and needs**

Outside Effects on Student Experience

Students absorb the culture and social environment around them. Often, they do so without deciphering the contextual meaning of the experiences. When provided with diverse cultural contexts, students are able to adapt and incorporate multiple meanings from cultural cues vastly different from their own. SOCIO-CULTURAL FACTORS have a definitive impact on a students' psychological, emotional, affective, and physiological development. They also affect a student's academic learning and future achievements.

SOCIO-CULTURAL FACTORS: the influences of the culture and social environment around the students

A complex experience

The educational experience for most students is complex. There are diverse, interlocking meanings and inferences. If one aspect of the complexity is altered, it affects other aspects. This, in turn, may impact how a student or teacher views a learning experience. Today's schools must be prepared to work with students who bring complex understandings, interpretations, and nuances. This diversity can provide many barriers to communication and learning, which, if not overcome, could impede student learning.

Physical health

In addition, health conditions affect student learning. To the extent possible, the teacher needs to know about any health issues that affect a student's performance and make accommodation for it in the classroom. Another concern is the students' food and clothing allowances. It is possible that a family is living in such poverty that the child may not have sufficient food or clothing. A teacher should call these matters to the attention of administrators and follow through to make sure the child is receiving appropriate attention.

Mental health

To learn and develop to their peak ability, students must have healthy self-images and self-worth. Students could reduce their focus on education when they are dealing with personal issues such as when they feel bullied or isolated. When a student is attending school from a homeless shelter or is lost in the middle of a parent's divorce, they are also less likely to prioritize school.

Health classes

Most schools will offer health classes that address issues including:

- Sexuality
- Self-image
- Peer pressure
- Nutrition

- Wellness
- Gang activity
- Drug engagement
- Other relevant teen experiences

In most districts, as part of a well-rounded core curriculum, students are required to take a health class. By setting this mandate, the school and district ensure that students are exposed to issues that directly affect them. In addition, by educating students in such issues, officials seek to prevent students from engaging in negative activities. Even though one health class is rarely enough to effectively address the multiplicity of such issues, in today's era of tight school budgets and financial issues, this is not likely to change.

Neglected and Abused Students

Unfortunately, many students are exposed to abuse and dangerous situations. Child abuse may manifest itself as a phenomenon known as chronic shock syndrome. The individual's nervous system becomes geared up to handle the extra flow of hormones and electrical impulses accompanying the fight or flight reaction. Each time the abuse happens, this occurs and creates a shift in the biology of the brain and allied systems. Essentially, the victim becomes allergic (hypersensitized) to stress of the kind that prevailed during the period of abuse. Recent research indicates such a shift is reflected in brain chemistry and structural changes and may last a lifetime.

Abused vs. neglected

The abused child differs from the neglected one. While the neglected child suffers from understimulation, the abused one suffers from overstimulation. The neglected child may be:

- Withdrawn

- Quiet

- Almost sedate

In contrast, the abused child may be:

- Angry

- Energetic

- Rebellious

- Aggressive

- Hard to control

In each case, the environment of abuse or neglect shapes the behavior of the child away from home. Often, out of reflex, the child will flinch when seeming to anticipate a blow, or may be unable to accept or understand healthy attention directed to him or her. To sense what the child's feelings and experiences may be, the teacher merely needs to watch the child's reaction to a loud noise, someone's aggression, or the response when offered some companionship by another child.

Signs of physical abuse

Obvious signs of physical abuse are marks from:

- Hand

- Fist

- Belt

- Coat hanger

- Kitchen utensil

- Extension cord

- Any other imaginable implement for striking and inflicting pain on a child

To effectively help the child, the suspicion has to be backed up with hard evidence. Unusual marks in geometric shapes may indicate the presence of an implement for spanking such as a spoon, homemade paddle, extension cord, or coat hanger. Marks on the arms and legs may indicate being whipped there. Teachers should always be suspicious about bruises.

Evaluating injuries

Bruises on the neck and face usually do not come from a child tripping and falling. Rather, they are usually the result of intentional hitting—and even choking. Noting the sizes and shapes of bruises and using simple imagination may reveal the source of the injury. The observer should notice whether the bruise has reddened areas, indicating ruptured capillaries, or is uniformly colored but shaded a darker color toward the perimeter. The rupture of capillaries indicates a strong hit, while the shaded bruise indicates a softer compression.

The educator who discovers any of these conditions should start with a reasonable suspicion that abuse is occuring. They would then gather specific indicators and firm evidence, not only for the sake of the child, but also when the report is scruitinized. Take note of the size of the injury, and describe it in concrete terms. For instance, describe a bruise as being the size of a quarter or an orange.

Signs of neglect

When identifying the neglected child, teachers can look for signs of malnourishment. For instance, a child may gorge at lunch, yet still be thin and underweight. This student may be quiet and shy, shabbily groomed, and unconcerned about his or her appearance. Poor nutrition at home may result in an unusually high number of colds. It is of utmost importance to guarantee that immunizations are current, as they probably have been overlooked. Children who are neglected are usually not very social, may isolate themselves, and may not respond to invitations to join other children in play. These are not necessarily signs of neglect since any child can display these traits from time to time. However, if they are accompanied by a persistant social anxiety, this may indicate that something is happening at home.

Signs of sexual abuse

In cases of sexual abuse the most blatant warning sign is the oversexualization of the child. These children become interested in sexually related matters long before his or her developmental stage would predict. The child may be seen to quietly masturbate at prepubescent ages and may even act out sexually with other children of their own age. If a child suddenly begins to engage in promiscuous sexual behavior, this is a sign that he or she is being molested. Sexual abuse of children is widespread and takes many forms. Kissing episodes by a parent or other adult, when out of normal context, are just as damaging as more overt forms of contact. The sexualized leer or stare by a perverted parent or adult can also be damaging. Deal with all situations of sexual abuse with extreme care. It is advised to wait for a trained professional who knows the methodology. Incorrectly conducted information gathering can be detrimental to a prosecution.

A Successful Environment

The student's capacity and potential for academic success is a product of his or her ability and the total environment, which is composed of the classroom and school system, home and family, and neighborhood and community. All of these segments are interrelated and can be supportive, one of the other, or divisive, one against the other. As a matter of course, the teacher will become familiar with all aspects of the system, the school, and the classroom. This would include not only processes and protocols but also the availability of resources provided to meet the academic, health, and welfare needs of students. But it is incumbent upon the teacher to look beyond the boundaries of the school system to identify additional resources as well as issues and situations that will effect (directly or indirectly) a student's ability to succeed in the classroom.

Resources for success

Initial contacts for resources outside of the school system will usually come from within the system itself—from administration, teacher organizations, department heads, and other colleagues. Resources can include libraries, museums, zoos, planetariums, etc. Teachers can obtain materials, media, speakers, and presenters from:

- Nonprofit organizations

- Social clubs

- Societies

- Civic organizations

- Community outreach programs of private businesses, corporations, and governmental agencies

Departments of social services can provide background and program information relevant to social issues, which may be impacting individual students. In turn, this can be a resource for classroom instruction regarding life skills, at-risk behaviors, and related areas.

The student's capacity and potential for academic success within the overall educational experience are products of her or his total environment: classroom and school system; home and family; neighborhood and community in general. All of these segments are interrelated and can be supportive, one of the other, or divisive, one against the other. As a matter of course, the teacher will become familiar with all aspects of the system, the school, and the classroom pertinent to the students' educational experience. This would include not only process and protocols but also the availability of resources provided to meet the academic, health, and welfare needs of students. It is incumbent upon the teacher to look beyond the boundaries of the school system to identify additional resources, as well as issues and situations, that will affect (directly or indirectly) a student's ability to succeed in the classroom.

> *It is incumbent upon the teacher to look beyond the boundaries of the school system to identify additional resources, as well as issues and situations, that will affect (directly or indirectly) a student's ability to succeed in the classroom.*

Examples of Issues or Situations

Students from multicultural backgrounds
Curriculum objectives and instructional strategies may be inappropriate and unsuccessful when presented in a single format that relies on the student's understanding and acceptance of the values and common attributes of a specific culture that is not his or her own.

Parental and family influences
Attitude, resources, and encouragement available in the home environment may contribute to a student's success or failure at school.

Family income level
Families with higher incomes are able to provide increased opportunities for students. Students from lower-income families will need to depend on the resources available from the school system and the community. These resources should be orchestrated by the classroom teacher in cooperation with school administrators and educational advocates in the community.

Family educational level
Family members with higher levels of education often serve as models for students and have high expectations for academic success. And families with specific aspirations for children (often regardless of their own educational background) encourage students to achieve academic success and are most often active participants in the process.

Family stability level

A family in crisis (caused by economic difficulties, divorce, substance abuse, physical abuse, etc.) creates a negative environment that may have a profound impact on all aspects of a student's life and particularly his or her ability to function academically. The situation may require professional intervention. It is often the classroom teacher who will recognize a family in crisis and instigate an intervention by reporting this to school or civil authorities.

Regardless of the positive or negative impacts on the student's education from outside sources, it is the teacher's responsibility to ensure that all students in the classroom have an equal opportunity for academic success.

Regardless of the positive or negative impacts on the student's education from outside sources, it is the teacher's responsibility to ensure that all students in the classroom have an equal opportunity for academic success. This begins with the teacher's statement of high expectations for every student and develops through planning, delivery, and evaluation of instruction that provides for inclusion and ensures that all students have equal access to the resources necessary for successful acquisition of the academic skills being taught and measured in the classroom.

Homogeneous Grouping

Classroom climate can have a significant influence on successful student learning. Interactions among and relationships between students are an important factor of a positive classroom climate. In past classroom practices, it was common for students to be grouped according to ability. This practice is sometimes referred to as tracking or HOMOGENOUS GROUPING. For example, students who found math challenging would be in the "low" math group, average math students would be in the "grade-level" math group, and excelling math learners would make up the "advanced" group.

HOMOGENOUS GROUPING: a classroom organizational concept where students are grouped according to ability

Drawbacks

This type of grouping can lead to problems with students' self-concept and motivation in class. Students who found themselves in the low group would feel ashamed or stupid. At the same time, students in the advanced group may feel superior and boast of their successes in front of other students, and they may feel stressed over needing to perform. In summary, this type of grouping typically leads to a combination of feelings including resentment, stress, inferiority, and failure—feelings that do not enhance learning.

Homogenous grouping typically leads to a combination of feelings including resentment, stress, inferiority, and failure—feelings that do not enhance learning.

HETEROGENEOUS GROUPING: a classroom organizational concept where students are grouped according to mixed ability

Heterogeneous Grouping

It's not that teachers can never group students by ability. Used once in a while, this method does allow students to work at a comfortable level. However, teachers often find that HETEROGENEOUS GROUPING (grouping by mixed abilities) allows all students to feel successful. In mixed groups, students can learn from more advanced students, while advanced students can still be provided with opportunities to excel in an activity.

Cooperative learning is an excellent setting for heterogeneous groups as students work together to solve problems or complete activities while benefitting from all learning abilities. In this setting, all students feel they are successful in their learning, and feelings of confidence, friendship, and achievement are experienced.

> *Cooperative learning is an excellent setting for heterogeneous groups as students work together to solve problems or complete activities while benefitting from all learning abilities.*

SKILL 2.5 **Identifying strategies for encouraging students to assume responsibility for shaping their learning tasks and outcomes**

MOTIVATION is an internal state that activates, guides, and sustains behavior. Research in educational psychology describes motivation as the volition or will that students bring to a task, their level of interest and intrinsic persistence, the personally held goals that guide their behavior, and their belief about the causes of their success or failure.

> **MOTIVATION:** an internal state that activates, guides, and sustains behavior

Motivational Theories

A form of attribution theory developed by Bernard Weiner (2000) describes how students' beliefs about the causes of academic success or failure affect their emotions and motivations: "Interpersonal and intrapersonal theories of motivation from an attributional perspective" (*Educational Psychology Review, 12*, pp. 1–14). For example, when students attribute failure to lack of ability, and ability is perceived as uncontrollable, they experience the emotions of shame and embarrassment and consequently decrease effort and show poorer performance. In contrast, when students attribute failure to lack of effort, and effort is perceived as controllable, they experience the emotion of guilt and consequently increase effort and show improved performance.

> **MASTERY GOALS:** characterized by students who strive to increase their ability and knowledge

Learners' goals in motivational theories

Motivational theories also explain how learners' goals affect the way they engage in academic tasks. Those who have MASTERY GOALS strive to increase their ability and knowledge. Those who have PERFORMANCE APPROACH GOALS strive for high grades and seek opportunities to demonstrate their abilities. Those who have PERFORMANCE AVOIDANCE GOALS are driven by fear of failure and avoid situations where their abilities are exposed. Research has found that mastery goals are associated with many positive outcomes such as persistence in the face of failure,

> **PERFORMANCE APPROACH GOALS:** characterized by students who strive for high grades and seek opportunities to demonstrate their abilities

> **PERFORMANCE AVOIDANCE GOALS:** characterized by students who are driven by fear of failure and avoid situations where their abilities are exposed

preference for challenging tasks, creativity, and intrinsic motivation. Performance avoidance goals are associated with negative outcomes such as poor concentration while studying, disorganized studying, less self-regulation, shallow information processing, and test anxiety. Performance approach goals are associated with positive outcomes and some negative outcomes such as an unwillingness to seek help and shallow information processing.

Applied behavior analysis is effective in a range of educational settings and is a set of techniques based on the behavioral principles of operant conditioning. For example, teachers can improve student behavior by systematically rewarding students who follow classroom rules with praise, stars, or tokens. These strategies are known as EXTRINSIC MOTIVATORS. Despite the demonstrated efficacy of awards in changing behavior, their use in education has been criticized by proponents of self-determination theory, who claim that praise and other rewards undermine intrinsic motivation. In addition, some educators argue that extrinsic motivation is not typically an effective strategy to build intrinsic motivation.

> **EXTRINSIC MOTIVATORS:** strategies that are characterized by motivating students through utilizing rewards for good behavior

Affecting intrinsic motivation

In fact, there is evidence that tangible rewards decrease intrinsic motivation in specific situations, such as when the student already has a high level of intrinsic motivation to perform the goal behavior. Results showing detrimental effects are counterbalanced by evidence that, in other situations, such as when rewards are given for attaining a gradually increasing standard of performance, rewards enhance intrinsic motivation.

> **SKILL 2.6** Demonstrating knowledge of how particular instructional methods and procedures, including the use of technology, can be expected to influence learning processes and outcomes

See Skill 2.3 for a discussion of instructional methods and procedure

See Skills 6.5 and 9.8 for a discussion of the use of technology

COMPETENCY 3

UNDERSTAND STUDENT DIVERSITY AND HOW TO PROVIDE INSTRUCTIONAL OPPORTUNITIES THAT MEET THE NEEDS OF STUDENTS WITH DIVERSE BACKGROUNDS AND EXCEPTIONALITIES AND PROMOTE ALL STUDENTS' LEARNING AND ACHIEVEMENT

SKILL Demonstrating knowledge of differences in approaches to learning
3.1 and performance *(e.g., variation in learning styles and preferred performance modes, multiple intelligences)* **and how to design instruction that is responsive to student needs and that uses student strengths to promote learning**

See Skill 1.2 for a discussion on developmental variation and instruction

---

SKILL Applying knowledge of areas of exceptionality *(e.g., learning*
3.2 *disabilities, perceptual difficulties, special physical or mental challenges, gifts, talents)* **and strategies for promoting learning for students with exceptionalities, including knowing when and how to access appropriate services and resources to meet student needs**

In student learning, there are many areas of exceptionalities. These areas can include students who are challenged, talented and gifted (TAG), and/or emotionally stressed or abused.

Students with Learning Disabilities

Teachers must be able to identify students with disabilities while maintaining their right to privacy. Often, students and their parents may be aware of a particular disability; however, they will not want peers or even teachers to know. Some disabilities necessitate special school care or medical attention by nurses or counseling staff. In these cases, administrators and teachers are often notified. Again, confidentiality and caution must be maintained.

There is significant disagreement over the term "disability," itself. Many people argue that it suggests a defect in a person's character. While disabilities can be physical, there are also learning disabilities, which can be related to an individual's ability to learn or communicate.

The term "students with disabilities" is quite broad; thus, there are few common characteristics among students with disabilities. In a generic sense, most disabilities hamper an individual's development or his or her ability to perform specific actions. For example, any degree of deafness will negatively affect auditory development; people with multiple sclerosis may have trouble with muscle function; and those who have Attention Deficit Hyperactivity Disorder (ADHD) may have trouble with concentration. It is important to remember that students with disabilities in one (or multiple) area(s) can still be highly functioning in other domains. In fact, even students with specific disabilities may not have all the possible challenges of that particular disability.

> The term "students with disabilities" is quite broad; thus, there are few common characteristics among students with disabilities. In a generic sense, most disabilities hamper an individual's development or his/her ability to perform specific actions.

Addressing disabled students' needs

Some disabilities may be obvious, particularly those that are physical. In such cases physical or behavioral abnormalities may be noticed by teachers and peers. Therefore, teachers must notice, correct, and reduce or eliminate teasing or bullying.

> **INDIVIDUAL EDUCATION PLAN (IEP):** a plan that provides an academic framework for a student with a disability

An INDIVIDUAL EDUCATION PLAN (IEP) provides an academic framework for a student with a disability. The IEP is developed by a team of educational professionals and is a tool by which teachers can ensure that a student diagnosed with a particular disability can maximize his or her potential.

Educators have become increasingly alert for and attentive to students with learning disabilities. These may include auditory or visual processing disabilities, attention deficit hyperactivity disorder, autism, and others. While educators and researchers are sensitive to all disabilities, the field has seen autism skyrocket among young children. This condition usually presents itself within the first three years of a child's life and hinders normal communication and social interactive behavior.

Emotional Stress and Abuse

Because all children experience stressful periods within their lives from time to time, all students may demonstrate some behaviors that indicate emotional distress. Emotionally healthy students can maintain control of their own behavior even during stressful times. The difference between typical stress-response behavior and severe emotional distress is determined by the frequency, duration, and intensity of stress-responsive behavior.

Signs of emotional distress

Lying, stealing, and fighting are maladaptive behaviors that any children may exhibit occasionally; however, if a child lies, steals, or fights regularly or blatantly, then these behaviors may be indicative of emotional distress. Lying can be especially common among young children who do so to avoid punishment or as a means to make themselves feel more important. As they move out of early childhood, lying can be a signal that children are feeling insecure. If feelings of insecurity escalate, lying may become habitual or obvious and that may indicate that the child is seeking attention because of emotional distress. Fighting, especially among siblings, is a common occurrence. However, if a child fights constantly, is unduly aggressive, or is belligerent toward others on a long-term basis, teachers and parents need to consider the possibility of emotional problems.

It is imperative that teachers are able to identify when children need help with their behavior. Therefore, educators must constantly monitor student behaviors; it is through actions that children will indicate that they need and/or want help. Repeatedly breaking established rules or destroying property can signify that a student is losing control. Other signs that a child needs help may include frequent bouts of crying, a quarrelsome attitude, and constant complaints about school, friends, or life in general. Any time a child's disposition, attitude, or habits change significantly, teachers and parents must seriously consider emotional difficulties.

> It is imperative that teachers are able to identify when children need help with their behavior. Therefore, educators must constantly monitor student behaviors; it is through actions that children will indicate that they need and/or want help.

Addressing emotionally distressed students

Classroom teachers have many safe and helpful interventions to assist them with students who are suffering serious emotional disturbances. First, the teacher must communicate the nature and extent of the suspected issues. Next, the school involves other professionals and parents/guardians in order to provide an appropriate safety net for the intervention. This is done unless the parents/guardians are suspected as the source of abuse. Finally, two-way communication constantly flows between the home and school, on a daily basis if necessary, to ensure that the student has a successful transition back to appropriate thoughts and behaviors.

By establishing environments that promote appropriate behavior for all students, teachers can reduce negative behaviors in the classroom. First, clear rules must be established and should include the understanding that students are to have respect for one another. If necessary, classmates may need to be informed of a students' special needs so they can give due consideration. For instance, if a student is blind, the teacher will need to explain the disability and specify that students keep the room in order at all times so that their classmate can navigate.

Behavior modification programs

For any student who might show emotional or behavioral disorders, a BEHAVIOR MODIFICATION PROGRAM is usually effective. Severe disorders may require that on a regular basis a school psychologist, guidance counselor, or behavior specialist is directly involved with the student and provides counseling and therapy. Frequently such interventions also involve the student's family. If deviant behavior does occur, the teacher should have a plan of action to difuse the situation and protect the student and other individuals. Such a plan could include a safe and secure time-out place where the student can go to regain self-control.

BEHAVIOR MODIFICATION PROGRAM: a course of action designed to help a student deal with emotional or behavioral disorders

Neurotic Disorders

Emotional disorders can escalate so severely that the child's well-being is threatened. Teachers and parents must recognize the signs of severe emotional stress, which may become detrimental to the child and others. During childhood, of the various forms of emotional disorders, neurotic disorders are the second most common group. Physical symptoms of NEUROSES include:

NEUROSIS: a psychological disorder that is characterized by general distress

- Extreme or ongoing anxiety
- Overdependence
- Social isolation
- Sleep problems

- Nausea
- Abdominal pain
- Diarrhea
- Headaches

Children may also have irrational fears of particular objects or situations or become consumed with obsessions, thoughts, or ideas. One of the most serious neuroses is depression. Signs that a child is depressed include:

- Ongoing sadness
- Crying
- Lack of interest in people or activities
- Eating and sleep disorders
- Talking about wanting to be dead

Teachers and other adults must listen to what the child is saying and should take these verbal expressions very seriously. Many school tragedies, including Columbine, CO, Jonesboro, AR, and Lake Worth, FL, may have been prevented if the signs of emotional issues had been recognized and treated.

Psychotic Disorders

Even more serious than neurosis is PSYCHOSIS, which is characterized by a loss of contact with reality. Psychosis is rare in childhood, but when it does occur, it is often difficult to diagnose. One fairly constant sign is failure to make normal emotional contact with other people. With schizophrenia, a common psychosis of childhood, the individual deliberately escapes from reality and withdraws from relationships with others. This disorder can be described as a person having contact with others, but through a curtain. Schizophrenia is more common in boys than in girls, and a major sign is a habitually flat or habitually agitated facial expression. Children suffering from schizophrenia are occasionally mute, but at times they talk incessantly using bizarre words in ways that make no sense. In a vicious cycle, their incoherent speech contributes to their frustration, and this compounds their fears and preoccupation.

> **PSYCHOSIS:** a psychological disorder that is characterized by a loss of contact with reality

Early Infantile Autism

The cause of EARLY INFANTILE AUTISM is unknown. In the past, some psychiatrists speculated that these children did not develop normally due to a lack of parental warmth. This has been dismissed as unlikely because the incidence of autism in families is usually limited to one child. While there are no scientific confirmations, some theorize that the disorder may be caused by metabolic or chromosomal defects.

> **EARLY INFANTILE AUTISM:** a disorder that is characterized by impaired social interaction and communication

Signs of early infantile autism

Early infantile autism may occur as early as the fourth month of life and may present itself as an infant lying apathetically and oblivious in the crib. In other cases, the baby appears to develop at a normal pace throughout infancy only to have the symptoms appear without warning at about eighteen months of age. Due to the nature of the symptoms, autistic children are often misdiagnosed as mentally retarded, deaf-mute, or organically brain-damaged. With this disorder as well, boys are twice as likely as girls to be diagnosed.

According to many psychologists who have been involved with treating autistic children, it seems that these children have built a wall between themselves and everyone else, including their families, and even their parents. They do not make eye contact with others and do not even appear to hear the voices of those who speak to them. They cannot empathize with others and have no ability to appreciate humor.

Autistic children usually have language disturbances. One-third never develop any speech; however, they may grunt or whine. Others may repeat the same word or phrase over and over or "parrot" what someone else has said. They often lack inner-language and cannot play by themselves above a primitive, sensory-motor level.

Frequently, autistic children will develop a preoccupation with objects; this appears to fill the void left by the absence of interpersonal relationships. They become compulsive about the arrangements of objects and often engage in simple, repetitive physical activities with objects for long periods of time. If these activities are interrupted, they may react with fear or rage. Others remain motionless for hours each day sometimes moving only their eyes or hands.

Socialization of autistic children

The developmental abilities of autistic children varies greatly. On intelligence tests they may score from severely subnormal to high average. Some exhibit astonishing abilities in isolated skill areas; for instance, one child may memorize volumes of material, another could sing beautifully, and a third could perform complicated mathematical problems. This phenomenon was popularized by the movie *Rain Man*.

The prognosis for autistic children is painfully discouraging. Only about five percent of autistic children become socially well-adjusted in adulthood. Another twenty percent make fair social adjustments. The remaining seventy-five percent are socially incapacitated and must be supervised for the duration of their lives.

Treatment may include outpatient psychotherapy, drugs, or long-term treatment in a residential center; however, for the long term, neither the presence nor absence of treatment appears to make a difference.

Behaviors Indicating Drug/Alcohol Abuse

Legally, the use of any illicit substance by a minor, including alcohol, is automatically considered abuse. This issue must be tackled by educators because illegal substances hamper and reduce social and academic functioning. The adage "Pot makes a smart kid average and an average kid dumb" is quite accurate with almost every controlled substance. There exist not a few families where substance abuse, such as pot smoking, is a known habit of the parents. Parental use hampers national drug and alcohol prevention efforts because children may start their dependency by stealing from parents. In addition, parental use negates the message that substance abuse is wrong.

Stages of substance abuse

Substance abuse, regardless of the substance, follows a pattern of withdrawal, blackouts, and tolerance. WITHDRAWAL occurs when the substance is removed from the blood stream and a metabolic craving is accompanied by:

- Sweating
- Nausea
- Dizziness
- Elevated blood pressure
- Seizures
- Death (in rare instances)

During the BLACKOUT stage an individual experiences serious physical symptoms but later doesn't remember anything of his or her actions. The anesthetized mind has eliminated conscious wakeful activity, functioning mainly on instinct. TOLERANCE is the final stage and changes over the course of the disease, increasing in the early stages and decreasing in the late chronic stage.

Dangers of unaddressed substance abuse

In the school setting, hard signs of dependency are rare and when seen, they must be considered very serious. Due to the danger of long-term injury or fatality, substance ingestion must be treated immediately by medical staff. Fatalities can occur in cases of seizures due to withdrawal, overdoses due to mixed substances, or overuse of a single substance including overdoses with alcohol alone. Never, under any circumstances, attempt to treat, protect, tolerate, or negotiate with a student who is showing signs of a physical crisis. It is advisable to find out the protocol for a particular school or district; however, most schools require the student to be isolated until they are removed from the school center by EMS or police.

Abuse vs. dependency

While there is a difference between abuse and dependency, for this age group they can be viewed in the same light. This is particularly true because for young people, addiction occurs at a high rate, rapidly after first use, and sometimes after only a few tries. Abuse is a lesser degree of involvement with substances; usually implying the person is not physically addicted. They may have just as many "soft signs" of involvement but lack true addiction. Dependency indicates a true physical addiction, characterized by several hard signs, some of which are less likely to be seen in a school setting. When deprived of the substance, the person may experience withdrawal symptoms, blackouts, tolerance, irresponsibility, and illogical behavior. Soft signs include declines in functioning in all domains including social and occupational, mental and emotional, and spiritual life.

WITHDRAWAL: a stage of substance abuse when substance is removed from the blood stream and a metabolic craving is accompanied by sweating, nausea, dizziness, elevated blood pressure, seizures, and, in rare instances, death

BLACKOUT: a stage of substance abuse when an individual experiences serious physical symptoms but later doesn't remember anything of his or her actions

TOLERANCE: the final stage of substance abuse characterized by a resistance to the effects of the substance

In the school setting, hard signs of dependency are rare and when seen, they must be considered very serious.

Social signs of substance abuse

Social decline is one of the signs of drug or alcohol abuse. In being acquainted with all students, educators will notice personality changes in any student. Characteristically, social withdrawal is first noticed when the student fails to say hello, avoids being near teachers, seems evasive or sneaky, and associates with a different, less academically focused, group of friends. Obviously, association with known substance abusers is almost always a warning sign. Adults must not accept the explanation that the suspected abuser is just being friends with the known abuser, or that the suspected abuser has other kinds of friends. There is a sharp demarcation between youth who abuse substances and those who do not.

The abuser will progressively disregard their appearance, showing up unclean, unkempt, and disheveled. Actual style of fashion may change to more radical trends such as nose rings, body piercings, and tattoos. Such fashion choices are used by nonabusing youth and, on their own, are not an indication of substance abuse. The socially impaired substance abuser will frequently be late for school, classes, and other appointments. The abuser seeks less and less satisfaction from traditional social activities such as school athletics, rallies, plays, student government, and after-school programs. In contrast, some abusers hide behind conformity, going to great pains to appear normal; these may be some of the most seriously impaired of all.

Mental/emotional signs of substance abuse

Mental and emotional impairments manifest as the addiction deepens. Academic indicators include declining school performance, standardized test scores, and interest in school. In addition, students with addictions may:

- Respond more slowly to prompts, sharp noises, or sudden actions

- Show emotional flattening and personality changes

- Have vacant expressions, hyperactivity, depression, psychosis, and a lack of motivation

- Discuss or attempt suicide

Students already having emotional problems (about three to six percent of any given population of youth) are more vulnerable to using drugs and alcohol than students who are well adjusted. Caution is recommended when educators question teenagers to ascertain drug and alcohol abuse. Students might have another psychiatric illness of which the school is not aware. They may appear to be high or intoxicated; but instead, they may be reacting to medications. Their odd behavior may be due to the psychiatric illness itself, not substance abuse. Thus, whenever possible, it is helpful to know a student's history.

Spiritual signs of substance abuse

The last step is spiritual decline, an even less obvious manifestation than the other signs of substance abuse. The broadest definition of SPIRITUALITY is the youth's existential relationship to the greater world around him or her. Attitudes of respect, humility, wonder, and affection indicate a person who has a sense of relationship to something greater. Attitudes of contempt, pride, ignorance, and arrogance indicate one who lacks an awareness of the enormity of existence. More specifically, a previously religious or reverent student may suddenly become blatantly disrespectful of organized religion. The inappropriate use of the cross or other religious symbol may also indicate spiritual decline.

> **SPIRITUALITY:** the youth's existential relationship to the greater world around him or her

Reasons for substance abuse

Although most students understand the dangers of drug and alcohol use, hard-core users cannot resist involvement. They may disregard the dangers because their emotional pain is so high. In today's complex world, many factors lead to high levels of emotional pain, not the least of which is family and community breakdown. Today, the divorce rate is extremely high and approximately one half of families are blended. Children are transported from parent to parent, often against their own wishes, and ex-spouses may retaliate against each other through children. Children from these families feel guilt, anger, and shame, feelings that can be dangerous as they usually remain unresolved. Once considered relatively harmless to children, divorce is now being reevaluated and is now viewed as a serious challenge.

Other causes of emotional pain to students include:

- Social awkwardness
- Depression
- Undiagnosed and/or untreated mental illnesses
- Personality disorders
- Learning disabilities
- ADHD
- Conduct disorders
- Substance abuse and dependency in family members

The most common manifestation of emotional pain are parent–child issues, which include deficits in communication, authority, and respect between parent(s) and child(ren). An equally common signal of emotional issues is conduct disorders, a behavior set characterized by:

- Aggression
- Exploitation
- Violence
- Defiance
- Running away
- Truancy

- Disregard for the rights of others
- Animal cruelty
- Fire-setting
- Bed-wetting
- Juvenile arrest records
- ADHD
- Substance abuse

Dealing with Giftedness and Disabilities

When giftedness is observed, teachers should also concern themselves with ensuring that such children receive the attention they need and deserve so they can continue to learn and grow.

The list of possible disabilities is almost endless. When noticed, teachers might seek the help of specialists within their school to determine if further testing or intervention is needed.

SKILL 3.3 Demonstrating knowledge of the process of second-language acquisition and strategies for supporting learning for students whose first language is not English, including knowing when and how to access appropriate services and resources to meet student needs

---

One of the most important things to know about the differences between first language (L1) and second language (L2) acquisition is that people usually will master L1, but they will almost never be fully proficient in L2.

One of the most important things to know about the differences between first language (L1) and second language (L2) acquisition is that people usually will master L1, but they will almost never be fully proficient in L2. However, if children can be trained in L2 before the age of seven, their chances at full mastery will be much higher. Children learn languages with little effort, which is why they can be babbling during one year and speaking with complete, complex ideas just a few years later. It is important to know that language is innate, meaning that our brains are ready to learn a language from birth. Yet a lot of language learning is behavioral, meaning that children imitate adults' speech.

L2 Acquisition

L2 acquisition is much harder for adults. Multiple theories of L2 acquisition have been developed by researchers such as Jim Cummins. Cummins argues that there are two types of language that usually need to be acquired by students learning English as a second language: Basic Interpersonal Communication Skills (BICS) and Cognitive Academic Language Proficiency (CALP). BICS is general, everyday language used to communicate simple thoughts. In contrast, CALP is the more complex, academic language used in school. It is harder for students to acquire CALP, and many teachers mistakenly assume that students can learn complex academic concepts in English if they have already mastered BICS. The truth is that CALP takes much longer to master, and in some cases, particularly with little exposure in certain subjects, it may never be mastered.

Five principles of L2 aquisition

Another set of theories is based on Stephen Krashen's research in L2 acquisition. Most people understand his theories based on five principles:

1. The ACQUISITION-LEARNING HYPOTHESIS: This states that there is a difference between learning a language and acquiring it. Children "acquire" a first language easily—it's natural. But adults often have to "learn" a language through coursework, studying, and memorizing. One can acquire a second language, but often it requires more deliberate and natural interaction with that language.

2. The MONITOR HYPOTHESIS: This is when the learned language "monitors" the acquired language. In other words, this is when a person's "grammar check" kicks in and keeps awkward, incorrect language out of a person's L2 communication.

3. The NATURAL ORDER HYPOTHESIS: This suggests that the learning of grammatical structures is predictable and follows a "natural order."

4. The INPUT HYPOTHESIS: Some people call this "comprehensible input." This means that a language learner will learn best when the instruction or conversation is just above the learner's ability. That way, the learner has the foundation to understand most of the language, but will still have to figure out, often in context, what the more difficult elements mean.

5. The AFFECTIVE FILTER HYPOTHESIS: This suggests that people will learn a second language when they are relaxed, have high levels of motivation, and have a decent level of self-confidence.

English as a Second Language

Teaching students who are learning English as a second language poses some unique challenges, particularly in a standards-based environment. The key is realizing that no matter how little English a student knows, the teacher should teach with the student's developmental level in mind. This means that instruction should not be "dumbed-down" for ESOL students. Different approaches should be used, however, to ensure that these students get multiple opportunities to learn and practice English and still learn content.

ACQUISITION-LEARNING HYPOTHESIS: suggests that there is a difference between learning a language and acquiring it

MONITOR HYPOTHESIS: suggests that the learned language "monitors" the acquired language; a person's "grammar check" kicks in and keeps awkward, incorrect language out of a person's L2 communication

NATURAL ORDER HYPOTHESIS: suggests that the learning of grammatical structures is predictable and follows a "natural order"

INPUT HYPOTHESIS: suggests that a language learner will learn best when the instruction or conversation is just above the learner's ability

AFFECTIVE FILTER HYPOTHESIS: suggests that people will learn a second language when they are relaxed, have high levels of motivation, and have a decent level of self-confidence

Approaches to ESOL students

Many ESOL approaches are based on social learning methods. By being placed in mixed level groups or by being paired with a student of another ability level, students will get a chance to practice English in a natural, non-threatening environment. Students should not be pushed into these groups to use complex language or to experiment with words that are too difficult. They should simply get a chance to practice with simple words and phrases.

Additional accommodations for ESOL students

ESOL students may need additional accommodations with assessments, assignments, and projects. For example, teachers may find that written tests provide little to no information about a student's understanding of the content. Therefore, an oral test may be better suited for ESOL students. When students are somewhat comfortable and capable with written tests, a shortened test may actually be preferable; take note that they will need extra time to translate.

Most lay people believe that in high school and college, learning a language involves strictly drills, memorization, and tests. While this is a common method used (some people call it a structural, grammatical, or linguistic approach), it certainly does not work for all students.

Motivational approaches to ESOL students

There are many approaches that are noted for their motivational purposes. In a general sense, when teachers work to motivate students to learn a language, they do things to help reduce fear and to assist students in identifying with native speakers of the target language. A very common method is often called the functional approach. In this approach, the teacher focuses on communicative elements. For example, a first-grade ESOL teacher might help students learn phrases that will assist them in finding a restroom, asking for help on the playground, etc. Many functionally based adult ESOL programs help learners with travel-related phrases and words.

Total physical response

TOTAL PHYSICAL RESPONSE: a kinesthetic approach that combines language learning and physical movement

Another very common motivational approach is TOTAL PHYSICAL RESPONSE. This is a kinesthetic approach that combines language learning and physical movement. In essence, students learn new vocabulary and grammar by responding to verbal commands with physical motion. Some people say it is particularly effective because the physical actions create good brain connections with the words.

In general, the best methods do not treat students as if they have a language deficit. Rather, the best methods build upon what students already know, and they help to instill the target language as a communicative process rather than a list of vocabulary words that have to be memorized.

SKILL 3.4 Demonstrating knowledge of how to use technological resources to facilitate learning for students with diverse backgrounds, characteristics, needs, and abilities

See Skill 6.5 for a discussion of technology in the classroom

See Skill 9.8 for a discussion of uses of assistive technology for students with diverse backgrounds, needs, and abilities

---

SKILL 3.5 Demonstrating knowledge of the contributions, characteristics, and lifestyles of various groups in U.S. society; the government, history, language, and culture of Minnesota-based American Indian groups; and ways to provide learning experiences that reflect and are responsive to students' diverse social, cultural, and family backgrounds

See Skill 1.6

Minnesota-based Native American Groups

Native American cultures have made significant contributions to cultures of the Americas and the world. Student recognition of these profound contributions, which have become an integral part of American life, is critical. When students understand the contributions of individual cultures, they learn to respect members of the unique cultural groups that make up their state.

It is important that students learn about the Native American contributions in fields of politics, American democracy, government, language, medicine, math, science, agriculture, technology, art, architecture, food, and sports.

As part of the Minnesota curriculum, students must demonstrate that they are able to analyze the effect past and current treaties, agreements, and congressional acts have had on Minnesota-based Native Americans. Also, to obtain a teaching license in the state of Minnesota, beginning elementary and social science teachers must have knowledge of Minnesota Tribal government, history, and culture.

SKILL 3.6 Demonstrating knowledge of cultural and community diversity and norms; how to learn about and incorporate students' experiences, cultures, and community resources into instruction; and how to bring multiple perspectives to content-area instruction

Diversity in the classroom includes race, ethnicity, gender, and varying socioeconomic situations but also includes students who are physically or intellectually challenged or who have exceptionalities. All students must be included in the learning process and all students can contribute and add value to the learning process. Acceptance of diversity and any specific requirements necessary to aid individuals to accomplish on a par with classmates must be incorporated in lesson planning, teacher presentation, and classroom activities.

Often, students absorb the culture and social environment around them without deciphering contextual meaning of the experiences. When provided with a diversity of cultural contexts, students are able to adapt and incorporate multiple meanings from cultural cues that are vastly different from their own socioeconomic backgrounds. Sociocultural factors provide a definitive impact on a student's psychological, emotional, affective, and physiological development, along with a student's academic learning and future opportunities.

Effective teaching begins with teachers who can demonstrate sensitivity for diversity in teaching and in relationships within school communities.

Effective teaching begins with teachers who can demonstrate sensitivity for diversity in teaching and in relationships within school communities. The teacher must take the time to know each student as an individual and demonstrate a sincere interest in each student. For example, it is important to know the correct spelling and pronunciation of each student's name and any preference in how the student would like to be addressed.

Teachers must plan time for interaction in the classroom when they and the class can become familiar with each student's interests and experiences. This will help the teacher and the students avoid making assumptions based on any individual's background or appearance.

INCLUSION: involving everyone in classroom discussions

Encourage all students to respond to each other's questions and statements in the classroom. Be prepared to respond, appropriately, should any issue or question regarding diversity arise during classroom discussions or activities. If necessary, to promote or control discussion in the classroom the teacher should provide the students with specific guidelines (which are easy to understand and follow) defining the intended objectives and any restrictions. INCLUSION means involving everyone in classroom discussions. The teacher should allow the students to volunteer and then call on the more reluctant students to provide additional information or opinions. All opinions that are not derogatory in case or by nature are valid and should be reinforced by the teacher's approval.

Teachers should also continually make cultural connections that are relevant and empowering for all students and that communicate academic and behavioral expectations. Cultural sensitivity is communicated beyond the classroom with parents and community members to establish and maintain relationships.

Rules in the classroom that respect all students regardless of background can make inroads on the thinking of children who may come from bigoted families. For example, projects that relate to people they don't know, such as the victims of a hurricane, will offer them an experience of caring for someone who is suffering. Trips to nursing homes and taking cards or gifts can have a great impact on children of all ages.

Cultural sensitivity is communicated beyond the classroom with parents and community members to establish and maintain relationships.

> ## SKILL 3.7 Demonstrating knowledge of how to recognize and respond to negative attitudes regarding diversity, including but not limited to bias, discrimination, prejudice, and institutional or personal racism and sexism, and how to create a learning community in which differences among groups and individuals are valued and respected

The primary responsibility of the classroom teacher is to ensure that all aspects of the educational process, and all information necessary to master specified skills, are readily accessible to all students in the classroom. The teacher must actively promote inclusion and should devise presentations that address commonalities among heterogeneous groups. In the development of lesson plans and presentation formats, this should be evident both in the concept and in the language used (e.g., incorporating ideas and phrases that suggest "we" rather than "they" whenever possible).

The prescribed teaching material in a given subject area will usually provide an adequate format appropriate to the grade level and the diversity of a general student population. By using additional content and instructional aides that are thematically the same as the prescribed material, the teacher can usually assure that these will also be lesson appropriate. The teacher is the final arbiter regarding content, format, and presentation in the classroom, so he or she must exercise judgment when reviewing all classroom materials, lesson plans, presentations, and activities against set criteria. For example:

The teacher is the final arbiter regarding content, format, and presentation in the classroom.

- **Offensive:** Anything which might be considered derogatory regarding any individual or group. Any comment or material which is insensitive to any nationality, religion, culture, race, family structure, etc. Regardless of the composition of a particular classroom, negativism about any group harbors an acceptance of such negativism and contributes to a "them" versus "us" attitude.

- **Exclusive:** Anything which ignores or nullifies the needs, rights, or value of an individual or any group. Anything which stratifies society, placing some group or groups above others in significance.

- **Inappropriate:** Below or beyond the suitable comprehension level. Imprecise, inadequate for mastery of specific skills within the subject matter. Fails to provide accurately measurable skill acquisition.

SKILL 3.8 Recognizing the importance for teachers of a belief in all students' ability to learn at the highest levels and a commitment to persist in helping all students achieve success as learners

---

Academic Expectations

In a document prepared for the Southern Regional Education Board, titled *Strategies for Creating a Classroom Culture of High Expectations*, Myra Cloer Reynolds summarized the process necessary to meet stated educational objective when she wrote, "Motivation and classroom management skills are essential to creating and sustaining an environment of high expectations and improvement in today's schools."

In some school systems, very high expectations are placed on certain students and minimal expectations placed on others. Often, the result is predictable: students achieve as they are expected to achieve. A teacher is expected to provide the same standards of excellence in education for all students. This standard cannot be met or upheld unless the teacher has (and conveys) high expectations for all students.

Student expectations affecting performance

Considerable research has been done, over several decades, regarding student performance. Time and again, a direct correlation has been demonstrated between the teacher's expectations for a particular student and that student's academic performance. This may be unintended and subtle, but the effects are manifested and measurable.

> A direct correlation has been demonstrated between the teacher's expectations for a particular student and that student's academic performance.

For example, a teacher may not provide the fullest effort on behalf of the student when he or she has low expectations of success. And the student may "buy into" this evaluation of his or her potential, possibly becoming scholastically further burdened by low self-esteem. Other students, with more self-confidence in their own abilities, might still go along with this "free ride"—willing to do only what is expected of them and unwittingly allowing this disservice to hamper their academic progress.

Employing high expectations in the classroom

A teacher can convey high expectations to students in a variety of ways. Much has to do with the attitude of the teacher and positive interactions with the students—clearly stating expectations and reinforcing this at every opportunity.

METHODS FOR IMPLEMENTING HIGH EXPECTATIONS	
Notify the class of your high expectations for their academic success	Let students know that they can acquire all the skills in which you will be instructing them and that you take personal responsibility and pride in their success.
Speak to the class about the opportunity to support your goals for their success	Let students know that you appreciate when they approach you with questions, problems, or doubts about their performance, understanding of class work, or ability to succeed. That sort of request enables you to help them directly, and helps you succeed as a teacher.
Never lower standards or "dilute" instruction for certain students	It is the teacher's responsibility to ascertain the means to bring the student's academic performance up to standard.
Use all forms of teacher communication with students to reinforce your high expectations for them—as a class and especially as individuals	What we internalize as individuals, we utilize in group settings.

The teacher should provide positive reinforcement about the progress that the student is making regarding the high expectations for his or her academic achievement. If the work itself is below expectations—perhaps even substandard—provide positive, constructive feedback about what should be done to meet expectations.

An example of an opportunity to communicate expectations might be when writing comments on exams and papers being returned to individual students.

Express your confidence in the student's ability. A negative comment, like a negative attitude, is unacceptable on the part of the teacher. The teacher may deem it necessary to speak one-on-one with the student regarding his or her performance. Remember, however, no student ever feels motivated when reading the words "*See me*" on an exam or assignment.

DOMAIN II
LEARNING
ENVIRONMENT

PERSONALIZED STUDY PLAN

KNOWN MATERIAL/ SKIP IT

PAGE	COMPETENCY AND SKILL	
55	**4: Understand how to establish a safe, inclusive, and positive learning environment that encourages positive social interaction, active engagement in learning, and self-motivation**	☐
	4.1: Demonstrating knowledge of how to establish a positive classroom climate	☐
	4.2: Demonstrating knowledge of how to help students work productively and cooperatively	☐
	4.3: Demonstrating knowledge of expectations for student interactions, academic discussions, and individual and group responsibility	☐
	4.4: Applying knowledge of human motivation, behavior, and social groups	☐
	4.5: Demonstrating knowledge of factors and situations that are likely to promote or diminish intrinsic motivation	☐
	4.6: Recognizing how intrinsic motivation promotes students' lifelong learning	☐
	4.7: Demonstrating knowledge of how to analyze the classroom and make adjustments to enhance social relationships and increase student motivation	☐
61	**5: Understand how to create an organized and productive learning environment that promotes all students' participation and learning**	☐
	5.1: Demonstrating knowledge of appropriate classroom routines and procedures	☐
	5.2: Applying knowledge of strategies for managing the instructional environment	☐
	5.3: Demonstrating knowledge of strategies for organizing the physical environment of the classroom	☐
	5.4: Demonstrating knowledge of how to organize, allocate, and manage resources to promote students' learning	☐
	5.5: Applying knowledge of how to design and manage learning communities	☐
	5.6: Applying knowledge of effective classroom management	☐
	5.7: Demonstrating knowledge of how to analyze the classroom environment and make decisions and adjustments to enhance productivity and participation	☐

PERSONALIZED STUDY PLAN

KNOWN MATERIAL/ SKIP IT

PAGE		COMPETENCY AND SKILL	
75	6:	**Understand how to use effective verbal, nonverbal, and media communication techniques to promote active inquiry, learning, collaboration, and supportive interaction in the classroom**	☐
	6.1:	Applying knowledge of communication theory, language development, the role of language in learning, and the use of language for various purposes	☐
	6.2:	Demonstrating knowledge of how various student characteristics may affect communication in the classroom	☐
	6.3:	Demonstrating knowledge of effective verbal, nonverbal, and media communication techniques	☐
	6.4:	Identifying strategies for supporting and expanding elementary students' expression in speaking, writing, and other media	☐
	6.5:	Demonstrating knowledge of how to use a variety of media and educational technologies to enrich learning opportunities	☐
	6.6:	Applying knowledge of strategies for adjusting communication to enhance student understanding and engagement	☐
	6.7:	Demonstrating knowledge of different purposes for questioning and techniques for effective questioning in various learning contexts	☐

COMPETENCY 4

UNDERSTAND HOW TO ESTABLISH A SAFE, INCLUSIVE, AND POSITIVE LEARNING ENVIRONMENT THAT ENCOURAGES POSITIVE SOCIAL INTERACTION, ACTIVE ENGAGEMENT IN LEARNING, AND SELF-MOTIVATION

> **SKILL 4.1** Demonstrating knowledge of how to establish a positive classroom climate and create a learning environment that promotes self-esteem, active engagement, and positive interpersonal relationships for all students

A positive self-concept for a child or adolescent is very important; in terms of the students' ability to learn and to be an integral member of society, self-concept and interpersonal skills provide the foundation upon which all learning is based. If students think poorly of themselves or have sustained feelings of inferiority, they may not be able to optimize their potential for learning. It is therefore part of the teacher's task to ensure that each student develops a positive self-concept.

A positive self-concept does not imply feelings of superiority, perfection, or competence/efficacy. Instead, a positive self-concept involves self-acceptance as a person, liking oneself, and having a proper respect for oneself. The teacher who encourages these qualities has contributed to the development of a positive self-concept in students.

Teachers can take a number of different approaches to enhancing the self-concept of students. One such scheme is called the process approach, which proposes a three-phase model for teaching. This model includes a sensing function, a transforming function, and an acting function. These three phases can be simplified into the words by which the model is usually given: reach, touch, and teach.

1. The sensing, or perceptual, function: Incorporates information or stimuli in an intuitive manner.

2. The transforming function: Conceptualizes abstracts, evaluates, and provides meaning and value to perceived information.

3. The acting function: Chooses actions from several different alternatives to be set forth overtly.

The process model may be applied to almost any curricular field.

INVITATIONAL EDUCATION: an approach that aims directly at the enhancement of self-concept

An approach that aims directly at the enhancement of self-concept is designated as INVITATIONAL EDUCATION. According to this approach, teachers and their behaviors may be inviting or they may be disinviting. Inviting behaviors enhance self-concept among students, while disinviting behaviors diminish self-concept.

Disinviting behaviors include those that demean students, as well as those that may be chauvinistic, sexist, condescending, thoughtless, or insensitive to student feelings. Inviting behaviors are the opposite of these and are characterized by teachers who act with consistency and sensitivity. Inviting teacher behaviors reflect an attitude of doing with rather than doing to. Students are invited or disinvited depending on the teacher behaviors.

Invitational teachers exhibit the following skills (Biehler and Snowman, 394):

- Reaching each student (learning names, having one-to-one contact)

- Listening with care (picking up subtle cues)

- Being real with students (providing only realistic praise, "coming on straight")

- Being real with oneself (honestly appraising your own feelings and disappointments)

- Inviting good discipline (showing students you have respect in personal ways)

- Handling rejection (not taking lack of student response in personal ways)

- Inviting oneself (thinking positively about oneself)

SKILL 4.2 Demonstrating knowledge of how to help students work productively and cooperatively with each other in various contexts and how to establish peer relationships that promote learning

Cooperative Learning

Cooperative learning situations, as practiced in today's classrooms, grew out of research conducted by several groups in the early 1970s. Cooperative learning situations can range from very formal applications such as Student Teams Achievement Divisions (STAD) and Cooperative Integrated Reading and Composition (CIRC) to less formal groupings known variously as group investigation, learning together, or discovery groups. Cooperative learning as a general term is now firmly recognized and established as a teaching and learning technique in American schools.

Since cooperative learning techniques are so widely diffused in the schools, it is necessary to orient students in the skills by which cooperative learning groups can operate smoothly. Students who cannot interact constructively with other students will not be able to take advantage of the learning opportunities provided by the cooperative learning situations and will furthermore deprive their fellow students of the opportunity for cooperative learning.

These skills form the hierarchy of cooperation in which students first learn to work together as a group, so they may then proceed to levels at which they can engage in simulated conflict situations. This cooperative setting allows different points of view to be constructively entertained.

SKILL Demonstrating knowledge of expectations for student interactions, 4.3 academic discussions, and individual and group responsibility that create a positive classroom climate of openness, mutual respect, support, inquiry, and learning

See Skill 4.1

SKILL Applying knowledge of human motivation, behavior, and social 4.4 groups, including principles of psychology, anthropology, and sociology, to identify effective strategies for promoting student learning and for organizing and supporting individual and group work

See Skill 2.5

SKILL Demonstrating knowledge of factors and situations that are likely 4.5 to promote or diminish intrinsic motivation and strategies for helping students become self-motivated *(e.g., relating lessons to students' personal interests, allowing students to have choices in their learning, leading students to ask questions and pursue problems that are meaningful to them)*

Teachers need to be aware that much of what they say and do can be motivating and may have a positive effect on students' achievement. Studies have been conducted to determine the impact of teacher behavior on student performance.

Teachers need to be aware that much of what they say and do can be motivating and may have a positive effect on students' achievement.

Surprisingly, a teacher's voice can make a real impression on students. The human voice has several dimensions, including volume, pitch, rate, etc. A recent study on the effects of speech rate indicates that, although both boys and girls prefer to listen at a rate of about 200 words per minute, boys tend to prefer slower rates than girls. This same study indicates that a slower rate of speech directly affects processing ability and comprehension.

Teachers as Motivators

Other speech factors correlate with teaching-criterion scores including:

- Communication of ideas

- Communication of emotion

- Distinctness/pronunciation

- Quality variation and phrasing

These scores show that "good" teachers ("good" meaning teachers who positively impact and motivate students) use more variety in speech than do less effective teachers. Thus, a teacher's speech skills can be strong motivating elements. Body language has an even greater effect on student achievement and ability to set and focus on goals. Smiles provide support and give feedback about the teacher's affective state—a deadpan expression can actually be detrimental to student progress, and frowns are perceived by students to mean displeasure, disapproval, and even anger. Studies also show that teacher posture and movement are indicators of their enthusiasm and energy, which emphatically influence student outcomes including learning, attitudes, motivation, and focus on goals. Teachers are second only to parents in their effect on student motivation.

Hands-on learning

Teachers can also enhance student motivation by planning and directing interactive, hands-on learning experiences. Research substantiates that cooperative group projects decrease student behavior problems and increase student on-task behavior. Students who are directly involved with learning activities are more motivated to complete a task to the best of their ability.

Also see Skill 2.5

SKILL 4.6	Recognizing how intrinsic motivation promotes students' lifelong learning and how the use of various motivational strategies can encourage continuous student development of skills and abilities

Types of Motivation

EXTRINSIC MOTIVATION is motivation that comes from the expectation of rewards or punishments. The rewards and punishments can be varied. For example, in social situations, most human beings are extrinsically motivated to behave in common, socially accepted ways. The punishment for *not* doing so might be embarrassment or ridicule. The reward for doing so might be the acceptance of peers. In the classroom, rewards might be grades, candy, or special privileges. Punishments might be phone calls to parents, detention, suspension, or poor grades.

INTRINSIC MOTIVATION is motivation that comes from within. For example, while some children only read if given extrinsic rewards (e.g., winning an award for the most pages read), other children read because they enjoy it.

There are benefits and drawbacks of both methods of motivation. In reality, it should be noted that in an ideal world, all motivation would be intrinsic. But this is not the case. Consider having to clean your apartment, dorm room, or house. We might appreciate the "reward" of a clean living space at the end of the activity, but most of us do not particularly enjoy the process of cleaning and we only put up with it so that we get the end result.

In learning, we want all students to be intrinsically motivated. We would want students to not care about grades or prizes as much as we might want them to do their work, listen attentively, and read just because they want to learn. And while all teachers should work tirelessly to ensure that they develop intrinsic motivation as much as possible within their students, everyone knows that for certain students and subjects, extrinsic motivators must be used.

Using extrinsic motivators

What extrinsic motivators are useful in the classroom? If things like candy and prizes are *always* used to get students to pay attention in class, soon they will expect these things and possibly not pay attention in their absence. Likewise, if punishment is always used as a motivator, students may be consumed with fear rather than have the frame of mind that is most conducive to learning.

Benchmarks and standards are indeed useful for many teachers. Punishments, if they are reasonable, applied consistently, and students know what to expect, can be useful in making sure students behave appropriately. The best punishments, though, are ones in which a whole school has decided will be consistently used from classroom to classroom and grade level to grade level.

EXTRINSIC MOTIVATION: motivation that comes from the expectation of rewards or punishments

INTRINSIC MOTIVATION: motivation that comes from within

In general, teachers must walk a careful line with motivation. They must utilize extrinsic motivators when all possible intrinsic motivators have failed to work.

Encouraging Intrinsic Motivation

As a rule, teachers should strive to encourage intrinsic motivation for students' learning. To do so lessens the need to use extrinsic motivators, such as frivolous rewards and harsh punishments.

Student engagement with the material

The best way to encourage intrinsic motivation is to engage students in the learning. Engagement happens most when students work with material that is of greatest interest to them and if they feel there is a useful application for such material. For example, teachers will notice intrinsic motivation in reading when students have found books that they relate to.

When teachers believe that certain students just will not read, often (though not always), those students have not found books that they like. Considering that hundreds of thousands of books are out there, most likely, each student can find at least one interesting book.

Extrinsic Motivators

Grades

The extrinsic motivator of grades can be a particularly large challenge for well-meaning high school teachers who have college-bound students. Such students may not care much about the learning as much as they do about the grades so that their college applications look more competitive. Unfortunately, across the country, this has resulted in very troubling behavior. Plagiarism and cheating have been noticed in high schools everywhere.

While teachers may want to encourage students to learn for the sake of the learning itself, they must contend with students who have been trained to "win at all costs." Teachers can therefore use many strategies—*not* to eradicate the very act of cheating, for example—but to encourage students to explore topics that are of interest to them or to create more meaningful, authentic assessments. Authentic assessments are those in which students have to use new learning in a real-world, deeply meaningful way.

Punishment

Finally, it must be noted that punishment as an extrinsic motivator, while necessary at some times, often creates greater problems in the future. Students who feel like they are constantly punished into better behavior or to do better academically lose interest in pleasing teachers, acting appropriately, or learning. It is always

> *Students who feel like they are constantly punished into better behavior or to do better academically lose interest in pleasing teachers, acting appropriately, or learning.*

better, whenever possible, for teachers to work at engaging students first and then punishing if all options have been exhausted.

SKILL 4.7 **Demonstrating knowledge of how to analyze the classroom environment and make decisions and adjustments to enhance social relationships and increase student motivation and engagement**

See Skill 4.5

COMPETENCY 5

UNDERSTAND HOW TO CREATE AN ORGANIZED AND PRODUCTIVE LEARNING ENVIRONMENT THAT PROMOTES ALL STUDENTS' PARTICIPATION AND LEARNING

SKILL 5.1 **Demonstrating knowledge of effective, developmentally appropriate classroom routines and procedures that promote an organized and productive learning environment and encourage purposeful learning and the full participation of all students in independent and group work**

Importance of Classroom Organization

Instructional momentum requires an organized system for material placement and distribution. Inability to find an overhead transparency, a necessary chart page, or the handout worksheet for the day not only stops the momentum but is very irritating to students. Disorganization of materials frustrates both teacher and students. Effective teachers deal with daily classroom procedures efficiently and quickly because then students will spend the majority of class time engaged in academic tasks, which will likely result in higher achievement.

Effective teachers deal with daily classroom procedures efficiently and quickly because then students will spend the majority of class time engaged in academic tasks, which will likely result in higher achievement.

Strategies for organization

In the lower grades, an organized system uses a classroom helper for effective distribution and collection of books, equipment, supplies, etc. At higher grade levels, the teacher is concerned with materials such as textbooks, written instructional aids, worksheets, computer programs, etc., which must be produced, maintained, distributed, and collected for future use.

One important consideration is the production of sufficient copies of duplicated materials to satisfy classroom needs. Another is the efficient distribution of worksheets and other materials. The teacher may decide to hand out materials as students are in their learning sites (desks, etc.) or have distribution materials at a clearly specified place (or small number of places) in the classroom. In any case, there should be firmly established procedures, completely understood by students, for receiving classroom materials.

Establishing a classroom routine

An effective teacher will also consider the needs and abilities of her students when developing routines or a daily schedule. For routines, a teacher might motivate a low-achieving student with a coveted task (such as taking down the attendance sheet or a recommendation for Safety Patrol) in order to increase confidence in that child. This increased confidence could lead to an increased interest in school and improved learning. Likewise, a teacher should also consider the needs of his or her students when developing the aspects of the daily schedule. For instance, if faced with a "hard to calm down" group, a teacher might schedule quiet reading time after recess. Being aware of their students' trends and characteristics in developing a classroom routine can significantly affect student learning.

* having a Routine is key to success

> An effective teacher will also consider the needs and abilities of her students when developing routines or a daily schedule.

SKILL 5.2 Applying knowledge of strategies for managing the instructional environment to maximize class time spent in learning *(e.g., creating expectations for communication and behavior, managing transitions, managing materials, implementing appropriate schedules)*

Effectives Use of Classroom Time

Effective teachers use class time efficiently. This results in higher student subject engagement and will likely result in more subject matter retention. One way that teachers use class time efficiently is through a smooth transition from one activity to another; this is also known as management transition.

Management transition

MANAGEMENT TRANSITION is defined as shifting from one activity to another in a systemic, academically oriented way. One factor that contributes to efficient management transition is the teacher's management of instructional material. Effective teachers gather their materials during the planning stage of instruction. Doing this, a teacher avoids flipping through things and looking for the items necessary for the current lesson. Momentum is lost and student concentration is broken when this occurs.

Additionally, teachers who keep students informed of the sequencing of instructional activities maintain systematic transitions because the students are prepared to move on to the next activity. For example, the teacher says, "When we finish with this guided practice together, we will turn to page twenty-three and each student will do the exercises. I will then circulate throughout the classroom helping on an individual basis. Okay, let's begin." Following an example such as this will lead to systematic smooth transitions between activities because the students will be turning to page twenty-three when the class finishes the practice without a break in concentration.

Group fragmentation

Another method that leads to smooth transitions is to move students in groups and clusters rather than one by one. This is called GROUP FRAGMENTATION. For example, if some students do seat work while other students gather for a reading group, the teacher moves the students in predetermined groups. Instead of calling the individual names of the reading group, which would be time consuming and laborious, the teacher simply says, "Will the blue reading group please assemble at the reading station. The red and yellow groups will quietly do the vocabulary assignment I am now passing out." As a result of this activity, the classroom is ready to move on in a matter of seconds rather than minutes.

Additionally, the teacher may employ academic TRANSITION SIGNALS, defined as teacher utterances that indicate movement of the lesson from one topic or activity to another by indicating where the lesson is and where it is going. For example, the teacher may say, "That completes our description of clouds, now we will examine weather fronts." Like the sequencing of instructional materials, this keeps the student informed on what is coming next so the students will move to the next activity with little or no break in concentration.

Therefore, effective teachers manage transitions from one activity to another in a systematically oriented way through efficient management of instructional matter, sequencing of instructional activities, moving students in groups, and by employing academic transition signals.

MANAGEMENT TRANSITION: shifting from one activity to another in a systemic, academically-oriented way

GROUP FRAGMENTATION: a method for ensuring smooth transitions, whereby a teacher moves students in groups and clusters rather than one by one

TRANSITION SIGNALS: a teacher utterance or gesture that indicates movement of the lesson from one topic or activity to another by indicating where the lesson is and where it is going

Through an efficient use of class time, achievement is increased because students spend more class time engaged in on-task behavior.

Examples of transitions

TRANSITIONS refer to changes in class activities that involve movement. Some examples are:

- Breaking up from large group instruction into small groups for learning centers and small-group instruction

- Classroom to lunch, to the playground, or to elective classes

- Finishing reading at the end of one period and getting ready for math the next period

- Emergency situations such as fire drills

Successful transitions are achieved by using proactive strategies. Early in the year, the teacher pinpoints the transition periods in the day and anticipates possible behavior problems, such as students habitually returning late from lunch. After identifying possible problems with the environment or the schedule, the teacher plans proactive strategies to minimize or eliminate those problems.

Proactive planning also gives the teacher the advantage of being prepared, addressing behaviors before they become problems, and incorporating strategies into the classroom management plan right away. Transition plans can be developed for each type of transition and the expected behaviors for each situation taught directly to the students.

SKILL 5.3 Demonstrating knowledge of strategies for organizing the physical environment of the classroom to facilitate student learning and achieve defined goals

---

Physical Attributes of the Classroom

The physical setting of the classroom contributes a great deal toward the propensity for students to learn. An adequate, well-built, and well-equipped classroom will invite students to learn. This has been called INVITATIONAL LEARNING.

Important classroom factors

Among the important factors to consider in the physical setting of the classroom are:

- Adequate physical space

- Repair status

- Lighting adequacy

- Adequate entry and exit access (including handicap accessibility)
- Ventilation/climate control
- Coloration

Adequate physical space

A classroom must have adequate physical space so students can conduct themselves comfortably. Some students are distracted by windows, pencil sharpeners, doors, etc. Some students prefer the front, middle, or back rows.

Repair status

The teacher has the responsibility to report any items of classroom disrepair to maintenance staff. Broken windows, falling plaster, exposed sharp surfaces, leaks in ceiling or walls, and other items of disrepair present hazards to students.

Lighting adequacy

Another factor that must be considered is adequate lighting. Report any inadequacies in classroom illumination. Florescent lights placed at acute angles often burn out faster. A healthy supply of spare tubes is a sound investment.

Adequate entry and exit access

Local fire and safety codes dictate entry and exit standards. In addition, all corridors and classrooms should be wheelchair accessible for students and others who use them. Older schools may not have this accessibility.

Ventilation/climate control

Another consideration is adequate ventilation and climate control. Some classrooms in some states use air conditioning extensively. Sometimes it is so cold as to be considered a distraction. Specialty classes such as science require specialized hoods for ventilation. Physical education classes have the added responsibility for shower areas and specialized environments that must be heated, such as pool or athletic training rooms.

Coloration

Classrooms with warmer subdued colors contribute to students' concentration on task items. Neutral hues for coloration of walls, ceiling, and carpet or tile are generally used in classrooms to minimize distractions.

Furniture

In the modern classroom, a great deal of furniture, equipment, supplies, appliances, and learning aids help the teachers teach and students learn. The classroom should be provided with furnishings that fit the purpose of the classroom. For example, the kindergarten classroom may have a reading center, a playhouse, a

A classroom must have adequate physical space so students can conduct themselves comfortably.

In the modern classroom, a great deal of furniture, equipment, supplies, appliances, and learning aids help the teachers teach and students learn.

puzzle table, student work desks and tables, a sandbox, and any other relevant learning and interest areas.

Whatever the arrangement of furniture and equipment, the teacher must provide for adequate traffic flow. Rows of desks must have adequate space between them to enable students to move and the teacher to circulate. All areas must be open to line-of-sight supervision by the teacher.

In all cases, proper care must be taken to ensure student safety. Furniture and equipment should be situated safely at all times. No equipment, materials, boxes, etc., should be placed where there is danger of them falling. Doors must have entry and exit accessibility at all times.

Emergency responses

The major emergency responses include two categories for student movement: tornado warning response, and building evacuation, which includes most other emergencies (fire, bomb threat, etc.).

Tornado warning response

For tornadoes, the prescribed response is to evacuate all students and personnel to the first floor of multistory buildings, and to place students along walls away from windows. All people, including the teacher, should then crouch on the floor and cover their heads with their hands. These are standard procedures for severe weather, particularly tornadoes.

Building evacuation

Teachers should be thoroughly familiar with evacuation routes established for each classroom in which they teach.

Most other emergency situations require evacuation of the school building. Teachers should be thoroughly familiar with evacuation routes established for each classroom in which they teach. Teachers should accompany and supervise students throughout the evacuation procedure and check to see that all students under their supervision are accounted for. Teachers should then continue to supervise students until the building may be reoccupied (upon proper school or community authority) or until other procedures are followed for students to officially leave the school area and cease to be the supervisory responsibility of the school. Elementary students evacuated to another school can wear nametags and parents or guardians should sign them out at a central location.

SKILL **Demonstrating knowledge of how to organize, allocate, and**
5.4 **manage resources** *(e.g., time, space, attention)* **to promote students'**
learning and active engagement in productive tasks

See Skills 5.1 and 5.2

SKILL **Applying knowledge of how to design and manage learning**
5.5 **communities in which students assume responsibility for**
themselves and one another, exhibit commitment, participate in
decision making, work both collaboratively and independently, and
engage in purposeful learning activities

Teaching social skills can be rather difficult because social competence requires a
repertoire of skills in a number of areas. The socially competent person must be
able to get along with family and friends, function in a work environment, take
care of personal needs, solve problems in daily living, and identify sources of help.
A class of students with emotional disabilities may present several deficits in a few
areas or a few deficits in many areas. Therefore, the teacher must begin with an
assessment of the skill deficits and prioritize the ones to teach first.

* Social
skills
are
important.

TYPE OF ASSESSMENT	DESCRIPTION
Direct Observation	Teacher observes student in various settings with a checklist
Role Play	Teacher observes students in structured scenarios
Teacher Ratings	Teacher rates student with a checklist or formal assessment instrument

Continued on next page

TYPE OF ASSESSMENT	DESCRIPTION
Sociometric Measures	*Peer Nomination:* Student names specific classmates who meet a stated criterion (i.e., playmate); score is the number of times a child is nominated
	Peer Rating: Students rank all their classmates on a Likert-type scale (e.g., 1–3 or 1–5 scale) on stated criterion; individual score is the average of the total ratings of their classmates
	Paired Comparison: Student is presented with paired classmate combinations and asked to choose who is most or least liked in the pair
Context Observation	Student is observed to determine if the skill deficit is present in one setting, but not others
Comparison with Other Student	Student's social skill behavior is compared to two other students in the same situation to determine if there is a deficit or if the behavior is not really a problem

Social skills instruction can include teaching conversation skills, assertiveness, play and peer interaction, problem solving and coping skills, self-help, task-related behaviors, self-concept-related skills (e.g., expressing feelings, accepting consequences), and job-related skills.

One advantage of schooling organizations for students is to facilitate social skills and social development. While teachers cannot take the primary role in developing such traits as honesty, fairness, and concern for others, they are extremely important in the process. The first recommendation is to be a very good role model. As we all know, actions do indeed speak louder than words.

Second, teachers need to communicate expectations and be firm about them. When teachers ignore certain "infractions" and make a big deal about others, they demonstrate to students that it isn't about manners and social skills, but rather discipline and favoritism. All students need to feel safe, cared about, and secure with their classmates. Teachers should be good examples of how to be generous, caring, considerate, and sociable individuals.

SKILL **Applying knowledge of effective classroom management,**
5.6 **including methods for encouraging students to monitor their own**
behavior and for promoting students' cooperation and sense of
responsibility and accountability in the classroom

Behavior Management Plan Strategies for Increasing Desired Behaviors

1. Prompt: A PROMPT is a visual or verbal cue that assists the child through the behavior-shaping process. In some cases, the teacher may use a physical prompt such as guiding a child's hand. Visual cues include signs or other visual aids. Verbal cues include talking a child through the steps of a task. The gradual removal of the prompt as the child masters the target behavior is called fading.

> **PROMPT:** a visual or verbal cue that assists the child through the behavior-shaping process

2. Modeling: In order for modeling to be effective, the child must be at a cognitive and developmental level to imitate the model. Teachers are behavior models in the classroom, but peers are powerful models as well, especially in adolescence. A child who does not perceive a model as acceptable will not likely copy the model's behavior. This is why teachers should be careful to reinforce appropriate behavior and not fall into the trap of attending to inappropriate behaviors. Children who see that the students who misbehave get the teacher's constant attention will most likely begin to model those students' behaviors.

3. Contingency contracting: Also known as the Premack Principle or "Grandma's Law," this technique is based on the concept that a less preferred behavior that occurs frequently can be used to increase a preferred behavior that has a lower rate of occurrence. In short, performance of X results in the opportunity to do Y, such as getting 10 minutes of free time for completing the math assignment with 85% accuracy.

   – The use of contingency contracts is a process that continues after formal schooling and into the world of work and adult living. Contracts can be individualized, be developed with input of the child, and accent positive behaviors. Contingencies can also be simple verbal contracts, such as the teacher telling a child that he or she may earn a treat or special activity for completion of a specific academic activity. Contingency contracts can be simple daily contracts or more formal, written contracts.

   – Written contracts last for longer periods of time and must be clear, specific, and fair. Payoffs should be deliverable immediately after the student completes the terms of the contract. An advantage of a written contract is that the child can see and reaffirm the terms of the contract. By being actively involved in the development of the contract with the teacher and/ or parent, the child assumes responsibility for fulfilling his or her share of the deal. Contracts can be renewed and renegotiated as the student progresses toward the target behavior goal.

4. Token Economy: A token economy mirrors the money system in that the students earn tokens (money) that are of little value themselves, but can be traded for tangible or activity rewards, just as currency can be spent for merchandise. Using stamps, stickers, stars, or point cards instead of items like poker chips decrease the likelihood of theft, loss, and noise in the classroom.

Tips for a token economy:

- Keep the system simple to understand and administer

- Develop a reward "menu" that is deliverable and varied

- Decide on the target behaviors

- Explain the system completely and in positive terms before beginning the economy

- Periodically review the rules

- Price the rewards and costs fairly, and post the menu where it can be easily read

- Gradually fade to a variable schedule of reinforcement

Behavior Management Plan Strategies for Decreasing Undesirable Behaviors

1. Extinction: Reinforcement is withheld for an unacceptable behavior. A common example is ignoring the student who calls out without raising his hand and recognizing the student who is raising his hand to speak. This would not be a suitable strategy for serious misbehaviors where others are in danger of being hurt.

2. Differential reinforcement of incompatible behaviors (DRI): In this method, the teacher reinforces an acceptable behavior that is not compatible with the target behavior. A child cannot be out of her seat and in her seat at the same time, so the teacher would reinforce the time when the child is in her seat.

3. Differential reinforcement of alternative behaviors (DRA): The student is rewarded for producing a behavior that is an alternative to the undesired target behavior, such as talking with a classmate instead of arguing.

4. Differential reinforcement of other behaviors (DRO): Reinforcement is provided for producing any appropriate behaviors except for the target behavior during a specified time interval. This technique works well with stereotypic, disruptive, or self-injurious behaviors.

5. Satiation or negative practice: This technique involves reinforcing the inappropriate behavior on a fixed reinforcement schedule until the student discontinues the behavior. The reinforcement must be consistently applied until the student does not want to do it. Behaviors suitable for satiation would be chronic "borrowing" of school supplies or getting up to go to the wastebasket or pencil sharpener. An example of satiation would be giving a student a pencil to sharpen at frequent intervals throughout the day so that the act of getting up to sharpen a pencil no longer has any appeal.

6. Verbal reprimands: Reprimands are best delivered privately, especially for secondary students, who may be provoked into more misbehavior if they are embarrassed in front of their peers. Verbal reprimands also may be a source of attention and reinforcement with some students.

Punishment as a "deterrent" to misbehavior

Punishment should not be the first strategy in behavior management plans because it tends to suppress behavior, not eliminate it. Punishment focuses on the negative rather than positive behaviors. There is also the chance that the child will comply out of fear, stress, or tension rather than a genuine behavior change. Furthermore, the punishment may be misused to the point where it is no longer effective. Forms of punishment include:

1. Adding an aversive event (e.g., detention, lunchroom cleanup, extra assignments)

2. Subtracting something that the child likes (e.g., recess)

   A. Response cost: In token economies, response cost results in loss of points or token. Response-cost or loss of privileges is preferred to adding aversives, but for long-term changes in behavior, punishment is less effective than other forms of decreasing misbehavior, such as extinction and ignoring.

   B. Time-out: Time-out is removing a child from the reinforcing situation to a setting that is not reinforcing. Time out may be observational (e.g., sitting at the end of the basketball court for five minutes or putting one's head down at the desk). The point is to have the child observe the others engaging in the appropriate behavior.

- Exclusion time-out: Placing a visual barrier between the student and the rest of the class. This could be a divider between the desks and the time-out area or removing the child to another room.

- Seclusion time-out: Necessitates a special time-out room that adheres to mandated standards, as well as a log of the children who are taken to time out, the reasons for their removal, and the time they spent there.

In order to be effective, time-out must be consistently applied, and the child must understand why he is being sent to the time-out area and for how long. The teacher briefly explains the reason for time-out, directs the child to the area, and refrains from long explanations, arguments, or debates. The time-out area should be as neutral as possible, away from busy areas, and easily observed by the monitor but not the rest of the class. The duration of time-out should vary with the age of the child and timed so the child knows when the end of time-out has arrived.

Time-out as part of a behavior management plan needs to be periodically evaluated for its effectiveness. By analyzing records of time-out (as required and directed by the school district), the teacher can see if the technique is working. If a student regularly goes to time-out at a certain time, the student may be avoiding a frustrating situation or a difficult academic subject. Seclusion time-out may be effective for children who tend to be group-oriented or aggressive and act out frequently. Isolation from the group is not rewarding for them. Shy, solitary, or withdrawn children may actually prefer to be in time-out and may increase the target behavior in order to go to time-out.

3. Overcorrection: Overcorrection is more effective with severe and profoundly handicapped students. The student is required to repeat an appropriate behavior for a specified number of times when the inappropriate behavior is exhibited.

4. Suspension: Suspension is the punishment of last resort. In addition to restrictions on suspension for students with disabilities, suspension translates into a "vacation" from school for many students with behavioral problems. Furthermore, suspension does not relieve the teacher from the responsibility of exploring alternatives that may be effective with the child. An alternative to out-of-school suspension is in-school suspension, where the student is placed in a special area to do his or her class work for a specified time and with minimal privileges. Extended suspensions (i.e., for drugs, weapons, or assault) or offenses punishable by expulsion result in a change of placement, which calls for special meetings to discuss alternative placement and/or services.

Group-Oriented Contingencies in Behavior Management

This strategy uses the power of the peer group to reinforce appropriate behavior. In one variation, dependent group-oriented contingencies, the rewards or consequences for the entire group depend upon the performance of a few members; for example, Susan's class receives a candy reward if she does not have a crying outburst for two days.

Interdependent group-oriented contingencies mean that each member of the group must achieve a specified level of performance in order for the group to get the reward. An example would be the entire class earning one period of free time if everyone passes the science test with at least 80%.

Other strategies for behavior management:

- Counseling techniques: These techniques include life-space interviewing, reality therapy, and active listening

- Realistic consequences: Consequences should be as close as possible to what may happen in the outside world, especially for adolescents

- Student participation: Students, especially older students, should participate as much as possible in the planning, goal-setting, and evaluation of their behavior management plans

- Contingency plans: Because adolescents frequently have a number of reinforcers outside of school, the teacher should try to incorporate contingencies for school behavior at home, since parents can control important reinforcers such as movies, going out with friends, car privileges, etc.

- Consistency: Consistency, especially with adolescents, reduces the occurrence of power struggles and teaches them that predictable consequences follow for their choice of actions

Initially, the target behavior may increase or worsen as the student realizes that the behavior is no longer reinforced. However, if the behavior management plan is properly administered, the teacher should begin to see results. Behavior management plan evaluation is a continuous process, because changes in behavior require changes in the target behavior, looking for outside variables that may account for behavior change, or changes in reinforcement schedules and menus.

It has already been established that appropriate verbal techniques include a soft, nonthreatening voice; avoidance of undue roughness, anger, or impatience, regardless of whether the teacher is instructing; providing a student alert; or giving a behavior reprimand.

Behavior management plan evaluation is a continuous process, because changes in behavior require changes in the target behavior, looking for outside variables that may account for behavior change, or changes in reinforcement schedules and menus.

Verbal Techniques and Body Language

Verbal techniques, which may be effective in modifying student behavior, can be as simple as stating the student's name, explaining briefly and succinctly what the student is doing that is inappropriate, and explaining what the student should be doing. Verbal techniques for reinforcing behavior include both encouragement and praise delivered by the teacher.

In addition, for verbal techniques to positively affect student behavior and learning, the teacher must give clear, concise directives while implying her warmth toward the students.

Other factors that contribute to enhanced student learning have to do with body language. The teacher needs to make eye contact with individual students; smile and nod approvingly; move closer to the students; give gentle pats on the shoulder, arm, or head; and bend forward so that the teacher is face to face with the children.

Some of these same techniques can be applied as a means of desisting student misbehaviors. Rather than smiling, the teacher may need to make eye contact first and then shake his or her head disapprovingly. Again, a gentle tap on the shoulder or arm can be used to get a student's attention in an attempt to stop deviancy.

It is also helpful for the teacher to prominently display the classroom rules. This will serve as a visual reminder of the students' expected behaviors. In a study of classroom management procedures, it was established that the combination of conspicuously displayed rules, frequent verbal references to the rules, and appropriate consequences led to increased levels of on-task behavior.

SKILL 5.7 **Demonstrating knowledge of how to analyze the classroom environment and make decisions and adjustments to enhance productivity and participation**

See Skill 5.3

COMPETENCY 6

UNDERSTAND HOW TO USE EFFECTIVE VERBAL, NONVERBAL, AND MEDIA COMMUNICATION TECHNIQUES TO PROMOTE ACTIVE INQUIRY, LEARNING, COLLABORATION, AND SUPPORTIVE INTERACTION IN THE CLASSROOM

* Age appropriate Communication

SKILL 6.1 Applying knowledge of communication theory, language development, the role of language in learning, and the use of language for various purposes *(e.g., to promote self-expression, identity development, learning)*

Student Age and Communication

Effective teachers are well versed in cognitive development, which is crucial to presenting ideas or materials to students at a level appropriate to their developmental maturity. These educators also have the ability to use nonverbal and verbal patterns of communications that focus on age-appropriate instructions and materials.

Consistent with Piaget's theory of cognitive development, younger children (below age eight) have limited language skills. Therefore, instructions and information should use simplified language. In contrast, older children (age eight and older) have a greater ability to understand language and are therefore capable of solving complex problems. These students should have more detailed instructions and materials that require more advanced language skills.

> *Effective teachers are well versed in cognitive development, which is crucial to presenting ideas or materials to students at a level appropriate to their developmental maturity.*

Communication in the Classroom

The classroom environment has become an increasing milieu of cognitive, social, emotional, and cultural diversity. The effective teacher must rise to the challenge of presenting ideas and materials appropriate for varying levels of students, while still being relevant to students as a whole. Research indicates that successful teachers first, ensure that assignments are understood and second, hold students responsible for assignments. The clearer the students' understanding of the objectives, the more effective instruction will be. Therefore, teachers must identify and articulate the specific behaviors that are expected during and after the completion of tasks.

Implementing successful communication

Learning will be increased if the teacher begins a lesson by providing orientation and direction, such as stating the objectives and outlining the lesson content. Besides telling the students what they are going to learn, teachers may choose to use advance organizers that include visual motivations such as:

- Outlines

- Graphs

- Models

J. M. Kallison, Jr. found that subject matter retention increased when lessons included an outline at the beginning of the lesson and a summary at the end. This type of structure is utilized in successful classrooms and is especially valuable to the visual learner and is a motivational factor for most students. Next, he or she must support the lesson's momentum by providing distinct explanations. The instructor must:

- Effectively transition from one part of the lesson to another

- Check for student comprehension

- Provide practice where it is appropriate

Specific questions asked at the beginning of a lesson can also help students focus on the content and be more attentive to instruction. Effective teachers also clearly explain difficult points during a lesson and then analyze problems utilizing questioning techniques with the students.

SKILL 6.2 Demonstrating knowledge of how various student characteristics *(e.g., age, gender, cultural background, linguistic background, exceptionality)* **may affect communication in the classroom and how to communicate effectively with all students** *(e.g., using active listening skills, appropriate vocabulary, nonverbal indicators)*

To create an effective learning culture, there must be a positive environment that facilitates discussion-oriented, nonthreatening communication among all students. The teacher must take the lead and model appropriate actions and speech, and intervene quickly when a student makes a misstep and offends another (this often happens inadvertently).

Possible Communication Issues

In a diverse classroom, the teacher should be aware of the following communication issues:

- Be sensitive to terminology and language patterns that may exclude or demean students. Regularly switch between the use of "he" and "she" in speech and writing. Know and use the current terms that ethnic and cultural groups use to identify themselves (e.g., "Latinos" [favored] vs. "Hispanics").

- Be aware of body language that is intimidating or offensive to some cultures, such as direct eye contact, and adjust accordingly.

- Monitor your own reactions to students to ensure equal responses to males and females, as well as differently performing students.

- Don't protect students from criticism because of their ethnicity or gender. Likewise, acknowledge and praise all meritorious work without singling out particular students. Both actions can make all students hyper-aware of ethnic and gender differences and cause anxiety or resentment throughout the class.

- Emphasize the importance of discussing and considering different viewpoints and opinions. Demonstrate and express value for all opinions and comments and lead students to do the same.

Student Differences

When teaching in diverse classrooms, teachers must also expect to be working and communicating with students who are diverse. Even without the typical classifications, each student is unique and this should be treated as an asset.

Gender

Another obvious difference among students is gender. Interactions with male students are typically viewed as being different from those with female students. Depending on the lesson, female students may be more interested in working with partners or perhaps even individually. On the other hand, male students may enjoy a more collaborative or hands-on activity. The gender of the teacher will also come into play, particularly with students of a different gender. Of course, every student is different and may not fit into a stereotypical role, and getting to know their students' preferences for learning will help teachers to truly enhance learning in the classroom.

Cultural background

Most class rosters will also consist of students from a variety of cultures. Teachers should get to know their learners (of all cultures) so that they may incorporate elements of the students' cultures into classroom activities and planning. Getting to know about their backgrounds and cultural traditions helps to build rapport with each student. This also educates the teacher about the world in which he or she teaches.

Language

For students still learning English, teachers must make every attempt to communicate with these learners daily. Whether it is through translation by another student who speaks the same language, word cards, computer programs, drawings, or other methods, teachers must find ways to encourage each student's participation. Of course, the teacher must also be sure the appropriate language services begin for the student in a timely manner.

Socioeconomic backgrounds

SOCIOECONOMIC BACKGROUND: the history of the economic and social life of a student

Another consideration is different SOCIOECONOMIC BACKGROUNDS. Research has shown that all students are equally capable of performing well in the classroom; unfortunately, students from lower socioeconomic backgrounds are faced with a number of challenges to reaching their full potential.

For instance, single parents may be less able to help their children in completing homework consistently. These families may need help formalizing a homework system, or perhaps the student would need more attention on study or test-taking skills. Teachers should encourage these students as much as possible and offer positive reinforcements when they meet or exceed classroom expectations. Educators should also watch these students carefully for signs of malnutrition, fatigue, and other impediments to learning.

SKILL 6.3 Demonstrating knowledge of effective verbal, nonverbal, and media communication techniques for conveying ideas and information and for achieving specified goals *(e.g., providing feedback, building student self-esteem)*

See Skill 6.1

> ## SKILL 6.4
> **Identifying strategies for supporting and expanding elementary students' expression in speaking, writing, and other media and for fostering sensitive communication by and among all students**

See Skills 6.1 and 6.2

> ## SKILL 6.5
> **Demonstrating knowledge of how to use a variety of media and educational technologies to enrich learning opportunities**

Technology and Communication

The number of tools that teachers have available to them to present information to students is always growing. Where just ten years ago teachers needed to only know how to use word processing programs, grading programs, and overhead projectors, today, electronic slideshows (most people think of PowerPoint) are becoming the new norm, and other methods of information distribution are expected by principals, parents, and students alike.

Videos

Many instructional programs include short video clips for students to help amplify ideas. For example, many science programs include very short clips to demonstrate scientific principles. Literature programs might include short dramatizations of stories or background information on a literature selection. These tools are particularly helpful to replace "prior knowledge" for students before embarking on new topics, and they are especially important for students who are strong visual learners.

Technology and communication with parents

In many schools, electronic and print information from teachers is necessary for communicating things to parents. For example, since many students' parents are at work all day long, it is more efficient for parents to look online for homework assignments rather than discuss certain homework issues. Many schools have instituted homework hotlines where teachers record homework assignments for parents or absent students to call in and access.

In general, we know that the more a teacher communicates with parents, the more likely parents will trust and assist the teacher in his methods and strategies. And parents are impressed by teachers who take the time to put together something in

In general, we know that the more a teacher communicates with parents, the more likely parents will trust the teacher and assist the teacher in his methods and strategies.

a professional manner. So, teachers will earn much more respect from families by providing information in a timely and professional manner.

Web sites

Many teachers now also have Web sites where they post:

- Assignments

- Exemplary student work

- Helpful links

- Other useful information

While this use of technology is good, teachers should double-check to ensure that sensitive student information is not included on the Web. Although most people would say that including a picture of the students at work in the classroom is acceptable, schools are finding that having *no* pictures of students—individually or in a group—is better for the protection of students.

Learning to use technology effectively

Teachers who do now know how to use these various tools have multiple learning options. Many community colleges specifically teach these skills, and many Web sites are available with video-based tutorials.

Incorporating technology effectively into a fully content- and skill-based curriculum requires a good understanding of lesson objectives and how those objectives can be met with the technology. While teachers should definitely consider technological integration as an important aspect of their work in any subject and at any grade level, teachers should not include technology simply for the sake of technology. The best approach, considering all subjects can in certain ways be enhanced with technology, is for the teacher to consider a variety of lessons and units and decide which focus areas can be enhanced with technological tools.

Technology and Group Situations

Using technology in collaborative student group situations is considered to be the most effective method for a few reasons. Practically, most teachers cannot assign one computer to each student in the class whenever the teacher would like to utilize computers in the classroom. But that should not matter. As technological tools are complicated and complex, pair and small group work better facilitates stronger, social-based learning.

Groups and addressing skill disparity

Even though teachers may assume all students know how to use various technological tools, they need to remember two very important things:

1. Not *all* students are proficient. Even though some highly proficient students lead teachers to believe that the entire generation of kids in schools today already understands technology, many students actually never learned it at home. Some actually do not have the tools at home because of the high costs and, therefore, have no opportunity to practice.

2. Not all technology skills transfer. While one student may navigate the Web easily, she may not be able to use a word processing program with a similar level of expertise.

Social opportunities to learn technology will help students to engage in a more productive, friendly, and help-centered fashion. Learning together, particularly in technology, can indeed reduce any anxiety or fear a student may have.

Enhancing lessons through technology and groups

Teachers can consider technology learning as a method to also teach cooperation, decision-making skills, and problem-solving skills. For example, as a small group of students work together on a project on a computer, they must decide together how they will proceed and create. Teachers can instruct students in good cooperative decision-making skills to make the process easier. Students can also engage in activities where they are required to solve problems, build real-life solutions to situations, and create real-world products. Doing so will only enhance content-area instruction.

> *Teachers can consider technology learning as a method to also teach co-operation, decision-making skills, and problem-solving skills.*

Assessing appropriate technology

Finally, it is important to remember that, as with all other learning, technological learning must be developmentally appropriate. Realize that while very young students can perform various functions on the computer, by virtue of development level, the time required for a particular activity may be greatly increased. Also, various technological tools are simply too advanced, too fast, and too complex for very young students. It may be best to introduce basic elements of technology in the earlier grades.

Applying knowledge of strategies for adjusting communication to enhance student understanding and engagement

Communicating with Students

While teachers should never consider that all students' learning is based on a teacher's communication to students, much valuable information does occur in the transmission of words between teacher and student. The problem, however, is in dealing with the various types of learning difficulties that students have, as well as with other environmental factors and learning preferences.

While teachers should never consider that all students' learning is based on teacher's communication to students, much valuable information does occur in the transmission of words between teacher and student.

Disabilities and communication

First, various disabilities, including hearing loss, Attention Deficit Hyperactivity Disorder, and others, can severely impact a student's ability to successfully listen to and comprehend what the teacher may be saying. In such cases, teachers should communicate with Special Education and other resource teachers about procedures and practices to follow. But teachers can also place these students in specific classroom locations, give them "partners" who can assist, and periodically walk near them to find out how they are doing.

Environment and communication

Environmental factors can inhibit a teacher's communication to students.

Environmental factors can inhibit a teacher's communication to students. Often, air conditioners and other room or building noises can impact students' understanding of course content. Students also have various preferences in how they best understand. Some need a lot of teacher explanation and assistance; others need very little. While a teacher can never judge how much students understand simply by looking at their expressions, the teacher may get a pretty good idea if the students are in need of a change of communication style, a new activity, or if they simply need further review.

> **SKILL Demonstrating knowledge of different purposes for questioning**
> **6.7** *(e.g., stimulating discussion, probing for student understanding, helping students articulate their ideas and thinking processes, promoting productive risk taking and problem solving, facilitating recall, encouraging convergent and divergent thinking, stimulating curiosity)* **and techniques for effective questioning in various learning contexts**

A Successful Teacher

Teachers who couple diversity in instructional practices with engaging and challenging curriculum and the latest advances in technology can create the ultimate learning environment for creative thinking and continuous learning for students. Teachers who are innovative and creative in instructional practices are able to model and foster creative thinking in their students. Encouraging students to maintain journals or portfolios of their valued work from projects and assignments will allow students to make conscious choices on including a diversity of their creative endeavors in a filing format that can be treasured throughout the educational journey.

Teachers who are innovative and creative in instructional practices are able to model and foster creative thinking in their students.

Questioning

When teachers are very deliberate about the questions they use with their students, amazing things in the classroom can happen. Most of us remember questions at the end of the chapter in the textbook, or we remember quiz or test questions. While these things potentially have value, they are completely useless if the questions are not well crafted, the purposes for the questions are not defined, and the methods by which students will answer the questions are not engaging.

Keep in mind that good questioning does not always imply that there are correct answers (note that yes or no questions in the classroom do not provide much in the way of stimulation and thought). Good questioning usually implies that teachers are encouraging deep reflection and active thinking in students. In general, we can say that through questioning, we want students to take risks, solve problems, recall facts, and demonstrate understanding.

Good questioning usually implies that teachers are encouraging deep reflection and active thinking in students.

Risk-taking questions

When we say that we want students to take risks, we mean that we want them to "try out" various answers and possibilities. By answering a risk-taking question, students experiment with their academic voices.

Problem-solving questions

Problem-solving questions provoke thought and encourage students to think of questions as entries into problems, not indicators that correct answers are always available in the world.

Factual recall questions

Even though factual recall questions should not be over-used, it is important to teach students how to comprehend reading, speech, film, or other media. It is also important that students remember certain facts—and questioning can bring on small levels of stress that potentially trigger memory. However, realize that stress may be very upsetting for some students and that such questions, particularly in public settings, may be inappropriate.

Finally, by questioning students, we see how much they know. All types of questioning can be done in a variety of formats. For example, we can question students out loud with a whole class. Teachers should refrain from calling on students too often, but occasionally it is an effective technique. Wait time is particularly important: When asking a question, a teacher should not assume that nobody will answer it if a couple seconds have elapsed. Often wait time encourages some students to answer, or it allows all students time to think about the question. Questioning can also take place in small groups or on paper.

DOMAIN III
INSTRUCTION AND ASSESSMENT

PERSONALIZED STUDY PLAN

KNOWN MATERIAL/ SKIP IT

PAGE		COMPETENCY AND SKILL	
89	7:	**Understand various types of assessment; relationships among assessment, instruction, and learning; and the use of assessment to ensure students' continuous development and achievement of defined standards and goals**	☐
	7.1:	Demonstrating knowledge of the characteristics, uses, advantages, and limitations of formal and informal assessment	☐
	7.2:	Demonstrating knowledge of measurement theory, central concepts in assessment, differences between assessment and evaluation, and the role of assessment	☐
	7.3:	Demonstrating knowledge of the purposes of assessment and how to select, construct, and use assessment strategies, instruments, and technologies	☐
	7.4:	Applying knowledge of strategies for integrating assessment and instruction and for using assessment	☐
	7.5:	Demonstrating knowledge of how to promote self-assessment to identify strengths and needs and set personal goals for learning	☐
	7.6:	Recognizing the importance of multiple assessments and strategies for modifying classroom assessments for diverse students	☐
	7.7:	Demonstrating knowledge of how to establish and maintain records of student performance	☐
102	8:	**Understand instructional planning procedures and how to use effective planning to design instruction that promotes learning and achievement for all students**	☐
	8.1:	Demonstrating knowledge of key factors to consider in planning instruction	☐
	8.2:	Applying knowledge of how to use different types of information and sources of data during planning	☐
	8.3:	Demonstrating knowledge of how to plan and implement learning experiences	☐

PERSONALIZED STUDY PLAN

KNOWN MATERIAL/ SKIP IT

PAGE	COMPETENCY AND SKILL	KNOWN MATERIAL/ SKIP IT
	8.4: Demonstrating knowledge of how to design lessons and activities that are differentiated	☐
	8.5: Applying knowledge of how to create short-range and long-range plans	☐
	8.6: Demonstrating knowledge of skills and strategies for engaging in effective planning in specified situations	☐
112	**9: Understand how to use a variety of instructional strategies to provide effective and appropriate learning experiences that promote all students' achievement and foster development of critical-thinking, problem-solving, and performance skills**	☐
	9.1: Demonstrating knowledge of various instructional strategies	☐
	9.2: Identifying cognitive processes associated with various kinds of learning and instructional strategies that stimulate these processes	☐
	9.3: Demonstrating knowledge of how to develop, implement, and evaluate lesson plans	☐
	9.4: Demonstrating knowledge of the importance of monitoring instructional effectiveness and responding to student needs	☐
	9.5: Applying knowledge of how to design teaching strategies that achieve different instructional purposes and meet varied student needs	☐
	9.6: Demonstrating knowledge of how to use multiple approaches to promote student engagement and learning	☐
	9.7: Demonstrating knowledge of how to develop clear, accurate presentations and representations of concepts	☐
	9.8: Applying knowledge of how to use educational technology	☐

COMPETENCY 7

UNDERSTAND VARIOUS TYPES OF ASSESSMENT; RELATIONSHIPS AMONG ASSESSMENT, INSTRUCTION, AND LEARNING; AND THE USE OF ASSESSMENT TO ENSURE STUDENTS' CONTINUOUS DEVELOPMENT AND ACHIEVEMENT OF DEFINED STANDARDS AND GOALS

* assessing student's Progress is always good

> **SKILL 7.1** **Demonstrating knowledge of the characteristics, uses, advantages, and limitations of different types of formal and informal assessment** *(e.g., criterion-referenced test, norm-referenced test, teacher-made test, performance-based assessment, portfolio, teacher observation, peer assessment, student self-assessment)*

In evaluating school reform efforts, students' performance measures must be assessed. These performance indicators are operationalized through the learning activities planned by the teacher. At varying stages of instruction, the intended outcome must be measured, the level of goal attainment established, and this continuous cycle of student evaluation proceeds. Many forms of assessments are objective, such as multiple choice, yes/no, true/false, and matching. Essays and portfolios, on the other hand, are considered open-ended and allow students to provide answers that are more authentic.

Assessments

The assessment of students is a very important aspect of the teaching and learning process. Periodic testing measures learning outcomes based on established objectives. It also provides information at various stages of learning to determine future student needs such as periodic reviews, reteaching, and enrichment. Educators may implement and assess student academic performance using norm-referenced, criterion-referenced, and performance-based assessments.

> *Educators may implement and assess student academic performance using norm-referenced, criterion-referenced, and performance-based assessments.*

Norm-referenced assessments

Standardized achievement tests can be norm-referenced or criterion-reference. In NORM-REFERENCED MEASUREMENTS the performance of the student is compared with the performance of other students who also took the same test. The original group of students who took the test establishes the norm. Norms can be based on age, sex, grade level, geographical location, ethnicity, or other broad classifications.

> **NORM-REFERENCED MEASUREMENTS:** analyze how a student's performance compares to that of other students who took a test

Standardized, norm-referenced achievement tests are designed to measure what a student knows in a particular subject in relation to other students of similar characteristics. The test batteries provide a broad scope of content area coverage so that it may be used on a larger scale in many different states and school districts. However, the questions may not measure the goals and content emphasized in a particular local curriculum. Therefore, using standardized tests to assess the success of the curriculum or teachers' effectiveness should be avoided (McMillan, 1997).

Uses of norm-referenced scores

Norm-referenced, standardized achievement tests produce different types of scores that are useful in different ways. The most common types of scores are the percentile ranks or percentile scores, grade equivalent scores, stanines, and percentage of items answered correctly.

Percentile scores

The PERCENTILE SCORE indicates how the students' performance compares to the norming group. It tells what percentage of the norming group was outscored by a particular student taking the test. For example, a student scoring at the eightieth percentile did better than eighty percent of the students in the norming group. Likewise, twenty percent of the norming group scored above the particular student, and eighty percent scored below. The scores are indicative of relative strengths and weaknesses. A student may show consistent strengths in language arts and consistent weakness in mathematics as indicated by the scores derived from the test. Yet one could not base remediation solely on these conclusions without a closer item analysis or a closer review of the objectives measured by the test.

Grade equivalency score

The GRADE EQUIVALENCY SCORE is expressed by year and month in school for each student. It is used to measure growth and progress. It indicates where a student stands in reference to the norming group. For example, a second-grade student who obtained a grade equivalent score of 4.5 on the language arts section of the test is really not achieving at the fourth grade five month level as one may think. The 4.5 grade equivalence means that the second grader has achieved at about the same level of the norming group who is in the fifth month of the fourth grade, if indeed such a student did take the test. However, when compared to other second graders in the norming group, the student may be about average.

A point of consideration with grade equivalence is that one may never know how well the second grader might do if placed in the fourth grade or how poorly the second grader might do if given the fourth grade test compared to other second graders in the norming group.

> **PERCENTILE SCORE:** indicates how the students' performance compares to the norming group

> **GRADE EQUIVALENCY SCORE:** this score indicates where a student stands in reference to the norming group

Stanines

STANINES indicate where the score is located on the normal curve for the norming group. Stanines are statistically determined but are not as precise as percentile ranking because it only gives the area in which the score is located, but not the precise location. Using stanines to report standard scores is still found to be practical and easy to understand for many parents and school personnel. Stanines range from one to nine (1–9) with five being the middle of the distribution.

STANINES: indicate where the score is located on the normal curve for the norming group

Percentage of items answered correctly

Finally, achievement test scores can be reported by percentage of items answered correctly. This form of reporting may not be very meaningful when there are only a few questions/items in a particular category. This makes it difficult to determine if the student guessed well at the items, was just lucky at selecting the right answers, or knowingly chose the correct responses.

Criterion-referenced assessments

CRITERION-REFERENCED ASSESSMENTS (or standardized achievement tests) are designed to indicate the student's performance that is directly related to specific educational objectives, thus indicating what the student can or cannot do. For example, the test may measure how well a student can subtract by regrouping in the tens place or how well a student can identify the long vowel sound in specific words.

CRITERION-REFERENCED ASSESSMENTS: assessments designed to indicate the student's performance that is directly related to specific educational objectives, thus indicating what the student can or cannot do

Criterion-referenced tests are specific to a particular curriculum, which allows the determination of the effectiveness of the curriculum, as well as specific skills acquired by the students. They also provide information needed to plan for future student needs. Because of the recognized value of criterion-referenced standardized achievement tests, many publishers have developed tailor-made tests to correlate with state and districts' general goals and specific learning objectives by pulling from a test bank of field-tested items. The test scores are reported by percentage of items answered correctly to indicate mastery or non-mastery.

Performance-based assessments

PERFORMANCE-BASED ASSESSMENTS are currently being used in a number of state testing programs to measure the learning outcomes of individual students in subject content areas. For example, to measure student-learning performance, Washington State uses the Washington Assessment of Student Learning (WASL) in Reading, Writing, Math and Science. This assessment became a high-stakes test when, for the class of 2008, passing it became a graduation requirement.

PERFORMANCE-BASED ASSESSMENTS: these assessments measure the learning outcomes of individual students in subject content areas

In today's classrooms, performance-based assessments in core subject areas must be monitored systematically. The process must include pretesting and daily or weekly gauging of student learning. Typical performance assessments include oral and written student work, which can take the form of:

- Research papers
- Oral presentations
- Class projects
- Journals
- Portfolios
- Community service projects

If they are effective, performance assessments will show the gaps or holes that can be then be filled through careful planning.

Summary

With today's emphasis on student learning accountability, the public and legislature demand effective teaching. Thus, assessment of student learning will remain a mandate in educational accountability. Each method, norm-referenced, criterion-referenced, and performance-based assessments, has costs and benefits. Before a state, district, or school community can determine which type of testing is the most effective, they must determine how the assessment will meet the learning goals and objectives of the students.

Purposes and Uses of Assessment

There are seven purposes of assessment:

1. To assist student learning

2. To identify students' strengths and weaknesses

3. To assess the effectiveness of a particular instructional strategy

4. To assess and improve the effectiveness of curriculum programs

5. To assess and improve teaching effectiveness

6. To provide data that assists in decision making

7. To communicate with and involve parents and other stakeholders

In a general sense, assessments can take four forms:

1. Observation: Noticing someone and judging their actions.

2. Informal continuous assessment: Not formal like a test or exam. It is continuous because it occurs periodically, such as on a daily or weekly basis.

3. Formal continuous assessment: More structured activity organized to measure learners progress, such as quizzes or group activities.

4. Formal assessment: Structured infrequent measure of learner achievement, such as tests and exams.

INFORMAL ASSESSMENTS help teachers measure how well the learners are processing information and progressing. Informal assessments can be in the form of homework assignments, field journals, and daily class work. Teachers then use the information gathered to tailor instruction to student needs.

On the other hand, FORMAL ASSESSMENTS are highly structured. They are conducted at regular intervals and if the progress is not satisfactory, interventions, including parent involvement, are absolutely essential. Tests, exams, and projects are types of formal assessments.

> **INFORMAL ASSESS-MENT:** a type of assessment that is more casual and not highly structured

> **FORMAL ASSESSMENT:** a type of assessment that is highly structured and usually graded or scored to evaluate student performance; these can be both continuous or periodic

Classification of Assessments

Assessments can be classified as follows:

- Diagnostic assessments: Determine individual strengths and weaknesses in specific areas.

- Readiness assessments: Measure prerequisite knowledge and skills.

- Interest and Attitude assessments: Attempt to identify topics of high interest or areas in which students may need extra motivational support.

- Evaluation assessments: Generally program- or teacher-focused.

- Placement assessments: Used for grouping students or determining where each student should begin in leveled materials.

- Formative assessments: Provide ongoing feedback on student progress and the effectiveness of instructional methods and materials.

- Summative assessments: Determine the degree of student mastery or learning that has taken place. Usually a value, such as a grade, is placed on the student's performance.

It is important to remember that in education, the main purpose of evaluation is to guide instruction. Therefore, tests must measure not only what a child has learned, but also what a child has yet to learn and what a teacher must teach. Although today's educators utilize many forms of assessment, testing remains an integral part of instruction and evaluation.

> **SKILL 7.2** Demonstrating knowledge of measurement theory, central concepts in assessment (*e.g., validity, reliability, bias*), differences between assessment and evaluation, and the role of assessment in teaching and learning

Accuracy in Student Evaluation

The accuracy of student evaluation is essential. ACCURACY is determined by the usability of the instrument and the consistency of measurement, which is observed through reliability and validity of the instruments.

VALIDITY is the extent to which a test measures what it is intended to measure. For example, a test may lack validity if it was designed to measure the creative writing of students, but it is also used to measure handwriting even though it was not designed for the latter.

RELIABILITY refers to the consistency of the test to measure what it should measure. For example, the items on a true or false quiz, given by a classroom teacher, are reliable if they convey the same meaning every time the quiz is administered to similar groups of students under similar situations. In other words, there is no ambiguity or confusion with the items on the quiz.

Difference between reliability and validity

The difference between validity and reliability can be visualized as throwing darts at a dartboard. There is validity if the dart hits the target (an assessment measures what it is intended to measure), it is reliable if the same spot is hit time after time (the assessment consistently measures what it should measure). The goal should be to develop assessments that are both valid and reliable (every time the assessment is administered, it measures what it is intended to measure).

ACCURACY: this is the usability of the instrument and the consistency of a measurement, which is observed through reliability and validity of the instruments

VALIDITY: the extent to which a test measures what it is intended to measure

RELIABILITY: the consistency of the test to measure what it should measure

Reliability versus Validity

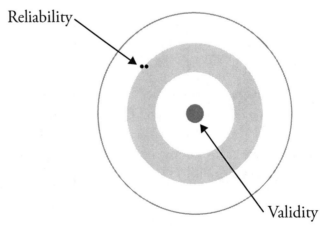

A perfect positive correlation equals +1.00 and a perfect negative correlation equals −1.00. The reliability of an assessment tool is generally expressed as a decimal to two places (e.g., 0.85). This decimal describes the correlation that would be expected between two scores if the same student took the test repeatedly.

Determining reliability

There are several ways to estimate the reliability of an instrument. The simplest approach is the TEST-RETEST METHOD. When the same test is administered again to the same students, if the test is perfectly reliable, each student will receive the same score each time. Even as the scores of individual students vary slightly from one time to the next, it is desirable for the rank order of the students to remain unchanged.

Other methods of estimating reliability rely on the same conceptual framework. SPLIT-HALF METHODS divide a single test into two parts and compare them. EQUIVALENT FORMS METHODS compare two versions of the same test. With some types of assessment, such as essays and observation reports, reliability also deals with the procedures and criteria used for scoring. The inter-rater reliability asks the question: How much will the results vary depending on who is scoring or rating the assessment data?

Determining validity

There are three common types of validity:

1. Content validity: describes the degree to which a test actually tests what it sets out to test. For example, in mathematics, a complex story problem will lower the validity of an arithmetic test because the story problem allows a student's reading ability to affect the results. However, note that it remains a valid test of the student's ability to solve story problems.

2. Criterion validity: deals with the test's ability to predict performance on another measure or test. For example, a college admissions test has high criterion validity if it accurately predicts those students who will attain high GPAs at a particular college. The criterion in this case is college GPA.

3. Construct validity: shows how well an assessment measures a particular theoretical concept such as intelligence or creativity. For example, intelligence is an idea or concept that is defined in many ways; therefore, an IQ test may have construct validity for someone who defines intelligence according to IQ. Conversely, someone who believes in multiple intelligences may say that an IQ test lacks construct validity. In either case, the validity is determined according to the definitions and dimensions of the construct being measured. First, the construct must be properly defined, then the assessment can be judged to see if it measures the construct in a valid way.

TEST-RETEST METHOD: a method of detemining reliability when the same test is administered again to the same students to ensure that the same scores are received

SPLIT-HALF METHOD: a method of dividing a single test into two parts and comparing them

EQUIVALENT FORMS METHOD: a method of comparing two versions of the same test

> **SKILL** **Demonstrating knowledge of the purposes of assessment**
> **7.3** *(e.g., monitoring, comparing, screening, diagnosing)* **and how to select, construct, and use assessment strategies, instruments, and technologies for different purposes and needs, including assessing student progress in achieving state standards**

See Skill 7.1

Subjective Tests and Rubrics

Subjective tests put the student in the driver's seat.

RUBRIC: a document that provides assessment criteria for high-scoring answers and projects

Subjective tests put the student in the driver's seat. These types of assessments usually consist of short answer questions, longer essays, or problem-solving items that require more critical thinking skills. Sometimes teachers provide RUBRICS that include assessment criteria for high-scoring answers and projects. Sometimes, the rubric is as simple as a checklist and, other times, a maximum point value is awarded for each item on the rubric. Either way, rubrics provide a guideline of the teacher's expectations for the specifics of the assignment. The teacher usually discusses and models what is expected to fulfill each guideline, as well as provides a detailed outline of these expectations for reference.

For example, students being asked to write a research paper might be provided with a rubric. An elementary teacher may assign a total of 50 points for the entire paper. The rubric may award 10 points for note taking quality, 10 points for research skills, 20 points for content covered, 5 points for creative elements, and 5 points for organization and presentation. Then a certain number of points will be awarded in accordance with the students' performance. Rubrics allow students to be scored in multiple areas, rather than simply on a final product.

Importance of Preparation

The bottom line is that studying and preparing for any type of test will equate to better student performance and achievement on tests.

The bottom line is that studying and preparing for any type of test will equate to better student performance and achievement on tests. In addition, as teachers evaluate the students' work, they are able to see each student's strengths and weaknesses. This information allows teachers to differentiate instruction for each student in order to maximize their learning.

SKILL **Applying knowledge of strategies for integrating assessment and**
7.4 **instruction and for using assessment to identify student strengths and needs, monitor student progress, evaluate and modify instruction, and promote student growth and access to effective learning opportunities**

The teacher appreciates the importance of knowing and understanding students in order to provide the most effective learning opportunities. Therefore, the teacher is aware of and uses a variety of strategies for developing this knowledge of students' strengths and weaknesses. In addition he or she is able to share this knowledge with the students, their parents, and others.

Tests

Tests are essential for the learner in understanding his/her current achievements and learning difficulties. Tests can have strong consequences for students, therefore, they should not be taken lightly, nor should they be given haphazardly. No longer can a teacher rely on ready-made tests to precisely assess what students know. To obtain an accurate measure of student progress, the teacher must know how to plan and construct tests. In addition, the teacher must know how to:

- Administer tests

- Arm students with test-taking skills

- Provide feedback on test performance

Research indicates that students do their best when they are motivated and aware of and able to apply test-taking skills. In addition, teachers must use test data as a meaningful aspect of instruction. For instance, it can be used to increase student motivation, especially when this information is available in the form of feedback. Using this strategy, teachers frequently administer tests and give immediate feedback, which is an effective way to increase achievement.

Standardized testing

Standardized testing is currently under great scrutiny; however, educators agree that all tests have a purpose. Each type serves as a means of gathering information about children's learning and most can provide accurate, helpful data for improving instruction. Notwithstanding, formative assessments should be the most common types administered. These are the basic, everyday types of assessments teachers continually use to understand students' growth and to help them achieve.

Observations

Valuable information can be obtained through teacher observations. Teachers are constantly observing students and making assessments about their performance, which in turn influences future instruction. INFORMAL OBSERVATIONS allow teachers to observe students with no predetermined focus. Through such observations, teachers may identify students who can work independently versus those who require a great deal of guidance. Informal observations can lead to more formal assessments, which can then lead to serious interventions and/or parent conferences.

Global and behavioral observations

A GLOBAL OBSERVATION is a teacher's written account of a student's interaction with peers, general attitude toward school and learning, overall ability to satisfactorily complete assignments, and typical behavior. It is written in lay terms without educational jargon and is therefore easily understood by parents. This document contains pertinent information about a child's class performance and is a valuable tool for school administrators, guidance counselors, psychologists, and other personnel who may be involved with the child.

A BEHAVIORAL OBSERVATION is a written anecdotal record of a child's behavior and activities for a specific period of time. The teacher records both the beginning and ending times for the observation and precisely indicates the child's every movement, utterance, and action during that designated time. This type of observation is valuable in determining a child's activity level and ability to attend to prescribed tasks.

Formal observations

Occasionally more FORMAL OBSERVATIONS are needed. In these cases, there is a specified focus, and predetermined, sample behavior is systematically observed. This is done because some goals or objectives can only be assessed by observation, such as those that occur during cooperative group activities. Formal observations often allow teachers to benefit from new information that may challenge some of their opinions about students.

Formal observations can be included in a student's record, as they add to the history of a child's education. Meaningful information such as the child's attendance, grade averages, and general health are also a part of the record. Some basic information about the child's family, current address, and schools attended is included. Standardized test scores and dates of administration are also an important aspect of the student's record.

INFORMAL OBSERVATION: allows teachers to observe students with no predetermined focus

GLOBAL OBSERVATION: a teacher's written account of a student's interaction with peers, general attitude toward school and learning, overall ability to satisfactorily complete assignments, and typical behavior

BEHAVIORAL OBSERVATION: a written anecdotal record of a child's behavior and activities for a specific period of time

FORMAL OBSERVATION: an observation where there is a specified focus, and predetermined, sample behavior is systematically observed

The narrative is a written record, which may be contained within a student's cumulative record. Teachers can use this information to set goals for individual students or to structure future activities. The information acquired through any of these tools can best be reported through a parent/student conference or a meeting with other educators. Although written reports could summarize the knowledge the teacher has gained, a more thorough explanation can be presented through a face-to-face meeting.

Student Records

The information contained within STUDENT RECORDS, teacher observations, and diagnostic tests are only as valuable as the teacher's ability to understand them. Although these data are contained in the student's cumulative record, it is the responsibility of each teacher to read and interpret the information.

> **STUDENT RECORDS:** a collection of documents about a certain student, including test scores and observations, that help an educator get a more accurate feel for a student's needs

Student test results

Diagnostic test results are somewhat uniform and easy to interpret. They usually include a scoring guide that tells the teacher what the numbers actually mean. Teachers also need to realize that these scores are not the ultimate indicator of a child's ability or learning needs. Many factors influence these scores including:

- How the child regarded the value or importance of the test
- How the child was feeling when the test was administered
- The rapport the child had with the tester

Therefore, the teacher should regard these scores as a "ballpark" figure.

Interpreting other teachers' observations

When a teacher reads another teacher's observations, it is important to keep in mind that each person brings certain biases to an observation. The reader may also influence the information contained within an observation with his/her own interpretation. It is necessary to be aware of these shortcomings when using teacher observations as a basis for designing learning programs.

Student records may provide the most assistance in guiding instruction. These records contain information that was gathered over a period of time and may show student growth and progress. They also hold information provided by several people including teachers, parents, and other educators or professionals. By reading this compilation of information, the teacher may get a more accurate feel for a student's needs, how he or she learns, what he or she knows, and what he or she needs to know to further his/her education.

Communicating Results

In addition to interpreting the results of ongoing assessments, it is also the teacher's job to communicate these results with the child's parents and future teachers. Just as the current teacher uses prior information to make instructional decisions, future teachers will also rely on the current teacher's records. Also, teachers should make themselves available if a future teacher needs clarification on a student's issue(s). Lastly, the teacher must ensure that parents receive the results of all assessments, and that they understand the results completely. Often, this can be accomplished through:

- Phone calls

- Letters

- Short meetings

- Special parent/teacher conferences

SKILL 7.5 Demonstrating knowledge of how to promote elementary students' use of self-assessment to identify their own strengths and needs and set personal goals for learning

SELF-ASSESSMENT: the process of students judging the quality of their work, based on given criteria, with the goal of improving performance in the future

Time allocated to self-assessment must also be considered in the course of designing a lesson or unit. SELF-ASSESSMENT is the process of students judging the quality of their work, based on given criteria, with the goal of improving performance in the future. The process of self-assessment itself also helps to teach students to think critically, so that they do not need someone else to tell them how well they are doing. There is a solid body of evidence that supports the use of self-assessment for improving student performance, particularly in writing. Additionally, students often like to do it and are more motivated to persist at difficult tasks! Research has also revealed that student attitudes toward evaluations are more positive when the students are involved in the assessment.

The process of self-assessment is a learning experience. The process must begin by involving students in defining the criteria on which they will be assessed. Teachers must then instruct students on how to apply that criteria to their own work. Teacher modeling, with examples, is crucial at this step. Students must then be given feedback on their self-evaluations so that they can learn how to most effectively use the process. Finally, students must be guided on how to use those self-evaluations to develop personal goals.

One popular method of self-assessment is using rubrics. Developing rubrics with students gives them the opportunity to participate in defining important criteria and also provides students with a tool to use during the learning task. Students can then systematically proceed through the assessment procedure, can discuss specific areas of strength and/or weakness, and can transition to goal setting in a more systematic and structured manner.

SKILL 7.6 **Recognizing the importance of using multiple assessments and strategies for modifying classroom assessments for students with various characteristics and needs** (e.g., English language learners, students with exceptionalities)

No single assessment can measure a student's abilities and progress. It is, therefore, necessary to use knowledge of the different assessment tools and their purposes when making decisions about a student's progress.

Testing Modifications

The intent of testing modifications is to minimize the effect of a student's disability or learning challenge. This provides an equal opportunity for students with disabilities to participate in assessments to demonstrate and express their knowledge and ability.

Testing modifications should be identified in the student's IEP, consistently implemented, and used to the least extent possible. Types of testing modifications include:

- Flexible scheduling: providing time extensions or altering testing duration (e.g., by inserting appropriate breaks)

- Flexible setting: using special lighting or acoustics, minimizing distractions (e.g., testing the student in a separate location), using adaptive equipment

- Alternate test format: using large print or Braille, increasing the space allocated for student response, realigning the format of question and answer selections (e.g., vertically rather than horizontally)

- Use of mechanical aids: tape recorders, word processors, visual and auditory magnification devices, calculators, spell check and grammar check software (where spelling and grammar are not the focus of the assessment)

> **SKILL** Demonstrating knowledge of how to establish and maintain records
> **7.7** of student performance, use technological resources to collect and
> analyze data and interpret results, and communicate responsibly
> and effectively with students, parents/guardians, and colleagues
> about performance and progress

See Skill 7.4

COMPETENCY 8

UNDERSTAND INSTRUCTIONAL PLANNING PROCEDURES AND HOW TO USE EFFECTIVE PLANNING TO DESIGN INSTRUCTION THAT PROMOTES LEARNING AND ACHIEVEMENT FOR ALL STUDENTS

> **SKILL** Demonstrating knowledge of key factors to consider in planning
> **8.1** instruction *(e.g., state standards; curriculum goals; nature of the subject
> matter; learning theory; students' development, characteristics, thinking, and prior
> experiences; students' current knowledge and skills; available time and resources)*

Understanding Standards and Planning Accordingly

The first step in planning successful instruction is having a firm grasp on the ending objectives for which the students will be held accountable. While teachers may have the best of intentions in teaching numerous, exciting topics, there are only so many days in a school year. Furthermore, the more content the teacher covers (skimmed over, so that students can be exposed to everything), the weaker the deep and lasting understandings of content by the students.

Aligning with standards

Teachers may benefit from laying out all crucial standards throughout the year and aligning them in a fashion that allows for conceptual growth.

So, with that in mind, teachers may benefit from laying out all crucial standards throughout the year and aligning them in a fashion that allows for conceptual growth. Conceptual growth refers to concepts building upon one another. Certain topics simply should be taught before other topics.

Demonstrating proficiency

Next, teachers should consider how students will be required to demonstrate proficiency of the various concepts presented. This is important, as all instruction needs to focus on making sure that students can indeed demonstrate proficiency.

Assessing understanding

Finally, as lessons and units are planned, to be most efficient with time, teachers should determine how much students already understand about the topics being taught. This will help the teacher to determine how long the concept will take to fully teach. This will allow the teacher to develop lessons that build on students' background knowledge without requiring them to repeat it. It will also help teachers manage their ability to teach all of the required standards in a one-year time period.

For information on readiness, see Skill 2.2

SKILL 8.2 **Applying knowledge of how to use different types of information and sources of data during planning to define learning goals, select appropriate instructional approaches and materials, and accommodate varied student learning styles, needs, and experiences**

Lesson Plans

Teaching was once seen as simply developing lesson plans, teaching, going home early, and taking the summer off. However, the demands of a classroom involve much more than grading papers. To begin with, writing lesson plans is very complicated. Lesson plans are crucial in guiding instruction within the classroom. The LESSON PLAN outlines the steps a teacher will implement and the forms of assessment that will be used in an instructional learning capacity. Teachers are able to both objectify and quantify learning goals and targets through the incorporating of effective performance-based assessments as well as the projected criteria for identifying when a student has learned the material presented.

LESSON PLAN: an outline of the steps a teacher will implement and the forms of assessment that will be used in an instructional learning capacity

Components

Components of a lesson plan include:

- The unit description
- Learning targets

- Learning experiences

- Explanation of learning rationale

- Assessments

These all must be present to provide both quantifiable and qualitative data. These two data sources help the teacher to ascertain whether student learning has taken place and whether effective teaching has occurred for the students. National and state learning standards must be considered, because not only will the teacher and the students be measured by the students' scores at the end of the year, the school will also. So, not only must the teacher be knowledgeable about state and local standards, she must structure her own classes in ways that will satisfy those frameworks.

Long-Term Considerations

On the large scale, the teacher must think about the scope of his ambitious plans for the day, the week, the unit, the semester, the year. The teacher must also decide on the subject matter for the unit, semester, and year, making certain that it is appropriate to the age of the students, relevant to their real lives, and in their realm of anticipated interest. Should he introduce politically controversial issues or avoid them? He must make these decisions deliberatively on the basis of feedback from his students, while at the same time keeping sight of his objectives.

Behavioral objectives

The teacher must be very knowledgeable about the writing of behavioral objectives that fall within the guidelines of both the state and local expectations.

The teacher must be very knowledgeable about the writing of behavioral objectives that fall within the guidelines of both the state and local expectations; additionally, the objectives must be measurable so he can know for sure whether he has accomplished what he set out to do.

Aligning goals with student needs

Once long-range goals have been identified and established, it is important to ensure that all goals and objectives are also in conjunction with student ability and needs. Some objectives may be too basic for a higher-level student, while others cannot be met by students with a lower level of knowledge. There are many forms of evaluating student needs to ensure that all goals set are challenging yet achievable.

Teachers should check a student's cumulative file for reading level and prior subject area achievement.

Teachers should check a student's cumulative file for reading level and prior subject area achievement. This provides a basis for goal setting but shouldn't be the only method used. Depending on the subject area, basic skills test, reading level evaluations, writing samples, and interest surveys can all be useful in determining if all goals are appropriate. Informal observation should always be used as well. Finally, it is important to take into consideration the student's level of motivation when addressing student needs.

Adjusting objectives to specific needs

When given objectives by the school or county, teachers may wish to adapt them so that they can better meet the needs of their individual student population. For example, if a higher-level advanced class is given the objective, "State five causes of World War II," a teacher may wish to adapt the objective to a higher level. "State five causes of World War II and explain how they contributed to the start of the war." Subsequently, objectives can be modified for a lower level as well: "From a list of causes, pick three that specifically caused World War II."

Constructing and Organizing Objectives

When organizing and sequencing objectives the teacher needs to remember that skills are building blocks. Taxonomy of educational objectives can be helpful to construct and organize objectives. Knowledge of material, for example, memorizing definitions or famous quotes, is low on the taxonomy of learning and should be worked with early in the sequence of teaching. Eventually, objectives should be developed to include higher-level thinking such as:

- Comprehension (being able to use a definition)

- Application (being able to apply the definition to other situations)

- Synthesis (being able to add other information)

- Evaluation (being able to judge the value of something)

Strategies

EMERGENT CURRICULUM describes the projects and themes that classrooms may pursue that have been inspired by the children's interests. The teacher uses all the tools of assessment available to her to learn as much as she can about her students and then continually assesses them over the period of the unit or semester. As she gets to know them, she listens to what their interests are and creates a curriculum in response to what she learns from her observations of her own students.

WEBBING is a recent concept related to the idea of emergent curriculum. The two main uses of webbing are planning and recording curriculum. Planning webs are used to generate ideas for activities and projects for the children from an observed interest such as rocks.

EMERGENT CURRICULUM: projects and themes that classrooms may pursue that have been inspired by the children's interests

WEBBING: a curriculum-planning strategy whereby activities are grouped by different areas of the room or by developmental domains and recorded in a web format

Teachers work together to come up with ideas and activities for the children and to record them in on a web format. Activities can be grouped by different areas of the room or by developmental domains. For example, clusters either fall under areas such as dramatic play or science areas or around domains such as language, cognitive, and physical development. Either configuration works; being consistent in each web is important.

This format will work as a unit, weekly, or monthly program plan. Any new activities that emerge throughout the unit can also be added to the web. The record will serve in the future to plan using activities that emerge from the children's play and ideas.

> **SKILL 8.3** **Demonstrating knowledge of how to plan and implement learning experiences that are appropriate for curriculum goals, relevant to students, and based on principles of effective instruction** *(e.g., activating students' prior knowledge, anticipating preconceptions, encouraging exploration and problem solving, building new skills on those previously acquired)*

To determine the abilities of incoming students, it may be helpful to consult their prior academic records. Letter grades assigned at previous levels of instruction as well as scores on standardized tests may be taken into account. In addition, the teacher may choose to administer pretests at the beginning of the school year and, perhaps, also at the initial stage of each new unit of instruction. The textbooks available for classroom use may provide suitable pretests, tests of student progress, and post-tests.

Selecting Assessments

In selecting tests and other assessment tools, the teacher should keep in mind that different kinds of tests measure different aspects of student development.

In selecting tests and other assessment tools, the teacher should keep in mind that different kinds of tests measure different aspects of student development. The tests included in most textbooks chosen for the classroom are usually achievement tests. Few of these are the type of tests intended to measure the students' inherent ability or aptitude. Teachers will find it difficult to raise students' scores based on ability tests, but students' scores on achievement tests may be expected to improve with proper instruction and application in the area being studied.

Using a variety of tasks

In addition to administering tests, the teacher may assess the readiness of students for a particular level of instruction by having them demonstrate their ability to perform some relevant task. In a class that emphasizes written composition, for example, students may be asked to submit writing samples. These may be used not only to ensure the placement of the students into the proper level but as a diagnostic tool to help them understand what aspects of their composition skills may need improvement. Similarly, students in a speech class may be asked to make an impromptu oral presentation before beginning a new level or specific level of instruction. Others may be asked to demonstrate their psychomotor skills in a physical education class, display their computational skills in a mathematics class, and so on. Whatever the chosen task, the teacher will need to select or devise an appropriate assessment scale and interpret the results with care.

> In addition to administering tests, the teacher may assess the readiness of students for a particular level of instruction by having them demonstrate their ability to perform some relevant task.

| SKILL 8.4 | Demonstrating knowledge of how to design lessons and activities that are differentiated to meet students' varied developmental and individual needs and to help all students progress |

Lesson plans are important in guiding instruction in the classroom. Incorporating the nuts and bolts of a teaching unit, the lesson plans outline the steps of teacher implementation, assessment of teacher instructional capacity, and student learning capacity. Teachers are able to objectify and quantify learning goals and targets in terms of incorporating effective performance-based assessments and projected criteria for identifying when a student has learned the material presented.

> Lesson plans are important in guiding instruction in the classroom.

Components of a Successful Lesson Plan

All components of a lesson plan—including the unit description, learning targets, learning experiences, explanation of learning rationale and assessments—must be designed to provide both quantifiable and qualitative data. These two data sources help the teacher ascertain whether student learning has taken place and whether effective teaching has occurred.

A typical format would include:

1. Written instructional lesson plan: Guidelines for what is being taught and how the students will be able to access the information. Subsequent evaluations and assessments will determine whether students have learned or correctly processed the subject content being taught.

detailed descriptions of lesson Plans are important.

2. Unit Description: Desribes the learning and classroom environment.

– Classroom Characteristics: The physical arrangements of the classroom, along with the student grouping patterns for the lesson being taught. Classroom rules and consequences should be clearly posted and visible.

– Student Characteristics: Demographics of the classroom, which include student number, gender, cultural and ethnic backgrounds, along with independent education students with IEPs (Individualized Education Plans).

3. Learning Goals/Targets/Objectives: What are the expectations of the lessons? Are the learning goals appropriate to the state learning standards and district academic goals? Are the targets appropriate for the grade level and, subject content area and do they include a multicultural perspective and global viewpoint?

4. Learning Experiences: How will student learning be supported using the learning goals?

– What prior knowledge or experiences will the students bring to the lesson? How will you check and verify that student knowledge?

– How will you engage all students in the classroom? How will students who have been identified as marginalized in the classroom be engaged in the lesson unit?

– How will the lesson plan be modified for students with IEPs and how will independent education students be evaluated for learning and processing of the modified lesson targets?

– How will the multicultural aspect be incorporated into the lesson plan?

– What interdisciplinary linkages and connections will be used to incorporate across other subject areas.

– What types of assessments and evaluations will be used to test student understanding and processing of the lesson plan?

– How will students be cooperatively grouped to engage in the lesson?

– What Internet links are provided in the lesson plan?

5. Rationales for Learning Experiences: Provide data on how the lesson plan addresses student learning goals and objectives. Address whether the lesson provides accommodations for students with IEPs and provides support for marginalized students in the classroom.

6. Assessments: Constructing pre- and post-assessments that evaluate student learning as it correlates to the learning goals and objectives. Do the assessments include a cultural integration that addresses the cultural needs and inclusion of students?

Differentiation

The effective teacher will seek to connect all students to the subject matter by using multiple techniques, with the goal being that each student, through his or her own abilities, will relate to one or more techniques and excel in the learning process. While all students need to have exposure to the same curriculum, not all students need to have the curriculum taught in the same way. DIFFERENTIATION is the term used to describe the variations of curriculum and instruction that can be provided to an entire class of students.

> **DIFFERENTIATION:** describes the variations of curriculum and instruction that can be provided to an entire class of students

Ways to differentiate

The following are three primary ways to differentiate:

THREE PRIMARY WAYS TO DIFFERENTIATE	
Content	The specifics of what is learned. Whole units or concepts should not be modified; however, within certain topics, specifics can be modified.
Process	The route to learning the content. This means that not everyone has to learn the content in exactly the same method.
Product	The result of the learning. Usually, a product is the result or assessment of learning. For example, not all students are going to demonstrate complete learning on a quiz; likewise, not all students will demonstrate complete learning on a written paper.

Keys to differentiation

There are two keys to successful differentiation:

TWO KEYS TO SUCCESSFUL DIFFERENTIATION	
Knowing what is essential in the curriculum	Although certain things can be modified, other things must remain in-tact in a specific order. Disrupting central components of a curriculum can actually damage a student's ability to learn something successfully.
Knowing the needs of the students	While this can take quite some time to figure out, it is very important that teachers pay attention to the interests, tendencies, and abilities of their students so that they understand how each of their students will best learn.

Keeping the Class as a Community

Many students will need certain concepts explained in greater depth; others may pick up on concepts rather quickly. For this reason, teachers will want to adapt the curriculum in a way that allows students with the opportunity to learn at their own pace, while also keeping the class together as a community. This can be difficult, but the more creative a teacher is with the ways in which students can demonstrate mastery, the more fun the experience will be for students and teachers. Furthermore, teachers who tailor lesson plans, activities, groupings, and other elements of curriculum to each student's need will reach students more successfully.

> **SKILL 8.5** **Applying knowledge of how to create short-range and long-range plans that are linked to student needs and performance, evaluate plans in relation to short-range and long-range goals, and adjust plans to meet student needs and enhance learning**

See Skill 8.2

> **SKILL 8.6** **Demonstrating knowledge of skills and strategies for engaging in effective planning in specified situations** *(e.g., collaborating with colleagues to plan instruction, integrating curricula and creating interdisciplinary units of study, managing technological resources during learning activities, managing student learning in a technology-integrated environment)*

Collaborative Learning

According to Walther-Thomas et al. (2000) *Collaboration for Inclusive Education,* ongoing professional development that provides teachers with opportunities to create effective instructional practice is vital and necessary: "A comprehensive approach to professional development is perhaps the most critical dimension of sustained support for successful program implementation." The inclusive approach incorporates learning programs that include all stakeholders in defining and developing high-quality programs for students. The figure below shows how an integrated approach of stakeholders can provide the optimal learning opportunity for all students.

Integrated Approach to Learning

The integrated approach

In the INTEGRATED APPROACH to learning, teachers, parents, and community support become the integral apexes to student learning. The focus and central core of the school community is triangular as a representation of how effective collaboration can work in creating success for student learners. The goal of student learning and achievement now become the heart of the school community. The direction of teacher professional development in constructing effective instruction is clearly articulated in a greater understanding of facilitating learning strategies that develop skills and education equity for students.

> **INTEGRATED APPROACH:** an approach to learning whereby teacher, parent, and community support become the integral apexes to student learning

Classroom application of collaborative learning

Teachers need diversity in their instructional toolkits, which can provide students with clear instruction, mentoring, inquiry, challenge, performance-based assessment, and journal reflections on their learning processes. For teachers, having a collaborative approach to instruction fosters for students a deeper appreciation of learning, subject matter, and knowledge acquisition. Implementing a consistent approach to learning from all stakeholders will create equitable educational opportunities for all learners.

The ability to gain additional insight into how students learn and modalities of differing learning styles can increase a teacher's capacity to develop proactive instruction methods. Teachers who team-teach or have daily networking opportunities can create a portfolio of curriculum articulation and inclusion for students.

> *Research has shown that educators who collaborate become more diversified and effective in implementation of curriculum and assessment of effective instructional practices.*

Networking

People in business are always encouraged to network in order to further their careers. The same can be said for teaching. If English teachers get together and discuss what is going on in their classrooms, those discussions make the whole much stronger than the parts. Even if there are no formal opportunities for such networking, it is wise for schools or even individual teachers to develop them and seek them out.

COMPETENCY 9

UNDERSTAND HOW TO USE A VARIETY OF INSTRUCTIONAL STRATEGIES TO PROVIDE EFFECTIVE AND APPROPRIATE LEARNING EXPERIENCES THAT PROMOTE ALL STUDENTS' ACHIEVEMENT AND FOSTER DEVELOPMENT OF CRITICAL-THINKING, PROBLEM-SOLVING, AND PERFORMANCE SKILLS

SKILL 9.1 **Demonstrating knowledge of various instructional strategies** *(e.g., cooperative learning, interdisciplinary instruction, hands-on activities, technology-based learning, guided discovery, guided practice, modeling)*; **their characteristics, advantages, and limitations; and their use in promoting student learning and achievement of state standards**

See Skill 2.3

SKILL 9.2 **Identifying cognitive processes associated with various kinds of learning and instructional strategies that stimulate these processes and nurture the development of students' critical-thinking, independent problem-solving, and performance capabilities**

Until they reach pre-adolescence, students do not think in abstract forms.

Until they reach pre-adolescence, students do not think in abstract forms. They are able to understand symbols, but deep symbolism is not yet comprehended. For example, language is a symbol, and they can understand that certain words symbolize things, actions, emotions, etc. But they do not yet have the same ability as an adolescent to see how symbolism works in a story.

When we say that young children are concrete thinkers, we mean that they are driven by senses. In other words, they are very literal thinkers. If they can see something, hear something, or feel something, they are more likely to believe it—and learn it.

Therefore, the more teachers can utilize this concrete thinking, the better their students will master grade-level standards at this age. Let's take the example of math. Ever wonder why young children always count with their fingers? This is because, even though they might be able to do it in their heads, seeing it (and feeling it, as they move their fingers) makes it more "real" to them. So, instead of teaching math through words and numbers on a chalkboard, teachers can be more effective by teaching math through manipulatives. By simply putting objects on a table, and then having students count the objects, take away a certain number and re-count the left-over objects, a teacher helps students understand the *concept* of subtraction more readily.

Many reading teachers have learned that students can comprehend stories more easily if they get a chance to dramatize the story. In other words, they "act out" a story, and thereby learn what the words mean more clearly than if they just read it and talked about it.

The whole concept of science laboratory learning in elementary school is founded on the idea that students will be more successful understanding concepts if they use their hands, eyes, ears, noses, etc., in the learning process. Many concepts that would otherwise be very difficult for students to learn can be attained very quickly in a laboratory setting.

See also Skills 1.1 and 1.2

> Young children are concrete thinkers; they are driven by senses.

> Many concepts that would otherwise be very difficult for students to learn can be attained very quickly in a laboratory setting.

SKILL 9.3 Demonstrating knowledge of how to develop, implement, and evaluate lesson plans that use various strategies, methods, and materials, including technological resources, to enhance student learning

Things to Consider when Planning a Lesson

— important

There are many things to consider when planning a lesson. First, lessons must have objectives. Those objectives state what students should be able to know and do by the time the lesson is finished. It is not good enough to simply know particular objectives for the sake of planning a lesson. If those objectives are not placed appropriately in the context of a coherent learning plan (i.e., a course of study, a unit, or an aligned curriculum), the lesson will mean very little in the overall depth of knowledge or skill of a student.

Second, when lessons have objectives, those objectives must be observable. To observe that an objective is accomplished, a teacher will need an assessment. Let's take an example of a seventh grade Language Arts teacher.

AN EXAMPLE OF LESSON PLANNING

This teacher has been working on a unit of argumentative writing. He wants his students at the end of the unit to be able to write a coherent, effective five-paragraph essay that argues an opinion about a current topic in the news. The lesson for the day is the thesis sentence. His objective is that students will be able to write a coherent thesis sentence that argues an opinion about a current issue. The assessment might be multi-faceted.

First, students are given four different sentences, three of which are potential thesis sentences, and one of which is an example sentence. If students can identify the sentence that is not a thesis sentence, they have been able to slightly show mastery of the objective. To continue ensuring that students have mastery of the objective, the assessment might also include a sample topic with some examples. Students would have to write a thesis sentence that could be supported by the given example sentences. Additionally, the students might be given another topic, and then they would have to consider their opinion on the topic and write a thesis sentence regarding that opinion. Having the assessment in mind before designing the lesson will ensure that the teacher is focusing exclusively on teaching material that is extremely pertinent to the objective(s).

Introducing a lesson

The introduction to a lesson is very important for three primary reasons. First, students need to be engaged. They need to know that the material they will be learning in the lesson is interesting and important. They need to be given a reason to motivate themselves to learn it.

Second, students need to know what they are going to study—they need to know what they are expected to learn. This is an area that teachers often forget. In their rush to get to the "meat" of the lesson, they forget that students may not really know what it is that they are going to be assessed on. Knowing this helps them focus.

Third, students need to have their background knowledge activated. If they have ways in which to attach new knowledge to existing knowledge throughout the lesson, they will be more successful in retaining and utilizing the new knowledge.

Concluding a lesson

Ending a lesson can be equally complex. This is where assessment comes into play. And even though teachers should constantly assess their students, even on a lesson-by-lesson basis, not all assessments need to be long, graded, something that students should prepare for, or something students should be worried about.

Some assessments should simply tell the teacher what students know and do not know about the lesson that has just been taught. Also, the end of lessons should help students know where the instruction will go next (i.e., the content of the next lesson, so they can see where their new knowledge is headed), and they should know how the new knowledge is valued and useful.

Some assessments should simply tell the teacher what students know and do not know about the lesson that has just been taught.

Inductive and deductive lessons

The difference between inductive and deductive lessons lies in the way in which the new learning is attained. DEDUCTIVE LESSONS move from the general to the specific, while INDUCTIVE LESSONS move in the opposite direction.

DEDUCTIVE LESSONS: lessons that move from the general to the specific

What does this mean for instruction? Sometimes, it is important for students to learn the small pieces first and then to understand that bigger picture. Other times, it is important for students to understand the bigger picture first and then learn the smaller pieces.

INDUCTIVE LESSONS: lessons that move from the specific to the general

When the students learn the smaller pieces first and then are exposed to the bigger picture this is inductive instruction. When the bigger picture is introduced first, and then the particulars are explained, that is deductive instruction.

Choosing inductive or deductive

How would the teacher decide what method to use? Let's take an example of the Civil War in a social studies class. The teacher wouldn't want to teach all the battles first and then inform students that these are part of a larger war. For this subject, he would probably use deductive instruction. However, when teaching students a second language, it might be more important to teach smaller pieces first and then, once those small pieces are mastered, ask the students to try to use those in a sentence for a real communicative purpose.

SKILL 9.4 **Demonstrating knowledge of the importance of continuously monitoring instructional effectiveness and responding flexibly to student understanding, ideas, needs, engagement, and feedback** *(e.g., by changing the pace of a lesson, using a different instructional approach, taking advantage of an unanticipated learning opportunity)*

Student learning is an intricate, multifaceted process. Teachers instruct based upon their students' background knowledge. The first step teachers may take in approaching a new topic or skill is to simply ask the students what they already know and list their responses. This will provide the teacher with a beginning point from which they can build instruction. The next step will include the teacher's delivery of the topic, subject matter, or skill information. Following these steps, the teacher will always provide the necessary time and resources for student practice. Student practice is perhaps the most crucial means by which information is internalized.

The Importance of Student Practice

There are unlimited forms of PRACTICE. Just as the teacher intricately planned her instructional delivery based upon student needs, the teacher will also carefully plan the practice activities necessary to enhance the learning experience. These practice activities will depend largely on the students' developmental stage and on the skill or knowledge being practiced. Although practice activities are intended to reinforce what the teacher has taught, for many students the practice—the interactive process of doing something—is the point at which learning occurs. Therefore, the importance of practice activities cannot be underestimated. Teachers must monitor students as they practice in order to observe both the difficulties that might arise as well as student proficiency. Based on the observations that teachers make during practice activities, it will be evident when additional instruction needs to occur and when the students are ready to go on to another concept or skill.

Repetition

Repetitive practice can occur in many forms. Sometimes the teacher will lead the students in choral chants whereby they repeat basic skills including addition, subtraction, and multiplication facts. This activity can also be effective in memorizing spelling words and academic laws. In addition to orally repeating information, these same kinds of skills can be acquired by students repeatedly writing multiplication tables, addition or subtraction facts, or spelling words. Older students may use these types of practice in memorizing algebraic formulas, geometric theorems, and scientific laws.

Repetitive practice may also occur over time. Teachers and students may revisit skills, concepts, or knowledge throughout a school year or even over several school years as a means of internalizing important information. Repetition may come in the form of discussing, rereading, or taking information to a higher level.

Short-term versus long-term retention

Most teachers are aware that short-term retention is the first phase of long-term retention. During the time period that short-term retention is being actualized, instruction and practice are ongoing. Once it appears that a skill or concept has become internalized, the teacher plans for future follow-up activities that will foster long-term retention. Long-term retention is not the result of

PRACTICE: the interactive process of doing something and the point at which learning occurs

Teachers must monitor students as they practice in order to observe difficulties that might arise as well as student proficiency.

Repetition may come in the form of discussing, rereading, or taking information to a higher level.

haphazard instruction, but rather is the result of deliberate and planned instruction. Just as assessment is ongoing, so is instruction and learning.

Practice time

One of the best uses of practice time is to assign homework activities that will permit students to both reinforce learning and revisit skills and concepts. This allows the teacher to use classroom time for instruction of new ideas, while giving the students opportunities and motivation to practice important skills or concepts. Sometimes, while working on homework assignments with the assistance of a parent, students will develop a broader comprehension of a concept. Also during this valuable time, students may realize valid questions that can then be addressed during class time.

Teacher observations

The value of teacher observations cannot be underestimated. It is through the use of observations that the teacher is able to informally assess the needs of the students during instruction. These observations will drive the lesson and determine the direction that future lessons will take. Teacher observations also set the pace of instruction and ascertain the flow of both student and teacher discourse. After a lesson is carefully planned, teacher observation is the single most important component of an instructional presentation.

It is through the use of observations that the teacher is able to informally assess the needs of the students during instruction.

Looking for on-task behavior

One of the primary behaviors that teachers look for in an observation is on-task behavior. There is no doubt that student time on-task directly influences student involvement in instruction and enhances student learning. If the teacher observes that a particular student is not on-task, he will change the method of instruction accordingly. He may change from a teacher-directed approach to a more interactive approach. Questioning will increase in order to cull the participation of the students. If appropriate, the teacher will introduce manipulative materials to the lesson. In addition, teachers may switch to a cooperative group activity thereby removing the responsibility of instruction from the teacher and putting it on the students.

Changing Approaches

Teachers will also change instructional strategies based on the questions and verbal comments of the students. If the students express confusion or doubt or are unclear in any way about the content of the lesson, the teacher will immediately take another approach in presenting the lesson. Sometimes this can be accomplished by simply rephrasing an explanation. At other times, it will be

Effective teachers are sensitive to the reactions and responses of their students and will almost intuitively know when instruction is valid and when it is not.

necessary for the teacher to use visual organizers or models for understanding to be clear. Effective teachers are sensitive to the reactions and responses of their students and will almost intuitively know when instruction is valid and when it is not. Teachers will constantly check for student comprehension, attention, and focus throughout the presentation of a lesson.

After the teacher has presented a skill or concept lesson, she will allow time for the students to practice the skill or concept. At this point, it is essential for the teacher to circulate among the students to check for understanding. If the teacher observes that any of the students did not clearly understand the skill or concept, then she must immediately readdress the issue using another technique or approach.

SKILL 9.5 **Applying knowledge of how to design teaching strategies that achieve different instructional purposes and meet varied student needs** *(e.g., using various grouping strategies; differentiating instruction; using multiple strategies for teaching the same content; using effective resources and materials, including computers and other technological resources)*

Curriculum Control

The degree to which the classroom teacher has control over the curriculum varies from setting to setting. Some schools have precisely defined curriculum plans and teachers are required to implement the instruction accordingly. A more common occurrence is that the textbooks become the default curriculum. A fourth-grade arithmetic book, for example, defines what must be taught in the fourth grade so that the fifth-grade teacher can continue the established sequence.

Whatever the source of limitations and requirements, the classroom teacher always has some control over the method of instructional delivery and the use of supplemental materials and procedures.

The teacher is responsible for implementing the formal curricula and for providing necessary scaffolding to enhance student learning. Since the basic element of educational structure is time, the teacher must distribute the necessary learning activities over the available amount of time. The teacher can do this by creating an overview of:

- What material is to be presented

- The total amount of time available (whether for the school year, grading period, unit, etc.)

- The relative importance of the components of the material

- The students' prior knowledge of portions of the material

Lesson planning and delivery

Planning an individual lesson is a continuation of the principles for curriculum design. The same considerations exist but on a smaller scale. Numerous lesson planning forms and guidelines are available and some may be mandated by schools or districts. Some procedures are restricted to lessons of a particular nature, such as teaching a skill. Others are more generally applicable and provide a framework appropriate for most instruction.

A typical lesson plan will include:

- Identification of objectives
- The content
- Materials and supplies
- Instructional delivery methods

- In-class reinforcement activities
- Homework assignments
- Evaluation of student learning
- Evaluation of the lesson and teacher effectiveness

Grouping for instruction

There are three common methods by which a teacher may address grouping for instruction:

THE COMMON METHODS FOR GROUPING	
Individualized Instruction	Individualization requires extensive assessment both for placement and, in an on-going capacity, to monitor student progress and to plan subsequent instructional activities. Few teachers have the resources and time necessary to fully individualize their instructional program.
Small Group Instruction	A compromise approach is to assign students to small groups and then modify the lesson plans to reflect the need of the group. This procedure offers some of the advantages of individualization without the extensive administrative demands. It is quite common, especially in content area instruction, for teachers to work with the whole class. This further reduces planning and management consideration and can ensure that all students are presented with the same information.
Whole Group Instruction	In whole group instruction, the teacher delivers the same content to the entire classroom. It requires the least amount of planning but meets the needs of the fewest students.

Addressing the varying needs of students

Teachers can use a number of procedures to address the varying needs of the students. Some of the more common procedures follow:

Keep in Mind

Vary assignments

A variety of assignments on the same content allows students to match learning styles and preferences with the assignment. If all assignments are writing assignments, for example, students who are hands-on or visual learners are at a disadvantage unrelated to the content base itself.

Cooperative learning

Cooperative learning activities allow students to share ideas, expertise, and insight within a nonthreatening setting. The focus tends to remain on positive learning rather than on competition.

Structured environment

Some students need and benefit from clear structure that defines the teacher's expectations and goals. The student who clearly understands expectations can work and plan accordingly.

Clearly stated assignments

Assignments should be clearly stated along with the expectation and criteria for completion. Reinforcement and practice activities should not be a guessing game for the students. The exception to this is, of course, those situations in which a discovery method is used.

Independent practice

Independent practice involving application and repetition is necessary for thorough learning. Students learn to be independent learners through practicing independent learning. These activities should always be within the students' abilities to perform successfully without assistance.

Repetition

Very little learning is successful with a single exposure. Learners generally require multiple exposures to the same information for learning to take place. However, this repetition does not have to be dull and monotonous. Varied assignments can provide repetition of content or skill practiced without repetition of specific activities. This helps keep learning fresh and exciting for the student.

Overlearning

As a principle of effective learning, overlearning recommends that students continue to study and review after they have achieved initial mastery. The use of repetition in the context of varied assignments offers the means to help students pursue and achieve overlearning.

See Skill 8.4

Demonstrating knowledge of how to use multiple approaches to promote student engagement and learning and how to vary the instructional process to achieve given purposes and respond to student needs

Folk wisdom says that the number of minutes a person is able to sit still and do one thing is typically equal to that person's age. While this might not have any scientific validity, most kindergarten teachers would probably agree that, yes, six minutes is about all their students can handle!

Mentally Taxing Activities

The truth of the matter is that most people, young or old, have a hard time concentrating on difficult mental tasks for too long. For children, such things as learning to read or do math are mentally taxing, and too much of one activity at one time can be detrimental. Students will not focus and the teacher will end up having to reteach the lesson.

For children, such things as learning to read or do math are mentally taxing, and too much of one activity at one time can be detrimental.

Varying activities

Generally, in younger grades, activities should change every 15–30 minutes. In older grades, activities should change every 20–40 minutes. The reason for this is not to encourage short attention spans but rather to encourage higher levels of intellectual focus for shorter periods of time, which can increase both retention and engagement.

It is important, however, for teachers in the younger grades to gradually increase the amount of time spent on reading or writing. In the younger grades, students will struggle to stay focused on a text, for example, simply because they have never been required to do such an activity. Their eyes in particular may get very tired. In writing, as well, hands and eyes will tire quickly, so gradual increases of time spent on these activities is a good idea. Over time, students will be able to handle more and more.

Example of varied activities

When designing and implementing lessons, it is crucial for teachers to develop multiple activities on the same content. For example, in a one-hour period to cover a reading lesson, a teacher can:

- Have a whole-class discussion
- Have students write independently

- Spend time reading aloud

- Have students read quietly

- Have students do an activity with the text

Not only will this change of activity keep students' attention, it will provide them with unique ways to think about, integrate, and learn the material.

SKILL 9.7
Demonstrating knowledge of how to develop clear, accurate presentations and representations of concepts, use alternative explanations to promote student understanding, and present varied perspectives to encourage critical thinking

Using Various Transmissions of Information

It is often the case that students may need to see or hear information in more than one manner (kinesthetically, spatially, visually) before it is truly internalized.

It is not always guaranteed that once a teacher instructs on a concept that students will automatically retain the information. It is often the case that students may need to see or hear information in more than one manner (kinesthetically, spatially, visually) before it is truly internalized. Therefore, teachers should present information to benefit various learning styles (or multiple intelligences), and use technologies (i.e., overhead projectors, related video clips, music, presentations) or other resources to supplement student learning and retention.

SKILL 9.8
Applying knowledge of how to use educational technology to deliver effective instruction to students working at different levels and paces, stimulate advanced levels of learning, and broaden students' knowledge about technology and its uses

Assistive Technology in the Classroom

Technology has advanced so rapidly in the last decade that many learning disabilities can be addressed, in part, with unique tools. Furthermore, in various situations, other technological tools can enhance and broaden students' exposure to concepts and modalities of learning.

Common examples of assistive technology

Some common tools for assisting students with disabilities are:

- Amplification devices that make computer content more clear

- Speech recognition devices that type in text as it is spoken by the student
- Large print keys for students who have trouble with hand-eye coordination
- Readers that read aloud alerts on screens

Other tools that have become very helpful for students are:

- Communication boards, which are asynchronous discussion or dialogue programs that allow students to post content in a discussion format. It is a particularly helpful way to encourage written discussion. It also is highly beneficial for students who have physical trouble getting to school.

- Wikis are tools that teachers are using more and more each day. Wikis are collaborative definitions, posted to computers, and often to the Web. After units, teachers might ask students in groups to post a wiki on a particular topic.

- Even though they are thought of as a tool for journalists, BLOGS have become popular in the classroom. Teachers often ask students to maintain blogs, or Web logs, on particular topics. Often, blogs are used for students to respond to classroom novels as students progress through books.

> **BLOGS:** short for web logs, places where people can post thoughts and opinions on particular topics in a journal or log format

Many additional tools are becoming available every day. It is a good idea to keep up-to-date on technological tools that can assist teachers in meeting all students' needs.

See also Skill 6.5

DOMAIN IV
PROFESSIONAL ROLES AND RESPONSIBILITIES

PERSONALIZED STUDY PLAN

KNOWN MATERIAL/ SKIP IT

PAGE	COMPETENCY AND SKILL	
129	**10: Understand how to communicate and interact effectively with families, colleagues, and the community to support and enhance student learning and well-being**	☐
	10.1: Applying knowledge of skills and strategies for establishing productive relationships with parents/guardians to support student learning and well-being	☐
	10.2: Demonstrating knowledge of and strategies for initiating and maintaining effective communication with families	☐
	10.3: Applying knowledge of skills and strategies for collaborating effectively with other professionals in the school	☐
	10.4: Demonstrating knowledge of skills and strategies for consulting with parents/guardians, counselors, other teachers, and professionals in community agencies	☐
	10.5: Demonstrating knowledge of community resources and strategies for using these resources to meet student needs	☐
136	**11: Understand professional development opportunities and resources and how to be a reflective practitioner who continually evaluates the effects of choices and actions on others, including students, parents/guardians, and colleagues, and who actively seeks out opportunities for professional growth**	☐
	11.1: Demonstrating knowledge of the role of reflection and self-assessment in continuous professional growth	☐
	11.2: Demonstrating knowledge of how to use classroom observation, information about students, and various types of research as sources for evaluating the outcomes of teaching and learning	☐
	11.3: Demonstrating knowledge of professional development opportunities and resources and how to use them	☐
	11.4: Demonstrating knowledge of the roles and responsibilities of members of the school community and methods for working effectively with others	☐

PERSONALIZED STUDY PLAN

✗
KNOWN MATERIAL/ SKIP IT

PAGE	COMPETENCY AND SKILL	
143	**12: Understand the historical and philosophical foundations of education; the rights and responsibilities of students, parents/guardians, and educators in various educational contexts; and legal and ethical guidelines for educators in minnesota**	☐
	12.1: Demonstrating knowledge of the historical and philosophical foundations of education, the purposes of educational organizations, and the operation of schools and school systems	☐
	12.2: Demonstrating knowledge of teachers' roles as public employees and their rights and responsibilities as professionals	☐
	12.3: Demonstrating knowledge of the standards of professional conduct in the Code of Ethics for Minnesota Teachers	☐
	12.4: Demonstrating knowledge of student rights in various contexts	☐

✗

COMPETENCY 10

UNDERSTAND HOW TO COMMUNICATE AND INTERACT EFFECTIVELY WITH FAMILIES, COLLEAGUES, AND THE COMMUNITY TO SUPPORT AND ENHANCE STUDENT LEARNING AND WELL-BEING

> **SKILL 10.1** Applying knowledge of skills and strategies for establishing productive relationships with parents/guardians to support student learning and well-being and for addressing parents'/guardians' concerns in given situations

Encouraging Parental and Family Involvement

Research proves that the more families are involved in a child's educational experience, the more that child will succeed academically. The problem is that often teachers assume that involvement in education simply means that the parents show up to help at school events or participate in parental activities on campus. In response, many teachers devise clever strategies to increase parental involvement at school. However, just because a parent shows up to school and assists with an activity does not mean that the child will learn more. Furthermore, many parents work during the day and cannot assist at the school. Teachers, therefore, have to think of different ways to encourage parental and family involvement in the educational process.

Newsletters

Quite often, teachers have great success involving families by just informing families of what is going on in the classroom. Newsletters are particularly effective for this purpose. Parents love to know what is going on in the classroom, and this way, they'll feel included. In newsletters, for example, teachers can provide suggestions on how parents can help with the educational goals of the school. Teachers can recommend that parents read with their children for twenty minutes per day or they can also provide suggestions on what to do when their children come across difficult words or when they ask a question about comprehension. These suggestions give parents practical strategies to use with their children.

Phone calls

Parents often equate phone calls from teachers with news about misbehaviors. Teachers can change that tone by calling parents with good news. Or they can send positive notes home with students. Thus, when they need to make negative phone calls, teachers will have greater success connecting with the parents.

Specific suggestions

Teachers can also provide very specific suggestions to individual parents. For example, let's say a student needs additional assistance in a particular subject. The teacher can provide tips to parents to encourage and increase deeper understandings in the subject outside of class.

Addressing Concerns with a Parent

When it is necessary to communicate (whether by phone, letter, or in person) with a parent regarding a concern about a student, the teacher should allow herself a "cooling off" period before making contact with the parent. It is important that the teacher remain professional and objective. The purpose for contacting the parent is to elicit support and additional information that may have a bearing on the student's behavior or performance. The teacher should be careful to not demean the child and not to appear antagonistic or confrontational. Be aware that the parent is likely to be quite uncomfortable with the bad news and will respond best if you take a cooperative, problem-solving approach to the issue. It is also a nice courtesy to notify parents of positive occurrences with their children. The teacher's communication with parents should not be limited to negative items.

> *The purpose for contacting the parent is to elicit support and additional information that may have a bearing on the student's behavior or performance.*

Parent conferences

The parent-teacher conference is generally for one of three purposes.

1. The teacher may wish to share information with the parents concerning the performance and behavior of the child.

2. The teacher may be interested in obtaining information from the parents about the child; such information may help answer questions or concerns that the teacher has.

3. The teacher may want to request parent support or involvement in specific activities or requirements; in many situations, more than one of the purposes may be involved.

Planning the conference

When a conference is scheduled, whether at the request of the teacher or parent, the teacher should allow sufficient time to prepare thoroughly. Collect all relevant information, samples of student work, records of behavior, and other items needed to help the parent understand the circumstances surrounding the issue. It is also a good idea to compile a list of questions or concerns you wish to address.

Arrange the time and location of the conference to provide privacy and to avoid interruptions.

Conducting the conference

Begin the conference by putting the parents as ease. Take the time to establish a comfortable mood, but do not waste time with unnecessary small talk. Begin your discussion with positive comments about the student. Identify strengths and desirable attributes, but do not exaggerate.

The teacher shoul address issues or areas of concern, being sure to focus on observable behaviors and concrete results or information. It is important to not make judgmental statements about parent or child. Sharing specific work samples, anecdotal records of behavior, etc., that clearly demonstrate the concerns is important as well. The teacher should be a good listener by hearing the parent's comments and explanations. Such background information can be invaluable in understanding the needs and motivations of the child.

Finally, end the conference with an agreed-upon plan of action between parents and teacher (and, when appropriate, the child). Bring the conference to a close politely but firmly, and thank the parents for their involvement.

After the conference

A day or two after the conference, it is a good idea to send a follow-up note to the parents. In this note, briefly and concisely reiterate the plan or step agreed to in the conference. Be polite and professional; avoid the temptation to be too informal or chatty. If the issue is a long-term, one such as the behavior or ongoing work performance of the student, make periodic follow-up contacts to keep the parents informed of the progress.

SKILL 10.2 Demonstrating knowledge of the importance of communicating with families on a regular basis and strategies for initiating and maintaining effective communication with families

See Skill 10.1

> ### SKILL 10.3 Applying knowledge of skills and strategies for collaborating effectively with other professionals in the school (e.g., teachers in other classrooms, special education teachers, media specialists, arts teachers, paraprofessionals) to improve student achievement and enhance the overall learning environment

While teachers often find that they spend considerable time in their classrooms with children, schools are organized in such a way that many groups of people have important and powerful roles. Some people are specialists and are meant to assist teachers in their work. Specialists are certified teachers who specialize in certain learning needs. Others are administrators (or various levels of administrators) who run the school programs. And others are board members or district officials who oversee all schools in the district. Let's look at each group individually.

Special Education and Child Study Teams

SPECIAL EDUCATION TEACHERS are specialists in teaching students who may have learning or physical disabilities. Reading specialists focus on students who need additional assistance in reading. Special education teachers work with regular education teachers, as well as other school staff, to develop, implement, and evaluate students with special needs. Special education teachers play an important role in the development and implementation of each student's 504 plan or Individualized Education Plan (IEP). These plans are legal documents stating the educational and behavioral objectives and goals for each student.

> **SPECIAL EDUCATION TEACHERS:** specialists in teaching students who may have learning or physical disabilities

> *Special education teachers work with regular education teachers, as well as other school staff, to develop, implement, and evaluate students with special needs.*

Teachers of gifted and talented students are included in this group because they oversee the individual needs of students with specific, advanced abilities.

Many schools have child study teams made up of additional professionals who aid students with various needs. These often include the students' teachers, parents, and the necessary professionals such as occupational therapists, special education teachers, speech therapists, guidance counselors, and school psychologists.

Curriculum Coordinator

Curriculum coordinators serve as the leaders in the development and implementation of a subject. These professionals work with teachers who are involved in the instruction of a particular subject. For example, the Language Arts Curriculum Coordinator would ensure that all the teachers who teach Language Arts understand the curriculum, have the materials to implement the curriculum, plan and conduct professional development, update curriculum, and so on.

Technology Coordinator

Technology coordinators work either entirely at one school or at multiple schools within a district. They develop programs and assist teachers in the use of technology or technologically specific curricular programs.

Administrators

While the roles of principal or assistant principal are readily identifiable, there are additional, more specific administrative positions. Sometimes, schools will hire people to administer programs such as Title I (additional resources for students who live in impoverished conditions). An "instructional coach" might have administrative duties, while also assisting teachers with particular areas of instruction. Administrators also work to ensure that parents and community members are satisfied with the local school system.

> SKILL 10.4 **Demonstrating knowledge of skills and strategies for consulting with parents/guardians, counselors, other teachers, and professionals in community agencies to link student environments and promote student development and learning**

Dealing with Demographics

According to Campbell, Campbell, and Dickinson (1992), *Teaching and Learning Through Multiple Intelligences*, "The changing nature of demographics is one of the strongest rationales for multicultural education in the United States." The Census Bureau predicts a changing demographic for the American population and school communities that will include a forecast between 1990 and 2030, that "while the white population will increase by 25%, the African American population will increase by 68%, the Asian-American, Pacific Island, and American Indian by 79%, and the Hispanic-American population by 187%." Reinforcing that learning beyond the classroom must include a diversity of instructional and learning strategies for adult role models in a student's life.

Mentoring

Mentoring has become an instrumental tool in addressing student achievement and access to learning. Adult mentors work individually with identified students on specific subject areas to reinforce the learning through tutorial instruction and application of knowledge. Providing students with adult role models to reinforce the learning has become a crucial instructional strategy for teachers seeking to maximize student learning beyond the classroom. Students who work with adult mentors from culturally diverse backgrounds are given a multicultural aspect of learning that is cooperative and multimodal in personalized instruction.

Technology and the Classroom

The use of technology provides a mentoring tutorial support system and different conceptual learning modalities for students seeking to understand classroom material. Technology provides a networking opportunity for students to find study buddies and peer study groups, along with free academic support to problem-solve and develop critical thinking skills that are imperative in acquiring knowledge and conceptual learning.

DISTANCE LEARNING is a technological strategy that keeps students and teachers interactively communicating about issues in the classroom and beyond. Students will communicate more freely using technology to ask teacher or adult mentors clarity questions than they will in a classroom of peers.

Community Resources

Connecting with community resources will also provide viable avenues of support in helping students who need additional academic remediation to access learning. Diversity programs are offered through the local universities and community agencies that connect college students or working adults with subject areas and classrooms in need of additional student interns and adult volunteers to support the academic programs in school communities.

> *The use of technology provides a mentoring tutorial support system and different conceptual learning modalities for students seeking to understand classroom material.*

> **DISTANCE LEARNING:** a technological strategy that keeps students and teachers interactively communicating about issues in the classroom and beyond

---

> **SKILL 10.5** **Demonstrating knowledge of resources in the community** *(e.g., cultural institutions, businesses, individuals, social service agencies)* **and strategies for using these resources to meet student needs and promote student development and learning**

Utilizing Community Resources

The community is a vital link to increasing learning experiences for students. Community resources can supplement the minimized and marginal educational resources of school communities. With state and federal educational funding becoming increasingly subject to legislative budget cuts, school communities welcome the financial support that community resources can provide in terms of discounted prices on high end supplies (e.g., computers, printers, and technology supplies), along with providing free notebooks, backpacks, and student supplies for low-income students who may have difficulty obtaining the basic supplies for school.

Community stores can provide cash rebates and teacher discounts for educators in struggling school districts and compromised school communities. Both professionally and personally, communities can enrich the student learning experiences by including the following support strategies:

- Provide programs that support student learning outcomes and future educational goals

- Create mentoring opportunities that provide adult role models in various industries to students interested in studying in that industry

- Provide financial support for school communities to help low-income or homeless students begin the school year with the basic supplies

- Develop paid internships with local university students to provide tutorial services for identified students in school communities who are having academic and social difficulties

- Provide parent-teen-community forums to create public voice of change in communities

- Offer parents who do not have computers or Internet connections stipends to purchase technology to create equitable opportunities for students to do research and complete requirements

- Visit classrooms and ask teachers and students what's needed to promote academic progress and growth

The commitment that a community shows to its educational communities is a valuable investment in the future. Community resources that are able to provide additional funding for tutors in marginalized classrooms or help schools reduce classrooms of students needing additional remedial instruction directly impact educational equity and facilitation of teaching and learning for both teachers and students.

Community resources are vital in providing the additional support to students, school communities, and families struggling to remain engaged in declining educational institutions competing for federal funding and limited district funding.

COMPETENCY 11

UNDERSTAND PROFESSIONAL DEVELOPMENT OPPORTUNITIES AND RESOURCES AND HOW TO BE A REFLECTIVE PRACTITIONER WHO CONTINUALLY EVALUATES THE EFFECTS OF CHOICES AND ACTIONS ON OTHERS, INCLUDING STUDENTS, PARENTS/GUARDIANS, AND COLLEAGUES, AND WHO ACTIVELY SEEKS OUT OPPORTUNITIES FOR PROFESSIONAL GROWTH

> **SKILL 11.1** Demonstrating knowledge of the role of reflection and self-assessment in continuous professional growth and of effective strategies for using reflection, self-assessment, critical thinking, problem solving, and self-directed learning to improve teaching practice and achieve professional goals

The Importance of Self Assessment

The very nature of the teaching profession—the yearly cycle of doing the same thing over and over again—creates the tendency to fossilize, to quit growing, to become complacent. Teachers who are truly successful are those who have built into their own approach safeguards against that tendency. They see themselves as constant learners. They believe that learning never ends. They are careful never to teach their classes the same as they did the last time. They build in a tendency to reflect on what is happening to the students under their care or what happened this year as compared to last year. They ask questions of themselves such as:

- What worked the best?

- What didn't work so well?

- What can be changed to improve success rates?

- What about continuing education?

- Should I go for another degree or should I enroll in more classes?

How to self-assess

There are several avenues a teacher might take in order to assess his own teaching strengths and weaknesses. Having several students who are unable to understand a concept might be an early indicator of the need for a self-evaluation. In such a case, a teacher might want to go over her lesson plans to make sure the topic is being covered thoroughly and in a clear fashion. Brainstorming other ways to tackle the content might also help. Speaking to other teachers, asking how they teach a certain skill, might give new insight to one's own teaching tactics.

Any good teacher will understand that he needs to self-evaluate and adjust his lessons periodically. Signing up for professional courses or workshops can also help a teacher assess her abilities by opening her eyes to new ways of teaching.

> **SKILL 11.2** **Demonstrating knowledge of how to use classroom observation, information about students, and various types of research as sources for evaluating the outcomes of teaching and learning and as a basis for reflecting on and modifying teaching practice**

There are many ways to evaluate a child's knowledge and to assess his or her learning needs. In recent years, the emphasis has shifted from "mastery testing" of isolated skills to authentic assessments of what children know. Authentic assessments allow the teacher to evaluate more precisely what each individual student knows, can do, and needs to do. Authentic assessments can help both the student and the teacher become more responsible for what is learned.

Authentic assessments allow the teacher to evaluate more precisely what each individual student knows, can do, and needs to do.

To determine the abilities of incoming students, it may be helpful to consult their prior academic records. Letter grades assigned at previous levels of instruction, as well as scores on standardized tests, may be taken into account. In addition, the teacher may choose to administer pre-tests at the beginning of the school year, and perhaps also at the initial stage of each new unit of instruction. The textbooks available for classroom use may provide suitable pre-tests, tests of student progress, and post-tests.

In addition to administering tests, the teacher may assess the readiness of students for a particular level of instruction by having them demonstrate their ability to perform some relevant task. In a class that emphasizes written composition, for example, students may be asked to submit writing samples.

Teachers should also gauge student readiness by simply asking them about their previous knowledge of the subject or task at hand. Though their comments may not be completely reliable indicators of what they know or understand, such discussions can provide an idea of the students' interest in what is being taught. Instruction has a greater impact when the material being introduced is of student interest and is relevant to the students' lives.

Instruction has a greater impact when the material being introduced is of student interest and is relevant to the students' lives.

After initial evaluations have been conducted and appropriate instruction follows, teachers will need to fine-tune individual evaluations in order to provide optimum learning experiences. Some of the types of evaluations that were used to determine initial general learning needs can be used on an ongoing basis to determine individual learning needs. It is somewhat more difficult to choose an appropriate evaluation instrument for elementary-aged students than for older students.

Therefore, teachers must be mindful of developmentally appropriate instruments. At the same time, teachers must be cognizant of the information that they wish to attain from a specific evaluation instrument. Ultimately, these two factors—students' developmental stage and the information to be derived—will determine which type of evaluation will be most appropriate and valuable. There are few commercially designed assessment tools that will prove to be as effective as a tool that is constructed by the teacher.

> *There are few commercially designed assessment tools that will prove to be as effective as a tool that is constructed by the teacher.*

The ability to create a personal and professional charting of students' academic and emotional growth, found within the performance-based assessment in individualized portfolios, becomes a tool for both students and teachers. Teachers can use semester portfolios to gauge student academic progress and the personal growth of students who are continually changing their self-images and worldviews. When a student is studying to master a math concept and is able to create visuals that show that what she or he has learned transcends the initial concept and connects to a higher level of thinking and application of knowledge, then the teacher can share an enjoyable moment of success with the student.

Teachers who are innovative and creative in instructional practices are able to model and foster creative thinking in their students. Encouraging students to maintain journals and portfolios of their valued work from projects and assignments will allow them the opportunity to preserve the diversity of their creative endeavors in a format that can be treasured throughout their educational journey.

Evaluating Teacher Effectiveness

It is important for teachers to involve themselves in constant periods of reflection and self-reflection to ensure they are meeting the needs of the students. There are several avenues a teacher might take in order to assess his or her own teaching strengths and weaknesses. Early indicators that self-evaluation might be necessary include having several students that do not understand a concept. In such a case, a teacher might want to go over his or her lesson plans to make sure the topic is being covered thoroughly and in a clear fashion. Brainstorming other ways to tackle the content might also help. Speaking to other teachers and asking how they teach a certain skill might give new insight to one's own teaching tactics.

Teachers will encounter situations daily where students have difficulty with a fact, task, concept or idea, when a student doesn't get it, doesn't acquire the skill, or can't internalize the information. As the teacher, what do you do? Repeat the instruction, verbatim, until it sinks in? Chastise or cajole the student into acknowledging an understanding? Since you are genuinely concerned about the student's acquisition of skills and academic success, you will immediately realize that the dilemma is yours, not the student's, and you will seek different ways to communicate an understanding of the information so that the student will completely comprehend it and will acquire a meaningful skill. After all, if the student does not succeed, it is the teacher who has failed.

In determining a better approach for providing an understanding to the student, you should consider many options for instruction. The process for identifying viable options would include answering the following questions:

- What different words or phrasing might be used to say the same thing?

- How would I explain an opposite condition or fact, and would a negative example provide an understanding through contrast?

- If I imagined that the problem/fact/skill which I want to teach was an object that I could move around in any direction, would I be able to identify the object's component parts? Could I revise my explanation to provide a better understanding by starting from a different component part, reordering the component parts, or redefining the component parts?

- Is there something preexisting in the student's acquired knowledge/skills that I can use to redirect or reinforce my explanation by making reference or demonstrating a link?

- Is there something specific to the student's culture or life experience that could inform my explanation/instruction?

In a student-centered learning environment, the goal is to provide the best education and opportunity for academic success for all students. Integrating the developmental patterns of physical, social, and academic norms for students will provide students with individualized learning plans that are specific to their skill levels and needs. Teachers who effectively develop and maximize a student's potential will use pre- and post-assessments to gain comprehensive data on the existing skill level of the student in order to plan and adapt curriculum to address and grow student skills. Maintaining communication with the student and parents will provide a community approach to learning in order to maximize student learning and growth.

See also Skill 11.1

> **SKILL 11.3** Demonstrating knowledge of various professional development opportunities and resources (*e.g., professional journals, educational research, online resources, workshops*) and how to use them to promote reflection, solve problems, and support professional growth, including continuous development of technology skills relevant to education

Professional Development

In order to promote the vision, mission, and action plans of school communities, teachers must be given the toolkits to maximize instructional performances. The development of student-centered learning communities that foster the academic capacities and learning synthesis for all students should be the fundamental goal of professional development for teachers.

Professional development requirements

The level of professional development may include traditional district workshops that enhance instructional expectations for teachers or the more complicated multiple-day workshops given by national and state educational organizations. Most workshops on the national and state level provide clock hours that can be used to renew certifications for teachers every five years. Typically, 150 clock hours is the standard certification number needed to provide a five-year certification renewal, so teachers must attend and complete paperwork for a diversity of workshops that range from one to fifty clock hours according to the timeframe of the workshops.

Most districts and schools provide in-service professional development opportunities for teachers during the school year dealing with district objectives and expectations and relevant workshops or classes that can enhance the teaching practices for teachers. Clock hours are provided with each class or workshop and the type of professional development being offered to teachers determines clock hours. Each year, schools are required to report the number of workshops, along with the participants attending the workshops, to the superintendent's office for filing. Teachers collecting clock hour forms are required to file the forms to maintain certification eligibility and job eligibility.

Practices needed for professional development

The research by the National Association of Secondary Principals, *Breaking Ranks II: Strategies for Leading High School Reform,* created the following multiple listing of educational practices needed for expanding the professional development opportunities for teachers:

- Interdisciplinary instruction among subject areas

Professional development opportunities for teacher performance improvement or enhancement in instructional practices are essential for creating comprehensive learning communities.

Most districts and schools provide in-service professional development opportunities for teachers during the school year dealing with district objectives and expectations and relevant workshops or classes that can enhance the teaching practices for teachers.

- Identifying of individual learning styles to maximize student academic performance

- Training teachers in understanding and applying multiple assessment formats and implementations in curriculum and instruction

- Looking at multiple methods of classroom management strategies

- Providing teachers with national, federal, state, and district curriculum expectations and performance outcomes

- Identifying the school communities' action plan of student learning objectives and teacher instructional practices

- Helping teachers understand how to use data to impact student learning goals and objectives

- Teaching teachers on how to disaggregate student data in improving instruction and curriculum implementation for student academic equity and access

- Developing leadership opportunities for teachers to become school and district trainers to promote effective learning communities for student achievement and success

In promoting professional development opportunities for teachers that enhance student achievement, the bottom line is that teachers must be given the time to complete workshops at no or minimal costs. School and district budgets must include financial resources to support and encourage teachers to engage in mandatory and optional professional development opportunities that create a win-win learning experience for students.

> *In promoting professional development opportunities for teachers that enhance student achievement, the bottom line is that teachers must be given the time to complete workshops at no or minimal costs.*

Using available data in professional development

Whether a teacher is using criterion-referenced, norm-referenced, or performance-based data to inform and impact student learning and achievement, the more important objective is ensuring that teachers know how to effectively use the data to improve and reflect upon existing teaching instruction. The goal of identifying ways for teachers to use the school data is simple: Is the teacher's instructional practice improving student learning goals and academic success?

School data can include:

- Demographic profiling
- Cultural and ethnic academic trends
- State and national assessments
- Portfolios
- Projects
- Disciplinary reports
- Academic subject pre- and post-assessments and weekly assessments

By looking at trends and discrepancies in school data, teachers can ascertain whether they are meeting the goals and objectives of the state, national, and federal mandates for school improvement reform and curriculum implementation.

Assessments and professional development

Assessments can be used to motivate students to learn and shape the learning environment to provide learning stimulation that optimizes student access to learning. Butler and McMunn (2006) have shown that factors that help motivate students to learn are:

- Involving students in their own assessment

- Matching assessment strategies to student learning

- Considering thinking styles and using assessments to adjust the classroom environment in order to enhance student motivation

Teachers can shape the way students learn by creating engaging learning opportunities that promote student achievement.

> **SKILL 11.4** **Demonstrating knowledge of the roles and responsibilities of various members of the school community and methods for working effectively with others in the school community** *(e.g., colleagues, mentors, principals, supervisors)* **to strengthen teaching knowledge, skills, and effectiveness**

Mentors

Part of being an effective teacher is to not only have students grow educationally, but to allow oneself to also continue to grow as a teacher. Working with other members of the school community—peers, supervisors, and other staff—will give the teacher the necessary grounding needed to increase skills and knowledge sets. When identifying possible mentors, teachers should choose fellow teachers who are respected and who should be emulated. Searching out other teachers who have had an amount of success in the area needing growth is another step. Asking them questions and for advice on brushing up lesson plans or techniques for delivery of instruction can be helpful. Talk to the supervisor or the principal when you are having difficulties or when you want to learn more about a topic. They may know of development training seminars, books, journals, or other resources that might be available. Teachers should remember that they are part of a team of professionals and that their personal success is part of a greater success that everyone hopes to achieve.

COMPETENCY 12
UNDERSTAND THE HISTORICAL AND PHILOSOPHICAL FOUNDATIONS OF EDUCATION; THE RIGHTS AND RESPONSIBILITIES OF STUDENTS, PARENTS/ GUARDIANS, AND EDUCATORS IN VARIOUS EDUCATIONAL CONTEXTS; AND LEGAL AND ETHICAL GUIDELINES FOR EDUCATORS IN MINNESOTA

> SKILL 12.1 Demonstrating knowledge of the historical and philosophical foundations of education, the purposes of educational organizations, and the operation of schools and school systems as organizations within the community

Historical Foundations of Education

The relationship between education and society is always evolving. Originally, schools were for the wealthy, as education was highly valued and also an expensive burden on local governments that were not equipped to educate every child. In poorer and more rural families, the children were needed to help the family either by working and bringing home a wage, or by helping to tend the house or farm. Large families might have older children watch the younger children—none of these children were typically able to get schooling or, if they did, it was intermittent. Thus, the schools reflected the social value of having a large, uneducated work force.

Integration of poor students

Around the time of the Great Depression, Franklin Roosevelt's New Deal increasingly helped keep young people in school while adults were given the menial tasks that children had once performed. While the primary reason for fuller schools was not education so much as a reorganization of workers—making room in the workforce for the out-of-work adults—the result was that poorer children began to be more evenly and regularly educated and this would eventually set the foundations for a middle class.

Integration of racially diverse students

After *Plessy* v. *Ferguson* in 1896 (but before *Brown* v. *The Board of Education* in 1954), "separate but equal" school facilities segregated the African-American children from white children. However, it was clear that African-American schools generally received less funding than schools for white children. *Brown* v. *Board of Education of Topeka* struck down segregation after the Supreme Court ruled that a separate but equal form of education would never truly give African-American children an equal foundation in learning. Society would begin to follow suit, albeit slowly, as segregated facilities began to fall away (in 1955, Rosa Parks would famously refuse to give up her seat on a bus for a white passenger).

Generally, schools and education are considered the great equalizer—giving each child a level start in life, the same tools to work with so that each might chisel out his future, regardless of class, color, religion, or other factors.

Generally, schools and education are considered the great equalizer—giving each child a level start in life, the same tools to work with so that each might chisel out his future, regardless of class, color, religion, or other factors.

Federal, State, and Local Involvement in Education

However, because schools depend largely on local funding from city and state budgets, not all schools are created equal. The tax money in poorer towns does not stretch as far as the money in wealthier neighborhoods, and schools and their facilities often suffer for it. Recently, the federal government has begun to step in and attempt to make schools throughout the nation more equal in standards, so that every child gets a solid grounding in learning. One proposal has been for school vouchers, which would allow parents to choose which school their children attend. This idea is based on the principle that if the local school does not have desirable facilities, then children could attend one that does. Contesters of this plan say that vouchers would only cause poor schools to become even less desirable as students flee and less tax money comes in.

NO CHILD LEFT BEHIND ACT: a federal act passed in 2001 that aims to improve schools by increasing educational standards and holding schools, school districts, and states accountable for performance and progress of students

No Child Left Behind Act

In 2001, the federal government implemented the NO CHILD LEFT BEHIND ACT, which aimed to improve schools by increasing educational standards and holding schools, school districts, and states accountable for performance and progress of students.

NEIGHBORHOOD SCHOOLS: those that students attend based on their home address

Types of schools

Another issue in governance has been the debate between local, neighborhood, and choice schools. NEIGHBORHOOD SCHOOLS are those that students attend based on their home address. For the past few decades, some school districts have provided students with the option of attending MAGNET SCHOOLS, or schools that are available to any student within the district. Usually, these schools have themes, such as business academies or college preparatory curricula.

MAGNET SCHOOLS: schools that are available to any student within the district

CHARTER SCHOOLS: schools that do not have to abide by the same policies as regular public schools

In addition to magnet schools, money is now available for CHARTER SCHOOLS, which do not have to abide by the same policies as regular public schools. Charter schools do not have to be run by school districts, but they take money from the districts in which their students originate. So, for example, if the local public school gets $5,000 per student per school year from local property taxes and the state (or however the state finances schools), that $5,000 would instead go to the charter school if one student opted to go there.

Finally, in some states and cities, VOUCHER MONEY is available for students attending private schools; in this plan, the government gives parents part or all of the money that would have been put into the local public district(s) so that they can use it to send their children to private schools. None of these options is without controversy in this country.

The Ideal Classroom

Ideally, a school gives every child a solid base of learning so that each child can compete equally in life and society. An ideal classroom has a mix of different types of students—different genders, different classes, and different races—so that the children in them learn to relate to all types of people, however different they may be. Unfortunately, this mix seldom happens in the classroom because people of different ethnicities, incomes, and religions typically live in different towns and neighborhoods; each neighborhood school reflects only the immediate area, which is typically a homogenous cross-section of society as a whole. No single plan (vouchers, No Child Left Behind) has managed to effect much change in this regard.

Ideally, a school gives every child a solid base of learning so that each child can compete equally in life and society.

To understand where we are today in American public education is to appreciate how politics, history, research, society, and the economy have all come together to develop a complex, sometimes bureaucratic, system of teaching and learning.

To understand where we are today in American public education is to appreciate how politics, history, research, society, and the economy have all come together to develop a complex, sometimes bureaucratic, system of teaching and learning.

Instructional Debates

Debates on instruction have typically focused on the role of the teacher. Some people argue that child-centered instruction is favorable, as it is more engaging for students. Others have advocated for more traditional methods, such as lecturing, note taking, and other teacher-centered activities.

Evolution of Education

Historically, public education has evolved from being something relegated to the wealthy. Education was usually private, tutor-based, and uneven. The concept of a free public education was developed in order to ensure that as many people in this country could participate in (and further develop) the nation's economy. Decades ago, a small one-room schoolhouse sufficed, but today, each neighborhood requires multiple schools to educate all of the local children. In these traditional settings, the teacher was the lecturer and leader of all instruction.

As the population has grown, the structure of public schooling has been shaped by bureaucracy. To accommodate all the children, the structures of public schools have changed so each child will have a similar, equal education no matter which school she attends. As classrooms and research grew and more beneficial instructional styles emerged, many classroom teachers began to incorporate cooperative learning, learning centers, reading and writing workshops, group projects (and other developmentally appropriate styles) into their classrooms.

> As the population has grown, the structure of public schooling has been shaped by bureaucracy.

SKILL 12.2 **Demonstrating knowledge of teachers' roles as public employees and their rights and responsibilities as professionals** *(e.g., obtaining and maintaining licensure, engaging in appropriate professional practices, addressing the needs of the whole learner, maintaining confidentiality, providing an appropriate education for students with disabilities, reporting cases of known or suspected abuse or neglect, using appropriate practices related to information and technology)*

One of the first things a teacher learns is how to obtain resources and help for his or her students. All schools have guidelines for receiving this assistance, especially since the implementation of the Americans with Disabilities Act. The first step in securing help is for the teacher to approach the school's administration or exceptional education department for direction in attaining special services or resources for qualifying students. Many schools have a committee designated for addressing these needs such as a Child Study Team or a Core Team. These teams are made up of both regular and exceptional education teachers, school psychologists, guidance counselors, and administrators. The particular student's classroom teacher usually has to complete some initial paperwork and will need to do some behavioral observations.

Family Involvement

Under the IDEA, parent/guardian involvement in the development of the student's IEP is required and absolutely essential for the advocacy of the disabled student's educational needs. IEPs must be tailored to meet the student's needs, and no one knows those needs better than the parent/guardian and other significant family members. Optimal conditions for a disabled student's education exist when teachers, school administrators, special education professionals, and parents/guardians work together to design and execute the IEP.

Due Process

Under the IDEA, Congress provides safeguards for students against schools' actions, including the right to sue in court, and encourages states to develop hearing and mediation systems to resolve disputes. No student, nor his or her parents/guardians, can be denied due process because of disability.

Abuse Situations

The child who is undergoing the abuse is the one whose needs must be served first. A suspected case gone unreported may destroy a child's life, and his or her subsequent life as a functional adult. It is the duty of any citizen who suspects abuse and neglect to make a report to their administrator/child protective services (an organization which identifies and handles cases of abuse), and it is especially important and required for State-licensed and certified persons to make a report. All reports can be kept confidential if required, but it is best to disclose your identity in case more information is required of you. This is a personal matter that has no impact on qualifications for licensure or certification. Failure to make a report when abuse or neglect is suspected is punishable by revocation of certification and license, a fine, and criminal charges.

Reporting suspected abuse

There is no time limit on an acceptable or safe period of time to wait before reporting, so hesitation to report may be a cause for action against you. Do not wait once your suspicion is firm. All you need to have is a reasonable suspicion, not actual proof. It is the job of investigators to determine the facts.

Do not wait once your suspicion is firm. All you need to have is a reasonable suspicion, not actual proof, which is the job for the investigators.

Permanent Records

Teachers must follow procedures and requirements for maintaining accurate student records.

The student permanent record is a file of the student's cumulative educational history. It contains a profile of the student's academic background as well as the student's behavioral and medical background. The purpose of the permanent record is to provide applicable information about the student so that the student's individual educational needs can be met. If any specialized testing has been administered, the results are noted in the permanent record. Any special requirements that the student may have are indicated in the permanent record. Highly personal information, including court orders regarding custody, is filed in the permanent record as appropriate. The importance and value of the permanent record cannot be underestimated. It offers a comprehensive picture of the student.

The purpose of the permanent record is to provide applicable information about the student so that the student's individual educational needs can be met.

Teachers must follow procedures for administering state- and district-mandated assessments.

State and federal law requires that public schools administer various assessments. Furthermore, most districts have additional assessments. While all assessments can provide information for teachers so that they can modify and improve instruction, all required assessments also provide the district, the state, and the federal government with information regarding the academic growth of students. Therefore, policies and procedures for administering tests must be followed carefully and thoroughly.

Whenever procedures are not followed carefully, the reliability and validity of the test scores are put into jeopardy. Reliability refers to the extent that assessments are consistent over time and setting. This essentially means that an assessment given at different times of day, on different days, in different classrooms, or by different administrators should all yield the same result. It is crucial that all teachers follow the same procedures so that all students get the same experiences and the test scores can be deemed reliable. By doing so, there is much less chance that differences in test scores occur because of conditions not pertaining to what students know.

Legal Responsibilities and Technology

In this technological age, it is important that teachers be aware of their legal responsibilities when using computers in the classroom. As public employees, teachers are particularly vulnerable to public scrutiny. Not only are teachers more likely to be caught if they are unethical in the use of computers in the classroom, but it is also the responsibility of educators to model, as well as teach, ethical computer behaviors.

Recent changes

In 1980, P. L.96-517, Section 117 of the copyright law was amended to cover the use of computers. The following changes were made:

1. The definition of a "computer program" was inserted and is now defined as "a set of statements or instructions to be used directly in a computer in order to bring about a certain result."

2. The owner of a copy of a computer program is not infringing on the copyright by making or authorizing the making of or adaptation of that program if the following criteria are met:

   – The new copy or adaptation must be created in order to be able to use the program in conjunction with the machine and is used in no other manner.

- The new copy or adaptation must be for archival purpose only and all archival copies must be destroyed in the event that continued possession of the computer program should cease to be rightful.

- Any copies prepared or adapted may not be leased, sold, or otherwise transferred without the authorization of the copyright owner.

Multiple copies of a program

The intent of this amendment to the copyright act is to allow an individual or institutional owner of a program to make "backup" copies in case of the destruction of the original program disk, while restricting the owner from making copies in order to use the program on more that one machine at a time or to share with other teachers. Under the Software Copyright Act of 1980, once a program is loaded into the memory of a computer, a temporary copy of that program is made. Multiple machine loading (moving from machine to machine and loading a single program into several computers for simultaneous use) constitutes making multiple copies, which is not permitted under the law.

Since the same is true of a networked program, it is necessary to obtain permission from the owner of the copyright or purchase a license agreement before multiple use of a program in a school setting.

Risks of ignoring the law

Infringement of copyright laws is a serious offense and can result in significant penalties if a teacher chooses to ignore the law. Not only does the teacher risk losing all personal computer equipment, but she is also placing her job as an educator in jeopardy.

> *Infringement of copyright laws is a serious offense and can result in significant penalties if a teacher chooses to ignore the law.*

SKILL 12.3 **Demonstrating knowledge of the standards of professional conduct in the Code of Ethics for Minnesota Teachers**

Minnesota teachers must comply with the Minnesota Teachers Code of Ethics (from Minnesota statute 8700.7500). The code contains specific rules regarding teachers' responsibilities and standards of conduct. The Code includes ten standards of professional conduct and rules for enforcement. Standards include provisions for nondiscrimination, health and safety, boundaries, misuse of relationships, reasonable discipline, confidentiality, suppression or distortion of subject matter, and false or misrepresentation of records or facts. It is imperative that all teachers familiarize themselves with the code.

> *The Code of Ethics for Minnesota Teachers can be found on the Web page below:*
>
> *https://www.revisor.mn .gov/rules/?id=8700.7500*

> **SKILL 12.4** **Demonstrating knowledge of student rights in various contexts** *(e.g., in relation to due process, discipline, privacy, free speech, equal educational opportunity)*

See also Skill 12.2

Inside the School System

The teacher will take this information to the appropriate committee for discussion and consideration. The committee will recommend the next step to be taken. Often, subsequent steps include a complete psychological evaluation along with certain physical examinations such as vision and hearing screening and a complete medical examination by a doctor.

The referral of students for this process is usually relatively simple for the classroom teacher and requires little more than some initial paper work and discussion. The services and resources the student receives as a result of the process typically prove to be invaluable to the student with a behavioral disorder.

Beyond the School System

An awareness of special services and resources and how to obtain them is essential to all teachers and their students.

At times, the teacher must go beyond the school system to meet the needs of some students. When the school system is unable to address the needs of a student, the teacher often must take the initiative and contact agencies within the community. Frequently, there is no special policy for finding resources. It is simply up to the individual teacher to be creative and resourceful and to find whatever help is available to meet the students' needs. Meeting the needs of all students is certainly a team effort that is most often spearheaded by the classroom teacher.

Inclusion, Mainstreaming, and Least Restrictive Environment

Inclusion, mainstreaming, and least restrictive environment are interrelated policies under the IDEA, with varying degrees of statutory imperatives.

Inclusion	The right of students with disabilities to be placed in the regular classroom
Least Restrictive Environment	The mandate that children be educated to the maximum extent appropriate with their nondisabled peers
Mainstreaming	A policy where disabled students can be placed in the regular classroom, as long as such placement does not interfere with the student's educational plan

Alcohol and Drug Abuse

There is a saying, *If you're going to be an alcoholic or drug addict in America, you will be.* Cynical but true, this comment implies that exposure to alcohol and drugs is 100 percent. We now have a widespread second generation of drug abusers in families. And alcohol is the oldest form of drug abuse known to humankind, with many families affected for three or more known generations. It's hard to tell youth to eschew drugs when even mom and dad, who grew up in the early illicit drug era, partake.

Dealing with student drug abuse

Educators, therefore, are not only likely to, but often do, face students who are high on something in school. Of course, they are not only a hazard to their own safety and those of others, but their ability to be productive learners is greatly diminished if not nonexistent. They show up instead of skip, because it's not always easy or practical for them to spend the day away from home but not in school. Unless they can stay inside they are at risk of being picked up for truancy. Some enjoy being high in school, getting a sense of satisfaction by putting something over on the system. Some just don't take drug use seriously enough to think use at school might be inappropriate.

Interventions

Many safe and helpful interventions are available to the classroom teacher when dealing with a student who is suffering from a serious emotional disturbance. First and foremost, the teacher must maintain open communication with the parents and other professionals who are involved with the student whenever overt behavior characteristics are exhibited. Students with behavior disorders need constant behavioral interventions, which may involve two-way communication between the home and school on a daily basis.

The teacher must establish an environment that promotes appropriate behavior for all students, as well as respect for one another. Classmates may need to be informed of a classmate's special needs to better understand behavioral interventions and outbursts that may occur in the classroom. The teacher should also initiate a behavior intervention program for any student who might demonstrate emotional or behavioral disorders. Such behavior modification plans can be an effective means of preventing deviant behavior. If deviant behavior does occur, the teacher needs to have previously arranged for a safe and secure time-out place where the student can go for a respite and an opportunity to regain self-control.

Program treatment

Often when a behavior disorder is more severe, the student must be involved in a more concentrated program aimed at alleviating deviant behavior, such as psychotherapy. In such instances, the school psychologist, guidance counselor, or behavior specialist should be directly involved with the student and provide counseling and therapy on a regular basis. Frequently, they are also involved with the student's family.

Drug therapy

Many families are turning to drug therapy. Once viewed as a radical step, administering drugs to children to balance their emotions or to control their behavior has become a widely used form of therapy. Of course, only a medical doctor can recommend or prescribe such drugs. Great care must be exercised when giving pills to children in order to change their behavior, especially since so many medicines have undesirable side effects. It is important to know that these drugs relieve only the symptoms of behavior and do not always eliminate the underlying causes. Parents and teachers need to be educated as to the side effects of these medications.

SAMPLE TEST

SAMPLE TEST

Student Development and Learning (Skills 1.1 – 3.8)

(Easy) (Skill 1.1)

1. Constructivist classrooms are considered to be:

    A. Student-centered

    B. Teacher-centered

    C. Focused on standardized tests

    D. Requiring little creativity

(Average) (Skill 1.1)

2. Which of the following is not a stage in Piaget's theory of child development?

    A. Sensory motor stage

    B. Preoptimal stage

    C. Concrete operational stage

    D. Formal operational stage

(Average) (Skill 1.1)

3. What developmental patterns should a professional teacher assess to meet the needs of the student?

    A. Academic, regional, and family background

    B. Social, physical, and academic

    C. Academic, physical, and family background

    D. Physical, family, and ethnic background

(Rigorous) (Skill 1.1)

4. According to Piaget, what stage is characterized by the ability to think abstractly and to use logic?

    A. Concrete operational

    B. Preoperational

    C. Formal operational

    D. Conservative operational

(Average) (Skill 1.1)

5. Students who can solve problems mentally have:

    A. Reached maturity

    B. Physically developed

    C. Reached the preoperational stage of thought

    D. Achieved the ability to manipulate objects symbolically

(Rigorous) (Skill 1.2)

6. Mr. Rogers describes his educational philosophy as eclectic, meaning that he uses many educational theories to guide his classroom practice. Why is this the best approach for today's teachers?

    A. Today's classrooms are often too diverse for one theory to meet the needs of all students

    B. Educators must be able to draw upon other strategies if one theory is not effective

    C. Both A and B

    D. None of the above

(Easy) (Skill 1.2)

7. **Who developed the theory of multiple intelligences?**

   A. Bruner

   B. Gardner

   C. Kagan

   D. Cooper

(Rigorous) (Skill 1.3)

8. **Which of the following statements MOST explains how philosophy has impacted other subject areas such as reading, math, and science?**

   A. Most subject areas emerged from Greek society and its great philosophers such as Plato and Aristotle

   B. Using philosophical arguments, experts have debated the best teaching strategies in various subject areas

   C. Philosophy drives the motivation and dedication of most great teachers

   D. A majority of the fifty states require students to take several years of philosophical courses

(Easy) (Skill 2.1)

9. **What is the most important benefit of students developing critical thinking skills?**

   A. Students are able to apply knowledge to a specific subject area as well as to other subject areas

   B. Students remember the information for testing purposes

   C. Students focus on a limited number of specific facts

   D. Students do not have to memorize the information for later recall

(Easy) (Skill 2.1)

10. **How can mnemonic devices be used to increase achievement?**

    A. They help students learn to pronounce assigned terms

    B. They provide visual cues to help students recall information

    C. They give auditory hints to increase learner retention

    D. They are most effective with kinesthetic learners

(Average) (Skill 2.3)

11. **Learning centers are unique instructional tools because they allow students to do all of the following except:**

    A. Learn through play

    B. Sit in their seats to complete assignments

    C. Select their own activities

    D. Set up the activity area under a teacher's guidance

(Rigorous) (Skill 2.3)

12. **Discovery learning is to inquiry as direct instruction is to:**

    A. Loosely developed lessons

    B. Clear instructions

    C. Random lessons

    D. Class discussion

(Easy) (Skill 2.3)

13. This instructional strategy engages students in active discussion about issues and problems of practical application:

   A. Case method

   B. Direct instruction

   C. Concept mapping

   D. Formative assessment

(Rigorous) (Skill 2.4)

14. Which of these is not a reason why schools offer health classes that address issues of sexuality, self-image, peer pressure, nutrition, wellness, gang activity, and drug engagement?

   A. In order to establish a core curriculum that is well-rounded

   B. Because health education is mandated by Title X

   C. To prevent students from engaging in negative activities

   D. So that students are exposed to issues that directly affect them

(Average) (Skill 2.4)

15. What do cooperative learning methods all have in common?

   A. Philosophy

   B. Cooperative task/cooperative reward structures

   C. Student roles and communication

   D. Teacher roles

(Rigorous) (Skill 2.5)

16. Mrs. Grant is providing her students with many extrinsic motivators in order to increase their intrinsic motivation. Which of the following best explains this relationship?

   A. This is a good relationship and will increase intrinsic motivation

   B. The relationship builds animosity between the teacher and the students

   C. Extrinsic motivation does not in itself help to build intrinsic motivation

   D. There is no place for extrinsic motivation in the classroom

(Average) (Skill 3.2)

17. This condition has skyrocketed among young children, usually presents itself within the first three years of a child's life, and hinders normal communication and social interactive behavior.

   A. ADHD

   B. Dyslexia

   C. Depression

   D. Autism

(Average) (Skill 3.2)

18. The difference between typical stress-response behavior and severe emotional distress can be identified by the:

   A. Situation, circumstances, and individuals around which the behavior occurs

   B. The family dynamics of the child

   C. Frequency, duration, and intensity of the stress-responsive behavior

   D. The child's age, maturity, and coping abilities

(Easy) (Skill 3.2)

19. It is essential that teachers develop relationships with their students and are aware of their personalities. Which of the following is an example of why this is important?

    A. Because most students do not have adult friends

    B. Because most teachers do not have friends who are children

    C. So that teachers can stay abreast of the social interaction among children

    D. Because then teachers can immediately identify behavioral changes and get the child help

(Average) (Skill 3.2)

20. You notice that one of your students is having a seizure and classmates inform you that this is because she was abusing drugs at her locker. What should you do immediately after contacting the main office about this emergency?

    A. Attempt to treat the student

    B. Find out the protocol for your school district

    C. Isolate the student until EMS or police arrive

    D. Interview classmates individually to gather the facts

(Easy) (Skill 3.3)

21. What is one of the most important things to know about the differences between first language (L1) and second language (L2) acquisition?

    A. A second language is easier to acquire than a first language

    B. Most people master a second language (L2), but rarely do they master a first language (L1)

    C. Most people master a first language (L1), but rarely do they master a second language (L2)

    D. Acquiring a first language (L1) is as difficult as acquiring a second language (L2)

(Easy) (Skill 3.3)

22. Before what age should children be trained to increase their chances at full mastery of a second language?

    A. Four

    B. Seven

    C. Twelve

    D. Sixteen

(Average) (Skill 3.6)

23. Taking students to visit the elderly in a nursing home helps students build which of the following?

    A. Cultural sensitivity

    B. Bias

    C. Gender sensitivity

    D. Honesty

(Average) (Skill 3.7)

24. When choosing new materials for the classroom, the teacher must review them to ensure that they are free of which of the following?

    A. Insensitivity to nationality

    B. That which nullifies the values of a group

    C. Development level

    D. All of the above

Learning Environment (Skills 4.1 – 6.7)

(Average) (Skill 4.1)

25. How can the teacher establish a positive climate in the classroom?

    A. Help students see the positive aspects of various cultures

    B. Use whole-group instruction for all content areas

    C. Help students divide into cooperative groups based on ability

    D. Eliminate teaching strategies that allow students to make choices

(Average) (Skill 4.1)

26. Invitational Education Approach includes which of the following?

    A. Sensing and perceptual function

    B. Superiority and perfection

    C. Inviting and disinviting behaviors

    D. Transforming and acting function

(Average) (Skill 4.1)

27. The process approach proposes which three-phase model for teaching?

    A. Explore, reach, and touch

    B. Reach, touch, and teach

    C. Reward, reach, and teach

    D. Reach, teach, and re-teach

(Rigorous) (Skill 4.2)

28. One higher level of cooperative learning groups is:

    A. Student Teams Achievement Divisions

    B. Discovery groups

    C. Learning together

    D. Simulated conflict situations

(Easy) (Skill 4.5)

29. A teacher's posture and movement affect the following student outcomes except:

    A. Student learning

    B. Attitudes

    C. Motivation

    D. Physical development

(Rigorous) (Skill 4.5)

30. What has been established to increase student originality, intrinsic motivation, and higher-order thinking skills?

    A. Classroom climate

    B. High expectations

    C. Student choice

    D. Use of authentic learning opportunities

(Average) (Skill 5.2)

31. **What would improve planning for instruction?**

    A. Describe the role of the teacher and student

    B. Evaluate the outcomes of instruction

    C. Rearrange the order of activities

    D. Give outside assignments

(Average) (Skill 5.2)

32. **How can student misconduct be redirected at times?**

    A. The teacher threatens the students

    B. The teacher assigns detention to the whole class

    C. The teacher stops the activity and stares at the students

    D. The teacher effectively handles changing from one activity to another

(Rigorous) (Skill 5.2)

33. **What have recent studies regarding effective teachers concluded?**

    A. Effective teachers let students establish rules

    B. Effective teachers establish routines by the sixth week of school

    C. Effective teachers state their own policies and establish consistent class rules and procedures on the first day of class

    D. Effective teachers establish flexible routines

(Average) (Skill 5.2)

34. **To maintain the flow of events in the classroom, what should an effective teacher do?**

    A. Work only in small groups

    B. Use only whole-class activities

    C. Direct attention to content rather than focusing the class on misbehavior

    D. Follow lectures with written assignments

(Rigorous) (Skill 5.2)

35. **The concept of efficient use of time includes which of the following?**

    A. Daily review, seatwork, and recitation of concepts

    B. Lesson initiation, transition, and comprehension check

    C. Review, test, and review

    D. Punctuality, management transition, and wait-time avoidance

(Average) (Skill 5.2)

36. **What is an example of an academic transition signal?**

    A. How do clouds form?

    B. Today we are going to study clouds.

    C. We have completed today's lesson.

    D. That completes the description of cumulus clouds. Now we will look at the description of cirrus clouds.

(Average) (Skill 5.5)

37. **What should the teacher do when a student is tapping a pencil on the desk during a lecture?**

    A. Stop the lesson and correct the student as an example to other students

    B. Walk over to the student and quietly touch the pencil as a signal for the student to stop

    C. Announce to the class that everyone should remember to remain quiet during the lecture

    D. Ignore the student, hoping he or she will stop

(Rigorous) (Skill 5.5)

38. **Why is punishment not always effective in managing student behavior?**

    A. It tends to suppress behavior, not eliminate it

    B. It focuses on the negative, rather than the positive

    C. Students may comply out of fear rather than a genuine behavior change

    D. All of the above

(Rigorous) (Skill 5.6)

39. **What is one way of effectively managing student conduct?**

    A. State expectations about behavior

    B. Let students discipline their peers

    C. Let minor infractions of the rules go unnoticed

    D. Increase disapproving remarks

(Average) (Skill 5.6)

40. **Robert throws a piece of paper across the room. The teacher ignores Robert. What is the teacher demonstrating?**

    A. Punishment

    B. Extinction

    C. Negative practice

    D. Verbal reprimand

(Average) (Skill 5.6)

41. **What is a prompt?**

    A. Reinforcement provided for producing any appropriate behavior during a specified time interval

    B. A token, such as a sticker or star, that can be traded for a reward

    C. A reward for producing a behavior that is an alternative to an undesired target behavior

    D. A visual or verbal cue that assists a child through the behavior-shaping process

(Rigorous) (Skill 5.6)

42. **What is most likely to happen when students witness a punitive or angry desist?**

    A. Respond with more behavior disruption

    B. All disruptive behavior stops

    C. Students align with teacher

    D. Behavior stays the same

(Easy) (Skill 5.6)

43. **What can be measured utilizing the following types of assessments: direct observation, role playing, context observation, and teacher ratings?**

    A. Social skills

    B. Reading skills

    C. Math skills

    D. Need for specialized instruction

(Rigorous) (Skill 5.6)

44. **What increases the likelihood that the response following an event will occur again?**

    A. Extinction

    B. Satiation

    C. Verbal reprimands

    D. Reinforcement

(Average) (Skill 5.6)

45. **Why is praise for compliance important in classroom management?**

    A. Students will continue deviant behavior

    B. Desirable conduct will be repeated

    C. It reflects simplicity and warmth

    D. Students will fulfill obligations

(Easy) (Skill 5.7)

46. **What might be a result if the teacher is distracted by some unrelated event in the instruction?**

    A. Students will leave the class

    B. Students will understand the importance of class rules

    C. Students will stay on-task longer

    D. Students will lose the momentum of the lesson

(Easy) (Skill 6.1)

47. **Outlines, graphs, and models are particularly good for which type of learners?**

    A. Auditory

    B. Kinestetic

    C. Visual

    D. Olfactory

(Average) (Skill 6.1)

48. **What has research shown to be the effect of using advance organizers in the lesson?**

    A. They facilitate learning and retention

    B. They allow teachers to use their planning time effectively

    C. They only serve to help the teacher organize the lesson

    D. They show definitive positive results on student achievement

(Average) (Skill 6.2)

49. To facilitate discussion-oriented, non-threatening communication among all students, teachers must do which of the following?

A. Model appropriate behavior

B. Allow students to express themselves freely

C. Show students that some views will not be tolerated

D. Explain that students should not disagree

(Average) (Skill 6.2)

50. In diverse classrooms, teachers must ensure that they neither protect students from criticism nor praise them because of their ethnicity or gender. Doing either action may result in which of the following outcomes?

A. Classmates may become anxious or resentful when dealing with the diverse students

B. Parents will appreciate their child being singled out

C. The child will be pleased to receive this attention

D. Other teachers will follow this example

(Easy) (Skill 6.5)

51. The use of technology in the classroom allows for:

A. More complex lessons

B. Better delivery of instruction

C. Variety of instruction

D. Better ability to meet more individual student needs

(Average) (Skill 6.7)

52. Wait-time has what effect?

A. Gives structure to the class discourse

B. Fewer chain and low-level questions are asked with more higher-level questions included

C. Gives the students time to evaluate the response

D. Gives the opportunity for in-depth discussion about the topic

Instruction and Assessment (Skills 7.1 – 9.8)

(Easy) (Skill 7.1)

53. Which of the following test items is not objective?

A. Multiple choice

B. Essay

C. Matching

D. True/false

(Rigorous) (Skill 7.1)

54. Of the following definitions, which best describes a standardized achievement test?

A. It measures narrow skills and abilities

B. It measures broad areas of knowledge

C. It measures the ability to perform a task

D. It measures performance related to specific, recently acquired information

(Rigorous) (Skill 7.1)

55. **Norm-referenced tests:**

    A. Provide information about how local test-takers performed compared to local test-takers from the previous year

    B. Provide information about how the local test-takers performed compared to a representative sampling of national test-takers

    C. Make no comparisons to national test takers

    D. None of the above

(Average) (Skill 7.1)

56. **It is most appropriate to use norm-referenced standardized tests for which of the following?**

    A. For comparison to the population on which the test was normed

    B. For teacher evaluation

    C. For evaluation of the administration

    D. For comparison to the school on which the test was normed

(Rigorous) (Skill 7.1)

57. **_____ is a standardized test in which performance is directly related to the educational objective(s).**

    A. Aptitude test

    B. Norm-referenced test

    C. Criterion-referenced test

    D. Summative evaluation

(Rigorous) (Skill 7.1)

58. **Which of the following is the least appropriate reason for teachers to be able to analyze data on their students?**

    A. To provide appropriate instruction

    B. To make instructional decisions

    C. To separate students into weaker and stronger academic groups

    D. To communicate and determine instructional progress

(Easy) (Skill 7.1)

59. **The seven purposes of assessment include all of the following except:**

    A. To identify students' strengths and weaknesses

    B. To assess the effectiveness of a particular instructional strategy

    C. To provide data that assists in decision making

    D. None of the above

(Average) (Skill 7.1)

60. **What is the best example of a formative assessment?**

    A. The results of an intelligence test

    B. Correcting tests in small groups and immediately recording the grades

    C. An essay that receives teacher feedback and can be corrected by students prior to having a grade recorded

    D. Scheduling a discussion prior to the test

(Rigorous) (Skill 7.2)

61. Fill in the blanks for I. _____ and II. _____ in the picture below:

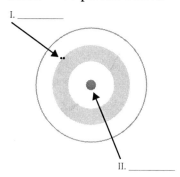

I. _____

II. _____

A. I. Reliability and II. Validity

B. I. Validity and II. Reliability

C. I. Reliability and II. Vigor

D. I. Rigor and II. Validity

(Rigorous) (Skill 7.2)

62. This method tests the validity and reliability of a test by dividing a single test into two parts and comparing them.

A. Split-half

B. Test-retest

C. Equivalent forms

D. Two-set

(Rigorous) (Skill 7.2)

63. An example of reliability in testing is _____.

A. items on the test produce the same response each time

B. the test was administered with poor lighting

C. items on the test measure what they should measure

D. the test is too long for the time allotted

(Easy) (Skill 7.3)

64. When a teacher wants to utilize an assessment that is subjective in nature, which of the following is the most effective method for scoring?

A. Rubric

B. Checklist

C. Alternative assessment

D. Subjective measures should not be utilized

(Rigorous) (Skill 7.6)

65. When students provide evidence of having special needs, standardized tests can be:

A. Given out with the same predetermined questions as what is administered to students without special needs

B. Exempted for certain children whose special-needs conditions would prevent them performing with any reliability or validity

C. Administered over a lengthier test period (i.e., four hours instead of three or two)

D. All of the above

(Average) (Skill 8.1)

66. Which of following is NOT the role of the teacher in the instructional process?

A. Instructor

B. Coach

C. Facilitator

D. Follower

(Rigorous) (Skill 8.2)

67. Discovery learning is to inquiry as direct instruction is to:

    A. Scripted lessons

    B. Well-developed instructions

    C. Clear instructions that eliminate all misinterpretations

    D. Creativity of teaching

(Rigorous) (Skill 8.6)

68. When developing lessons it is imperative teachers provide equity in pedagogy so:

    A. Unfair labeling of students will not occur

    B. Student experiences will be positive

    C. Students will achieve academic success

    D. All of the above

(Average) (Skill 8.6)

69. Which of the following is a good reason to collaborate with a peer?

    A. To increase your knowledge in areas where you feel you are weak, but the peer is strong

    B. To increase your planning time and that of your peer by combining the classes and taking more breaks

    C. To have fewer lesson plans to write

    D. To teach fewer subjects

(Rigorous) (Skill 8.6)

70. Which of the following are ways a professional can assess her teaching strengths and weaknesses?

    A. Examining how many students were unable to understand a concept

    B. Asking peers for suggestions or ideas

    C. Self-evaluation/reflection on lessons taught

    D. All of the above

(Rigorous) (Skill 8.6)

71. Mr. German is a math coach. He is the only math coach in his building and within his district. Mr. German believes it is imperative to seek out the support of colleagues to work in a more collaborative manner. Which of the following would be an appropriate step for him to take?

    A. Collaborating with other teachers in his building regardless of their skill level knowledge in his area

    B. Asking the administration to find colleagues with whom he can collaborate

    C. Joining a professional organization such as the National Council of Teachers of Mathematics (NCTM)

    D. Searching the Internet for possible collaboration opportunities

(Average) (Skill 9.1)

72. Why is it important for a teacher to pose a question before calling on students to answer?

    A. It helps manage student conduct

    B. It keeps the students as a group focused on the class work

    C. It allows students time to collaborate

    D. It gives the teacher time to walk among the students

(Rigorous) (Skill 9.1)

73. What would be espoused by Jerome Bruner?

    A. Thought depends on the acquisition of operations

    B. Memory plays a significant role in cognitive growth

    C. Genetics is the most important factor for cognitive growth

    D. Enriched environments have significant effects on cognitive growth

(Easy) (Skill 9.1)

74. When asking questions of students it is important to:

    A. Ask questions the students can answer

    B. Provide numerous questions

    C. Provide questions at various levels

    D. Provide only a limited number of questions

(Rigorous) (Skill 9.3)

75. Mr. Smith is introducing the concept of photosynthesis to his class next week. In preparing for this lesson, he considers that this concept will be new to many of his students. Mr. Smith understands that his students' brains are like filing cabinets and that there is currently no file for photosynthesis in those cabinets. What does Mr. Smith need to do to ensure his students acquire the necessary knowledge?

    A. Help them create a new file

    B. Teach the students the information; they will organize it themselves in their own way

    C. Find a way to connect the new learning to other information they already know

    D. Provide many repetitions and social situations during the learning process

(Rigorous) (Skill 9.3)

76. Curriculum mapping is an effective strategy because it:

    A. Provides an orderly sequence to instruction

    B. Provides lesson plans for teachers to use and follow

    C. Ties the curriculum into instruction

    D. Provides a clear map so all students receive the same instruction across all classes

(Rigorous) (Skill 9.5)

77. The teacher states that the lesson the students will be engaged in will consist of a review of the material from the previous day, demonstration of the scientific of an electronic circuit, and small group work on setting up an electronic circuit. What has the teacher demonstrated?

    A. The importance of reviewing

    B. Giving the general framework for the lesson to facilitate learning

    C. Giving students the opportunity to leave if they are not interested in the lesson

    D. Providing momentum for the lesson

(Average) (Skill 9.5)

78. What is an effective way to prepare students for testing?

    A. Minimize the importance of the test

    B. Orient the students to the test by telling them of the purpose, how the results will be used, and how it is relevant to them

    C. Use the same format for every test are given

    D. Have them construct an outline to study from

(Rigorous) (Skill 9.8)

79. What are wikis?

    A. Electronic communication boards

    B. Speech recognition devices that type text as it is spoken by the student

    C. Collaborative definitions posted to computers

    D. Readers that read aloud alerts on screens

Professional Roles and Responsibilities (Skills 10.1 – 12.4)

(Average) (Skill 10.1)

80. Which of the following should NOT be a purpose of a parent-teacher conference?

    A. To involve the parent in their child's education

    B. To establish a friendship with the child's parents

    C. To resolve a concern about the child's performance

    D. To inform parents of positive behaviors by the child

(Easy) (Skill 10.1)

81. Mr. Brown wishes to improve his parent communication skills. Which of the following is a strategy he can utilize to accomplish this goal?

    A. Hold parent-teacher conferences

    B. Send home positive notes

    C. Have parent nights where the parents are invited into his classroom

    D. All of the above

(Easy) (Skill 10.1)

82. Tommy is a student in your class, and his parents are deaf. Tommy is struggling with math and you want to contact the parents to discuss the issue. How should you proceed?

    A. Limit contact because of the parents' inability to hear

    B. Use a TTY phone to communicate with the parents

    C. Talk to your administrator to find an appropriate interpreter to help you communicate with the parents personally

    D. Both B and C

(Easy) (Skill 10.1)

83. When communicating with parents for whom English is not the primary language you should:

    A. Provide materials whenever possible in their native language

    B. Use an interpreter

    C. Provide the same communication as you would to native English speaking parents

    D. All of the above

(Average) (Skill 11.1)

84. What is a benefit of frequent self-assessment?

    A. Opens new venues for professional development

    B. Saves teachers the pressure of being observed by others

    C. Reduces time spent on areas not needing attention

    D. Offers a model for students to adopt in self-improvement

(Average) (Skill 11.1)

85. Which of the following could be used to improve teaching skills?

    A. Developing a professional development plan

    B. Using self-evaluation and reflection

    C. Building professional learning communities

    D. All of the above

(Average) (Skill 11.3)

86. Which of the following is NOT a sound educational practice for expanding the professional development opportunities for teachers?

    A. Looking at multiple methods of classroom management strategies

    B. Training teachers in understanding and applying multiple assessment formats and implementations in curriculum and instruction

    C. Having the students complete professional development assessments on a regular basis

    D. Teaching teachers how to disaggregate student data in improving instruction and curriculum implementation for student academic equity and access

(Average) (Skill 11.4)

87. What would happen if a school utilized an integrated approach to professional development?

    A. All stakeholders' needs are addressed

    B. Teachers and administrators are on the same page

    C. High-quality programs for students are developed

    D. Parents drive the curriculum and instruction

(Average) (Skill 12.2)

88. Which of the following statements is true about computers in the classroom?

    A. Computers are simply a glorified game machine and just allow students to play games

    B. The computer should replace traditional research and writing skills taught to school-age children

    C. Computers stifle the creativity of children

    D. Computers allow students to access information they may otherwise be unable to

(Average) (Skill 12.2)

89. While an asset to students, technology is also important for teachers. Which of the following can be taught using technology to students?

    A. Cooperation skills

    B. Decision-making skills

    C. Problem-solving skills

    D. All of the above

(Easy) (Skill 12.2)

90. As a classroom teacher, you have data on all of your students that you must track over the remainder of the school year. You will need to keep copies of the scores students receive and then graph their results to share progress with the parents and administrators. Which of the following software programs will be most useful for this?

    A. Word processing program

    B. Spreadsheet

    C. Database

    D. Teacher utility and classroom management tools

(Average) (Skill 12.2)

91. Which of the following statements is NOT true?

    A. Printing and distributing material off of the Internet breaks the copyright law

    B. Articles are only copyrighted when there is a © in the article

    C. E-mail messages that are posted online are considered copyrighted

    D. It is not legal to scan magazine articles and place on your district Web site

(Average) (Skill 12.2)

92. Which is true of child protective services?

    A. They have been forced to become more punitive in their attempts to treat and prevent child abuse and neglect

    B. They have become more a means for identifying cases of abuse and less an agent for rehabilitation because of the large volume of cases

    C. They have become advocates for structured discipline within the school

    D. They have become a strong advocate in the court system

(Average) (Skill 12.4)

93. Which of the following increases appropriate behavior more than 80 percent?

    A. Monitoring the halls

    B. Having class rules

    C. Having class rules, giving feedback, and having individual consequences

    D. Having class rules and giving feedback

(Average) (Skill 12.4)

94. A 16-year-old girl who has been looking sad writes an essay in which the main protagonist commits suicide. You overhear her talking about suicide. What do you do?

   A. Report this immediately to school administration and talk to the girl, letting her know you will talk to her parents about it

   B. Report this immediately to authorities

   C. Report this immediately to school administration, make your own report to authorities if required by protocol in your school, and do nothing else

   D. Just give the child some extra attention, as it may be that's all she's looking for

(Rigorous) (Skill 12.4)

95. Jeanne, a bright, attentive student, is in her first hour English class. She is quiet, but very alert, often visually scanning the room in random patterns. Her pupils are dilated, and she has a slight but noticeable tremor in her hands. She fails to note a cue given from her teacher. At odd moments, she will act as if responding to stimuli that aren't there by suddenly changing her gaze. When spoken to directly, she has a limited response, but her teacher has a sense she is not herself. What should the teacher do?

   A. Ask the student if she is all right, then let it go, as there are not enough signals to be alarmed

   B. Meet with the student after class to get more information before making a referral

   C. Send the student to the office to see the nurse

   D. Quietly call for administration, remain calm, and be careful not to alarm the class

(Average) (Skill 12.4)

96. In successful inclusion of students with disabilities:

   A. A variety of instructional arrangements are available

   B. School personnel shift the responsibility for learning outcomes to the student s

   C. The physical facilities are used as they are

   D. Regular classroom teachers have sole responsibility for evaluating student progress

(Average) (Skill 12.4)

97. How may a teacher use a student's permanent record?

   A. To develop a better understanding of the needs of the student

   B. To record all instances of student disruptive behavior

   C. To brainstorm ideas for discussing with parents at parent-teacher conferences

   D. To develop realistic expectations of the student's performance early in the year

(Rigorous) (Skill 12.4)

98. You receive a phone call from a person who indicates she is now tutoring a student in your class. She would like you to provide an overview of the academic areas in which the student is having difficulties. What is the first thing you should do?

   A. Find a time and talk with the tutor about issues you see within the classroom

   B. Call the parents

   C. Put together a packet of information to share with the tutor

   D. Offer to invite the tutor in to have a discussion and observe the child

(Rigorous) (Skill 12.4)

99. Marcus is a first-grade boy of good developmental attainment. His learning progress is good the first half of the year. He shows no indicators of emotional distress. After the holiday break, he returns much changed. He is quieter, sullen even, tending to play alone. He has moments of tearfulness, sometimes almost without cause. He avoids contact with adults as often as he can. Even play with his friends has become limited. He has episodes of wetting not seen before and often wants to sleep in school. What approach is appropriate for this sudden change in behavior?

   A. Give him some time to adjust; the holiday break was probably too much fun to come back to school from

   B. Report this change immediately to administration; do not call the parents until administration decides a course of action

   C. Document his daily behavior carefully as soon as you notice such a change, and report to administration the next month or so in a meeting

   D. Make a courtesy call to the parents to let them know he is not acting like himself, being sure to tell them he is not making trouble for others

(Rigorous) (Skill 12.4)

100. Andy shows up to class abusive and irritable. He is often late, sleeps in class, sometimes slurs his speech, and has an odor of alcohol. What is the first intervention to take?

   A. Confront him, relying on a trusting relationship you think you have

   B. Do a lesson on alcohol abuse, making an example of him

   C. Do nothing; it is better to err on the side of failing to identify substance abuse

   D. Call administration, avoid conflict, and supervise others carefully

Answer Key

ANSWER KEY						
1. A	16. C	31. B	46. D	61. A	76. A	91. B
2. B	17. D	32. D	47. C	62. A	77. B	92. B
3. B	18. C	33. C	48. A	63. A	78. B	93. C
4. C	19. D	34. C	49. A	64. A	79. C	94. C
5. D	20. C	35. D	50. A	65. D	80. B	95. D
6. C	21. C	36. D	51. D	66. D	81. D	96. A
7. B	22. B	37. B	52. B	67. C	82. D	97. A
8. B	23. A	38. D	53. B	68. D	83. D	98. B
9. A	24. D	39. A	54. B	69. A	84. A	99. B
10. B	25. A	40. B	55. B	70. D	85. D	100. D
11. B	26. C	41. D	56. A	71. C	86. C	
12. A	27. B	42. A	57. C	72. B	87. C	
13. A	28. D	43. A	58. C	73. D	88. D	
14. B	29. D	44. D	59. D	74. C	89. D	
15. B	30. C	45. B	60. C	75. C	90. B	

Rigor Table

RIGOR TABLE	
Rigor level	**Questions**
Easy 21%	1, 7, 9, 10, 13, 19, 21, 22, 29, 43, 46, 47, 51, 53, 59, 64, 74, 81, 82, 83, 90
Average 44%	2, 3, 5, 11, 15, 17, 18, 20, 23, 24, 25, 26, 27, 31, 32, 34, 36, 37, 40, 41, 45, 48, 49, 50, 52, 56, 60, 66, 69, 72, 78, 80, 84, 85, 86, 87, 88, 89, 91, 92, 93, 95, 96, 97
Rigorous 36%	4, 6, 8, 12, 14, 16, 28, 30, 33, 35, 38, 39, 42, 44, 54, 55, 57, 58, 61, 62, 63, 65, 67, 68, 70, 71, 73, 75, 76, 77, 79, 94, 98, 99, 100

Sample Test with Rationales

Student Development and Learning (Skills 1.1 – 3.8)

(Easy) (Skill 1.1)

1. **Constructivist classrooms are considered to be:**

    A. Student-centered

    B. Teacher-centered

    C. Focused on standardized tests

    D. Requiring little creativity

    Answer: A. Student-centered

    Student-centered classrooms are considered to be "constructivist," in that students are given opportunities to construct their own meanings onto new pieces of knowledge.

(Average) (Skill 1.1)

2. **Which of the following is not a stage in Piaget's theory of child development?**

    A. Sensory motor stage

    B. Preoptimal stage

    C. Concrete operational stage

    D. Formal operational stage

Answer: B. Preoptimal stage

Jean Piaget believed children pass through a series of stages to develop from the most basic forms of concrete thinking to sophisticated levels of abstract thinking. His developmental theory consists of four learning stages, which can be remembered with the pneumonic, Stages Precious Children Follow (SPCF):

1. Sensory motor stage (from birth to age 2)

2. Preoperation stage (ages 2 to 7 or early elementary)

3. Concrete operational stage (ages 7 to 11 or upper elementary)

4. Formal operational stage (ages 7 to 15 or late elementary/high school)

(Average) (Skill 1.1)

3. **What developmental patterns should a professional teacher assess to meet the needs of the student?**

    A. Academic, regional, and family background

    B. Social, physical, and academic

    C. Academic, physical, and family background

    D. Physical, family, and ethnic background

Answer: B. Social, physical, and academic

The effective teacher applies knowledge of physical, social, and academic developmental patterns and individual differences to meet the instructional needs of all students in the classroom. The most important premise of child development is that all domains of development (physical, social, and academic) are integrated. The teacher has a broad knowledge and thorough understanding of the development that typically occurs during the student's current period of life. More important, the teacher understands how children learn best during each period of development. An examination of the student's file coupled with ongoing evaluation assures a successful educational experience for both teacher and students.

(Rigorous) (Skill 1.1)

4. **According to Piaget, what stage is characterized by the ability to think abstractly and to use logic?**

   A. Concrete operational

   B. Preoperational

   C. Formal operational

   D. Conservative operational

Answer: C. Formal operations

The four development stages are described in Piaget's theory:

1. *Sensorimotor stage*: from birth to age 2 years (children experience the world through movement and senses)

2. *Preoperational stage*: from ages 2 to 7 (acquisition of motor skills)

3. *Concrete operational stage*: from ages 7 to 11 (children begin to think logically about concrete events)

4. *Formal operational stage*: after age 11 (development of abstract reasoning)

These chronological periods are approximate and, in light of the fact that studies have demonstrated great variation between children, cannot be seen as rigid norms. Furthermore, these stages occur at different ages, depending upon the domain of knowledge under consideration. The ages normally given for the stages reflect when each stage tends to predominate even though one might elicit examples of two, three, or even all four stages of thinking at the same time from one individual, depending upon the domain of knowledge and the means used to elicit it.

(Average) (Skill 1.1)

5. **Students who can solve problems mentally have:**

   A. Reached maturity

   B. Physically developed

   C. Reached the preoperational stage of thought

   D. Achieved the ability to manipulate objects symbolically

Answer: D. Achieved the ability to manipulate objects symbolically

When students are able to solve mental problems, it is an indication to the teacher that they have achieved the ability to manipulate objects symbolically and should be instructed to continue to develop their cognitive and academic skills.

(Rigorous) (Skill 1.2)

6. **Mr. Rogers describes his educational philosophy as eclectic, meaning that he uses many educational theories to guide his classroom practice. Why is this the best approach for today's teachers?**

   A. Today's classrooms are often too diverse for one theory to meet the needs of all students

   B. Educators must be able to draw upon other strategies if one theory is not effective

   C. Both A and B

   D. None of the above

Answer: C. Both A and B

No one theory will work for every classroom; a good approach is for an educator to incorporate a range of learning theories in his or her practice. Still, under the guidance of any theory, good educators will differentiate their instructional practices to meet the needs of individual students' abilities and interests using various instructional practices.

(Easy) (Skill 1.2)

7. **Who developed the theory of multiple intelligences?**

   A. Bruner

   B. Gardner

   C. Kagan

   D. Cooper

Answer: B. Gardner

Howard Gardner's most famous work is probably *Frames of Mind*, which details seven dimensions of intelligence (visual/spatial intelligence, musical intelligence, verbal intelligence, logical/mathematical intelligence, interpersonal intelligence, intrapersonal intelligence, and bodily/kinesthetic intelligence). Gardner's claim that pencil and paper IQ tests do not capture the full range of human intelligences has garnered much praise within the field of education but has also been met with criticism, largely from psychometricians. Since the publication of *Frames of Mind*, Gardner has additionally identified the eighth dimension of intelligence, naturalist intelligence, and is still considering a possible ninth—existentialist intelligence.

(Rigorous) (Skill 1.3)

8. **Which of the following statements MOST explains how philosophy has impacted other subject areas such as reading, math, and science?**

   A. Most subject areas emerged from Greek society and its great philosophers such as Plato and Aristotle

   B. Using philosophical arguments, experts have debated the best teaching strategies in various subject areas

   C. Philosophy drives the motivation and dedication of most great teachers

   D. A majority of the fifty states require students to take several years of philosophical courses

Answer: B. Using philosophical arguments, experts have debated the best teaching strategies in various subject areas

Academic subject areas have also added to the philosophical debate on teaching. For example, reading teachers have long debated whether phonics or whole language was more appropriate as an instructional method. Language Arts teachers have debated the importance of a prescribed canon (famous works of literature) versus teaching literature simply to teach thinking skills and an appreciation of good literature. Math teachers have debated the extent to which application is necessary in math instruction; while some feel that it is more important to teach structure and process, others suggest that it is only relevant if math skills are taught in context.

(Easy) (Skill 2.1)

9. **What is the most important benefit of students developing critical thinking skills?**

   A. Students are able to apply knowledge to a specific subject area as well as to other subject areas

   B. Students remember the information for testing purposes

   C. Students focus on a limited number of specific facts

   D. Students do not have to memorize the information for later recall

Answer: A. Students are able to apply knowledge to a specifc subject area as well as to other subject areas

When a student learns to think critically he or she learns how to apply knowledge to a specific subject area, but more importantly, the student knows how to apply that information to other subject areas.

(Easy) (Skill 2.1)

10. **How can mnemonic devices be used to increase achievement?**

    A. They help students learn to pronounce assigned terms

    B. They provide visual cues to help students recall information

    C. They give auditory hints to increase learner retention

    D. They are most effective with kinesthetic learners

Answer: B. They provide visual cues to help students recall information

Mnemonics rely not only on repetition to remember facts, but also on associations between easy-to-remember constructs and lists of data. It is based on the principle that the human mind can more easily recall insignificant data when it is attached (in a logical way) to spatial, personal, or otherwise meaningful information.

(Average) (Skill 2.3)

11. Learning centers are unique instructional tools because they allow students to do all of the following except:

A. Learn through play

B. Sit in their seats to complete assignments

C. Select their own activities

D. Set up the activity area under a teacher's guidance

Answer: B. Sit in their seats to complete assignments

Learning centers are extremely important in flexible classrooms. In this setup, students have some time during which they can choose their own activity. Under a teacher's guidance, learners can even create the centers, collecting the necessary items, and then set up the area.

(Rigorous) (Skill 2.3)

12. Discovery learning is to inquiry as direct instruction is to:

A. Loosely developed lessons

B. Clear instructions

C. Random lessons

D. Class discussion

Answer: A. Loosely developed lessons

Direct instruction is a teaching method that emphasizes well-developed and carefully planned lessons with small learning increments. It assumes that learning outcomes are improved through clear instruction that eliminates misinterpretations.

(Easy) (Skill 2.3)

13. This instructional strategy engages students in active discussion about issues and problems of practical application:

A. Case method

B. Direct instruction

C. Concept mapping

D. Formative assessment

Answer: A. Case method

The case method is an instructional strategy that engages students in active discussion about issues and problems of practical application.

(Rigorous) (Skill 2.4)

14. Which of these is not a reason why schools offer health classes that address issues of sexuality, self-image, peer pressure, nutrition, wellness, gang activity, and drug engagement?

A. In order to establish a core curriculum that is well-rounded

B. Because health education is mandated by Title X

C. To prevent students from engaging in negative activities

D. So that students are exposed to issues that directly affect them

Answer: B. Because health education is mandated by Title X

Most schools will offer health classes that address issues of sexuality, self-image, peer pressure, nutrition, wellness, gang activity, drug engagement, and a variety of other relevant teen experiences. In most districts, as part of a well-rounded core-curriculum, students are required to take a health class. By setting this mandate, the school and district ensure that students are exposed to issues that directly affect them. In addition, by educating students in such issues, officials seek to prevent students from engaging in negative activities. Even though one health class is rarely enough to effectively address the multiplicity of such issues, in today's era of tight school budgets and financial issues, this is not likely to change.

(Average) (Skill 2.4)

15. **What do cooperative learning methods all have in common?**

    A. Philosophy

    B. Cooperative task/cooperative reward structures

    C. Student roles and communication

    D. Teacher roles

Answer: B. Cooperative task/cooperative reward structures.

Cooperative learning situations, as practiced in today's classrooms, grew out of searches conducted by several groups in the early 1970s. Cooperative learning situations can range from very formal applications such as STAD (Student Teams-Achievement Divisions) and CIRC (Cooperative Integrated Reading and Composition) to less formal groupings known variously as "group investigation," "learning together," and "discovery groups." Cooperative learning as a general term is now firmly recognized and established as a teaching and learning technique in American schools. Because cooperative learning techniques are so widely diffused in the schools, it is necessary to orient students in the skills by which cooperative learning groups can operate smoothly and thereby enhance learning. Students who cannot interact constructively with other students will not be able to take advantage of the learning opportunities provided by the cooperative learning situations and will furthermore deprive their fellow students of the opportunity for cooperative learning.

(Rigorous) (Skill 2.5)

16. **Mrs. Grant is providing her students with many extrinsic motivators in order to increase their intrinsic motivation. Which of the following best explains this relationship?**

    A. This is a good relationship and will increase intrinsic motivation

    B. The relationship builds animosity between the teacher and the students

    C. Extrinsic motivation does not in itself help to build intrinsic motivation

    D. There is no place for extrinsic motivation in the classroom

    Answer: C. Extrinsic motivation does not in itself help to build intrinsic motivation

    There are some cases where it is necessary to utilize extrinsic motivation; however, the use of extrinsic motivation is not typically an effective strategy to build intrinsic motivation. Intrinsic motivation comes from within students themselves, while extrinsic motivation comes from external individuals/forces.

(Average) (Skill 3.2)

17. **This condition has skyrocketed among young children, usually presents itself within the first three years of a child's life, and hinders normal communication and social interactive behavior.**

    A. ADHD

    B. Dyslexia

    C. Depression

    D. Autism

Answer: D. Autism

Educators and researchers are sensitive to all disabilities; however, the field has seen autism skyrocket among young children. This condition usually presents itself within the first three years of a child's life and hinders normal communication and social interactive behavior.

(Average) (Skill 3.2)

18. **The difference between typical stress-response behavior and severe emotional distress can be identified by the:**

    A. Situation, circumstances, and individuals around which the behavior occurs

    B. The family dynamics of the child

    C. Frequency, duration, and intensity of the stress-responsive behavior

    D. The child's age, maturity, and coping abilities

Answer: C. Frequency, duration, and intensity of the stress-responsive behavior

Because all children experience stressful periods within their lives from time to time, all students may demonstrate some behaviors that indicate emotional distress. Emotionally healthy students can maintain control of their own behavior even during stressful times. The difference between typical stress-response behavior and severe emotional distress is determined by the frequency, duration, and intensity of stress-responsive behavior.

(Easy) (Skill 3.2)

19. It is essential that teachers develop relationships with their students and are aware of their personalities. Which of the following is an example of why this is important?

   A. Because most students do not have adult friends

   B. Because most teachers do not have friends who are children

   C. So that teachers can stay abreast of the social interaction among children

   D. Because then teachers can immediately identify behavioral changes and get the child help

Answer: D. Because then teachers can immediately identify behavioral changes and get the child help

Social decline is one of the signs of drug or alcohol abuse. Being acquainted with all students, educators will notice personality changes in any student. Characteristically, social withdrawal is first noticed when the student fails to say hello, avoids being near teachers, seems evasive or sneaky, and associates with a different, less academically focused, group of friends. Obviously, association with known substance abusers is almost always a warning sign. Adults must not accept the explanation that the suspected abuser is just being friends with the known abuser, or that the suspected abuser has many kinds of friends. There is a sharp demarcation between youth who abuse substances and those who do not.

(Average) (Skill 3.2)

20. You notice that one of your students is having a seizure and classmates inform you that this is because she was abusing drugs at her locker. What should you do immediately after contacting the main office about this emergency?

   A. Attempt to treat the student

   B. Find out the protocol for your school district

   C. Isolate the student until EMS or police arrive

   D. Interview classmates individually to gather the facts

Answer: C. Isolate the student until EMS or police arrive

Never, under any circumstances, attempt to treat, protect, tolerate, or negotiate with a student who is showing signs of a physical crisis. It is advisable to find out the protocol for a particular school or district; however, most schools require the student to be isolated until they are removed from the school center by EMS or police.

(Easy) (Skill 3.3)

21. **What is one of the most important things to know about the differences between first language (L1) and second language (L2) acquisition?**

    A. A second language is easier to acquire than a first language

    B. Most people master a second language (L2), but rarely do they master a first language (L1)

    C. Most people master a first language (L1), but rarely do they master a second language (L2)

    D. Acquiring a first language (L1) is as difficult as acquiring a second language (L2)

    Answer: C. Most people master a first language (L1), but rarely do they master a second language (L2)

    One of the most important things to know about the differences between first language (L1) and second language (L2) acquisition is that people usually will master L1, but they will almost never be fully proficient in L2.

(Easy) (Skill 3.3)

22. **Before what age should children be trained to increase their chances at full mastery of a second language?**

    A. Four

    B. Seven

    C. Twelve

    D. Sixteen

Answer: B. Seven

It is difficult for children to become fully proficient in a second language. However, if they can be trained before the age of seven, their chances at full mastery will be much higher. Young children learn languages with little effort.

(Average) (Skill 3.6)

23. **Taking students to visit the elderly in a nursing home helps students build which of the following?**

    A. Cultural sensitivity

    B. Bias

    C. Gender sensitivity

    D. Honesty

Answer: A. Cultural sensitivity

Reaching out into the community beyond their own group helps students make cultural connections. Interacting with the elderly, with whom many students have little contact, broadens their understanding and makes them more sensitive to a culture outside of their own.

(Average) (Skill 3.7)

24. **When choosing new materials for the classroom, the teacher must review them to ensure that they are free of which of the following?**

    A. Insensitivity to nationality

    B. That which nullifies the values of a group

    C. Development level

    D. All of the above

Answer: D. All of the above

The textbook companies and publishers of educational materials provide a wide range of content. They strive to create materials free of bias and prejudices, but it is ultimately the teacher's responsibility to review all materials used in the classroom for appropriateness.

Learning Environment (Skills 4.1 – 6.7)

(Average) (Skill 4.1)

25. **How can the teacher establish a positive climate in the classroom?**

    A. Help students see the positive aspects of various cultures

    B. Use whole-group instruction for all content areas

    C. Help students divide into cooperative groups based on ability

    D. Eliminate teaching strategies that allow students to make choices

Answer: A. Help students see the positive aspects of various cultures

An important purpose of education is to prepare students to live successfully in the real world and appreciating different cultures will prepare them for a wide range of contexts and interactions. Additionally, the most fertile learning environment is one in which all viewpoints and backgrounds are respected.

(Average) (Skill 4.1)

26. **Invitational Education Approach includes which of the following?**

    A. Sensing and perceptual function

    B. Superiority and perfection

    C. Inviting and disinviting behaviors

    D. Transforming and acting function

Answer: C. inviting and disinviting behaviors

Invitational Education is an approach that aims at the enhancement of students' self-concepts. According to his approach, teachers and their behaviors may be inviting or they may be disinviting.

(Average) (Skill 4.1)

27. **The process approach proposes which three-phase model for teaching?**

    A. Explore, reach, and touch

    B. Reach, touch, and teach

    C. Reward, reach, and teach

    D. Reach, teach, and re-teach

Answer: B. Reach, touch, and teach

The process approach proposes a three-phase model for teaching. This model includes a sensing function, a transforming function, and an acting function. These three phases can be simplified into the words by which the model is usually given: reach, touch, and teach.

(Rigorous) (Skill 4.2)

28. **One higher level of cooperative learning groups is:**

    A. Student Teams Achievement Divisions

    B. Discovery groups

    C. Learning together

    D. Simulated conflict situations

Answer: D. Simulated conflict situations

Working within structured groups is the first step to cooperative learning. These skills then form the hierarchy of cooperation in which students proceed to levels at which they can engage in simulated conflict situations. In these higher level cooperative groups, students can constructively discuss different points of view.

(Easy) (Skill 4.5)

29. **A teacher's posture and movement affect the following student outcomes except:**

    A. Student learning

    B. Attitudes

    C. Motivation

    D. Physical development

Answer: D. Physical development

Studies show that a teacher's posture and movement are indicators of their enthusiasm and energy, which emphatically influence student outcomes including learning, attitudes, motivation, and focus on goals.

(Rigorous) (Skill 4.5)

30. **What has been established to increase student originality, intrinsic motivation, and higher-order thinking skills?**

    A. Classroom climate

    B. High expectations

    C. Student choice

    D. Use of authentic learning opportunities

Answer: C. Student choice

While all of the descriptors are good attributes for students to demonstrate, it has been shown through research that providing student choice can increase all of the described factors.

(Average) (Skill 5.2)

31. **What would improve planning for instruction?**

    A. Describe the role of the teacher and student

    B. Evaluate the outcomes of instruction

    C. Rearrange the order of activities

    D. Give outside assignments

Answer: B. Evaluate the outcomes of instruction

Important as it is to plan content, materials, activities, and goals and then take into account learner needs in order to base what goes on in the classroom on the results of that planning, it makes no difference if students are not able to demonstrate improvement in the skills being taught. An important part of the planning process is for the teacher to constantly adapt all aspects of the curriculum to what is actually happening in the classroom. Planning frequently misses the mark or fails to allow for unexpected factors. Evaluating the outcomes of instruction regularly and making adjustments accordingly will have a positive impact on the overall success of a teaching methodology.

(Average) (Skill 5.2)

32. **How can student misconduct be redirected at times?**

    A. The teacher threatens the students

    B. The teacher assigns detention to the whole class

    C. The teacher stops the activity and stares at the students

    D. The teacher effectively handles changing from one activity to another

Answer: D. The teacher effectively handles changing from one activity to another

Appropriate verbal techniques include a soft nonthreatening voice void of undue roughness, anger, or impatience regardless of whether the teacher is instructing, providing student alerts, or giving a behavior reprimand. Verbal techniques that may be effective in modifying student behavior include simply stating the student's name and explaining briefly and succinctly what the student is doing that is inappropriate and what the student should be doing. Verbal techniques for reinforcing behavior include both encouragement and praise delivered by the teacher. In addition, for verbal techniques to positively affect student behavior and learning, the teacher must give clear, concise directives while implying her warmth toward the students.

(Rigorous) (Skill 5.2)

33. **What have recent studies regarding effective teachers concluded?**

    A. Effective teachers let students establish rules

    B. Effective teachers establish routines by the sixth week of school

    C. Effective teachers state their own policies and establish consistent class rules and procedures on the first day of class

    D. Effective teachers establish flexible routines

Answer: C. Effective teachers state their own policies and establish consistent class rules and procedures on the first day of class

The teacher can get ahead of the game by stating clearly, on the first day of school, exactly what the rules are. These should be stated firmly but unemotionally. When one of those rules is broken, he can then refer to the rules, rendering enforcement much easier to achieve. It's extremely difficult to achieve goals with students who are out of control. Establishing limits early and consistently enforcing them enhances learning. It is also helpful for the teacher to prominently display the classroom rules. This will serve as a visual reminder of the students' expected behaviors. In a study of classroom management procedures, it was established that the combination of conspicuously displayed rules, frequent verbal references to the rules, and appropriate consequences for appropriate behaviors led to increased levels of on-task behavior.

(Average) (Skill 5.2)

34. **To maintain the flow of events in the classroom, what should an effective teacher do?**

    A. Work only in small groups

    B. Use only whole-class activities

    C. Direct attention to content rather than focusing the class on misbehavior

    D. Follow lectures with written assignments

Answer: C. Direct attention to content rather than focusing the class on misbehavior

Students who misbehave often do so to attract attention. Focusing the attention of the misbehaver as well as the rest of the class on the real purpose of the classroom sends the message that misbehaving will not be rewarded with class attention to the misbehaver. Engaging students in content by using the various tools available to the creative teacher goes a long way in ensuring a peaceful classroom.

(Rigorous) (Skill 5.2)

35. **The concept of efficient use of time includes which of the following?**

    A. Daily review, seatwork, and recitation of concepts

    B. Lesson initiation, transition, and comprehension check

    C. Review, test, and review

    D. Punctuality, management transition, and wait-time avoidance

Answer: D. Punctuality, management transition, and wait-time avoidance

The "benevolent boss" applies here. One who succeeds in managing a business follows these rules; so does the successful teacher.

(Average) (Skill 5.2)

36. **What is an example of an academic transition signal?**

    A. How do clouds form?

    B. Today we are going to study clouds.

    C. We have completed today's lesson.

    D. That completes the description of cumulus clouds. Now we will look at the description of cirrus clouds.

Answer: D. That completes the description of cumulus clouds. Now we will look at the description of cirrus clouds.

Transitions are language bridges between one topic and another. The teacher should thoughtfully plan transitions when several topics are going to be presented in one lesson to be sure that students are carried along. Without transitions, sometimes students are still focused on a previous topic and are lost in the discussion.

(Average) (Skill 5.5)

37. **What should the teacher do when a student is tapping a pencil on the desk during a lecture?**

    A. Stop the lesson and correct the student as an example to other students

    B. Walk over to the student and quietly touch the pencil as a signal for the student to stop

    C. Announce to the class that everyone should remember to remain quiet during the lecture

    D. Ignore the student, hoping he or she will stop

Answer: B. Walk over to the student and quietly touch the pencil as a signal for the student to stop

If the teacher acknowledges inappropriate behavior, it can embarrass the student and provoke further misconduct in retaliation or encourage attention-seeking behaviors. An effective method for redirecting misconduct is to silently signal to the student that the behavior is inappropriate without stopping the flow of instruction.

(Rigorous) (Skill 5.5)

38. **Why is punishment not always effective in managing student behavior?**

    A. It tends to suppress behavior, not eliminate it

    B. It focuses on the negative, rather than the positive

    C. Students may comply out of fear rather than a genuine behavior change

    D. All of the above

Answer: D. All of the above

When punishment is the first and only strategy in behavior management plans, it may be misused to the point where it is no longer effective.

Punishment tends to suppress behavior, not eliminate it. Punishment focuses on the negative rather than positive behaviors. There is also the chance that the child will comply out of fear, stress, or tension rather than a genuine behavior change. The use of social skills instruction, prompts, modeling, and reward systems in addition to punishment will yield the biggest changes in student behaviors.

(Rigorous) (Skill 5.6)

39. **What is one way of effectively managing student conduct?**

    A. State expectations about behavior

    B. Let students discipline their peers

    C. Let minor infractions of the rules go unnoticed

    D. Increase disapproving remarks

Answer: A. State expectations about behavior

The effective teacher makes clear, concise statements about what is considered appropriate and inappropriate behavior in the classroom, making sure to clearly outline the consequences for inappropriate behavior. It is helpful to prominently display classroom rules once they have been explicitly discussed.

(Average) (Skill 5.6)

40. **Robert throws a piece of paper across the room. The teacher ignores Robert. What is the teacher demonstrating?**

    A. Punishment

    B. Extinction

    C. Negative practice

    D. Verbal reprimand

Answer: B. Extinction

When a teacher uses extinction, reinforcement is withheld for an unacceptable behavior. This would not be a suitable strategy for serious misbehaviors where others are in danger of being hurt.

(Average) (Skill 5.6)

41. **What is a prompt?**

    A. Reinforcement provided for producing any appropriate behavior during a specified time interval

    B. A token, such as a sticker or star, that can be traded for a reward

    C. A reward for producing a behavior that is an alternative to an undesired target behavior

    D. A visual or verbal cue that assists a child through the behavior-shaping process

Answer: D. A visual or verbal cue that assists a child through the behavior-shaping process

A prompt is a visual or verbal cue that assists a child through the behavior-shaping process. Visual cues include signs or other visual aids. Verbal cues include talking a child through the steps of a task.

(Rigorous) (Skill 5.6)

42. **What is most likely to happen when students witness a punitive or angry desist?**

    A. Respond with more behavior disruption

    B. All disruptive behavior stops

    C. Students align with teacher

    D. Behavior stays the same

Answer: A. Respond with more behavior disruption

When the teacher becomes angry, several things happen. Students feel that the one who made her angry has achieved his or her goal by misbehaving. They also feel that the teacher is not in control. Because the teacher has become emotional, students feel that they may also react emotionally. Students tend to sympathize with the target of the teacher's anger.

(Easy) (Skill 5.6)

43. **What can be measured utilizing the following types of assessments: direct observation, role playing, context observation, and teacher ratings?**

    A. Social skills

    B. Reading skills

    C. Math skills

    D. Need for specialized instruction

Answer: A. Social skills

Social skills can be measured using the listed types of assessments. They can also be measured using sociometric measures, including peer nomination, peer rating, and paired-comparison.

(Rigorous) (Skill 5.6)

44. **What increases the likelihood that the response following an event will occur again?**

    A. Extinction

    B. Satiation

    C. Verbal reprimands

    D. Reinforcement

Answer: D. Reinforcement

If a child misbehaves and his peers laugh, the behavior has been reinforced and is likely to happen again. The teacher needs to stop misbehaviors before they start when at all possible. However, the same principle applies with appropriate behavior. The teacher can influence repetitions of the behaviors she wants by reinforcing them when they occur. She can also create circumstances where she has an opportunity to reinforce good behavior.

(Average) (Skill 5.6)

45. **Why is praise for compliance important in classroom management?**

    A. Students will continue deviant behavior

    B. Desirable conduct will be repeated

    C. It reflects simplicity and warmth

    D. Students will fulfill obligations

Answer: B. Desirable conduct will be repeated

The tried-and-true principle that behavior that is rewarded will be repeated is demonstrated here. If other students laugh at a child's misbehavior, he will repeat it. Similarly, if the teacher rewards the behaviors she wants to see repeated, it is likely to happen.

(Easy) (Skill 5.7)

46. **What might be a result if the teacher is distracted by some unrelated event in the instruction?**

    A. Students will leave the class

    B. Students will understand the importance of class rules

    C. Students will stay on-task longer

    D. Students will lose the momentum of the lesson

Answer: D. Students will lose the momentum of the lesson

The teacher who can attend to a task and an extraneous situation simultaneously without becoming immersed in either one is said to have "with-it-ness"; this ability is absolutely imperative for teacher effectiveness and success because it prevents students from becoming sidetracked.

(Easy) (Skill 6.1)

47. **Outlines, graphs, and models are particularly good for which type of learners?**

    A. Auditory

    B. Kinestetic

    C. Visual

    D. Olfactory

Answer: C. Visual

Teachers may choose to use advance organizers that include outlines, graphs, and models. This practice is especially valuable to the visual learner and is a motivational factor for most students.

(Average) (Skill 6.1)

48. **What has research shown to be the effect of using advance organizers in the lesson?**

    A. They facilitate learning and retention

    B. They allow teachers to use their planning time effectively

    C. They only serve to help the teacher organize the lesson

    D. They show definitive positive results on student achievement

Answer: A. They facilitate learning and retention

J.M. Kallison, Jr. found that subject matter retention increased when lessons included an outline at the beginning of the lesson and a summary at the end. This type of structure is utilized in successful classrooms and is especially valuable to the visual learner and is a motivational factor for most students.

(Average) (Skill 6.2)

49. **To facilitate discussion-oriented, non-threatening communication among all students, teachers must do which of the following?**

    A. Model appropriate behavior

    B. Allow students to express themselves freely

    C. Show students that some views will not be tolerated

    D. Explain that students should not disagree

Answer: A. Model appropriate behavior

To facilitate discussion-oriented, non-threatening communication among all students, teacher must take the lead and model appropriate actions and speech. They must also intervene quickly when a student makes a misstep and offends another (this often happens inadvertently).

(Average) (Skill 6.2)

50. **In diverse classrooms, teachers must ensure that they neither protect students from criticism nor praise them because of their ethnicity or gender. Doing either action may result in which of the following outcomes?**

    A. Classmates may become anxious or resentful when dealing with the diverse students

    B. Parents will appreciate their child being singled out

    C. The child will be pleased to receive this attention

    D. Other teachers will follow this example

Answer: A. Classmates may become anxious or resentful when dealing with the diverse students

Don't "protect" students from criticism because of their ethnicity or gender. Likewise, acknowledge and praise all meritorious work without singling out particular students. Both actions can make all students hyper-aware of ethnic and gender differences and cause anxiety or resentment throughout the class.

(Easy) (Skill 6.5)

51. **The use of technology in the classroom allows for:**

    A. More complex lessons

    B. Better delivery of instruction

    C. Variety of instruction

    D. Better ability to meet more individual student needs

Answer: D. Better ability to meet more individual student needs

The utilization of technology provides the teacher with the opportunity to incorporate more than one learning style into a lesson. In this way, the teacher is better able to meet the individual needs of his or her students.

(Average) (Skill 6.7)

52. **Wait-time has what effect?**

    A. Gives structure to the class discourse

    B. Fewer chain and low-level questions are asked with more higher-level questions included

    C. Gives the students time to evaluate the response

    D. Gives the opportunity for in-depth discussion about the topic

Answer: B. Fewer chain and low-level questions are asked with more higher-level questions included

One part of the questioning process for the successful teacher is wait time: the time between the question and either the student response or your follow-up. Many teachers vaguely recommend some general amount of wait-time (until the student starts to get uncomfortable or is clearly perplexed), but we focus here on wait-time as a specific and powerful communicative tool that speaks through its structured silences. Embedded in wait-time are subtle clues about your judgments of a student's abilities and your expectations of individuals and groups. For example, the more time you allow a student to mull over a question, the more you trust his or her ability to answer that question without getting flustered. As a rule, the practice of prompting is not a problem. Giving support and helping students reason through difficult conundrums is part of being an effective teacher.

Instruction and Assessment (Skills 7.1 – 9.8)

(Easy) (Skill 7.1)

53. **Which of the following test items is not objective?**

    A. Multiple choice

    B. Essay

    C. Matching

    D. True/false

Answer: B. Essay

Many forms of assessments are objective, such as multiple choice, yes/no, true/false, and matching. Essays and portfolios, on the other hand, are considered open-ended and allow students to provide answers that are more authentic.

(Rigorous) (Skill 7.1)

54. **Of the following definitions, which best describes a standardized achievement test?**

    A. It measures narrow skills and abilities

    B. It measures broad areas of knowledge

    C. It measures the ability to perform a task

    D. It measures performance related to specific, recently acquired information

Answer: B. It measures broad areas of knowledge

Standardized achievement tests measure a broad scope of content area knowledge. In this way it may be used on a larger scale in many different states and school districts.

(Rigorous) (Skill 7.1)

55. **Norm-referenced tests:**

    A. Provide information about how local test-takers performed compared to local test-takers from the previous year

    B. Provide information about how the local test-takers performed compared to a representative sampling of national test-takers

    C. Make no comparisons to national test takers

    D. None of the above

Answer: B. Provide information about how the local test-takers performed compared to a representative sampling of national test-takers

Norm-referenced tests are designed to measure what a student knows in a particular subject in relation to other students of similar characteristics. They typically provide information about how the local test-takers did compared to a representative sampling of national test-takers.

(Average) (Skill 7.1)

56. **It is most appropriate to use norm-referenced standardized tests for which of the following?**

    A. For comparison to the population on which the test was normed

    B. For teacher evaluation

    C. For evaluation of the administration

    D. For comparison to the school on which the test was normed

Answer: A. For comparison to the population on which the test was normed

While the efficacy of norm-referenced standardized tests have come under attack recently, they are currently the best device for determining where an individual student stands compared to a wide range of peers. They also provide a measure for a program or a school to evaluate how their own students are doing as compared to the populace at large. Even so, they should not be the only measure upon which decisions are made or evaluations drawn. There are many other instruments for measuring student achievement that the teacher needs to consult and take into account.

(Rigorous) (Skill 7.1)

57. _____ is a standardized test in which performance is directly related to the educational objective(s).

    A. Aptitude test

    B. Norm-referenced test

    C. Criterion-referenced test

    D. Summative evaluation

Answer: C. Criterion-referenced test

A criterion-referenced test takes the educational objectives of a course and rewrites them in the form of questions. The questions on the test are directly related to the objectives upon which the instruction is based. Thus the results of a criterion-referenced test will tell which objectives of the course a student has mastered and which he or she has not mastered.

(Rigorous) (Skill 7.1)

58. **Which of the following is the least appropriate reason for teachers to be able to analyze data on their students?**

    A. To provide appropriate instruction

    B. To make instructional decisions

    C. To separate students into weaker and stronger academic groups

    D. To communicate and determine instructional progress

Answer: C. To separate students into weaker and stronger academic groups

Especially in today's high-stakes environment, it is critical that teachers have a complete understanding of the process involved in examining student data in order to make instructional decisions, prepare lessons, determine progress, and report progress to stakeholders.

(Easy) (Skill 7.1)

59. The seven purposes of assessment include all of the following except:

   A. To identify students' strengths and weaknesses

   B. To assess the effectiveness of a particular instructional strategy

   C. To provide data that assists in decision making

   D. None of the above

Answer: D. None of the above

The seven purposes of assessment are:

- To assist student learning
- To identify students' strengths and weaknesses
- To assess the effectiveness of a particular instructional strategy
- To assess and improve the effectiveness of curriculum programs
- To assess and improve teaching effectiveness
- To provide data that assists in decision making
- To communicate with and involve parents and other stakeholders

(Average) (Skill 7.1)

60. What is the best example of a formative assessment?

   A. The results of an intelligence test

   B. Correcting tests in small groups and immediately recording the grades

   C. An essay that receives teacher feedback and can be corrected by students prior to having a grade recorded

   D. Scheduling a discussion prior to the test

Answer: C. An essay that receives teacher feedback and can be corrected by students prior to having a grade recorded

Formative assessments provide ongoing feedback on student progress and the effectiveness of instructional methods and materials. An example is an essay that receives teacher feedback and that can be corrected by students prior to having a grade recorded.

(Rigorous) (Skill 7.2)

61. Fill in the blanks for I. _____ and II. _____ in the picture below:

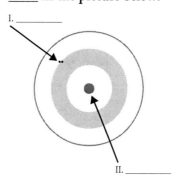

   A. I. Reliability and II. Validity

   B. I. Validity and II. Reliability

   C. I. Reliability and II. Vigor

   D. I. Rigor and II. Validity

Answer: A. I. Reliability and II. Validity

This picture represents I. Reliability and II. Validity.

(Rigorous) (Skill 7.2)

62. **This method tests the validity and reliability of a test by dividing a single test into two parts and comparing them.**

    A. Split-half

    B. Test-retest

    C. Equivalent forms

    D. Two-set

Answer: A. Split-half

There are several ways to estimate the reliability of an instrument. The simplest approach is the test-retest method. When the same test is administered again to the same students, if the test is perfectly reliable, each student will receive the same score each time. Even as the scores of individual students vary slightly from one time to the next, it is desirable for the rank order of the students to remain unchanged. Other methods of estimating reliability rely on the same conceptual framework. Split-half methods divide a single test into two parts and compare them. Equivalent forms methods compare two versions of the same test.

(Rigorous) (Skill 7.2)

63. **An example of reliability in testing is _____.**

    A. items on the test produce the same response each time

    B. the test was administered with poor lighting

    C. items on the test measure what they should measure

    D. the test is too long for the time allotted

Answer: A. items on the test produce the same response each time

When a test is reliable, it produces the same response each time. A test should give the same results when administered under the same conditions and to the same types of groups of students. This occurs when the items on the test are clear, unambiguous, and not confusing for the students. When items on the test measure what they should measure, this is called validity.

(Easy) (Skill 7.3)

64. **When a teacher wants to utilize an assessment that is subjective in nature, which of the following is the most effective method for scoring?**

    A. Rubric

    B. Checklist

    C. Alternative assessment

    D. Subjective measures should not be utilized

Answer: A. Rubric

Rubrics are the most effective tool for assessing items that can be considered subjective. They provide the students with a clearer picture of teacher expectations and provide the teacher with a more consistent method of comparing this type of assignment.

(Rigorous) (Skill 7.6)

65. **When students provide evidence of having special needs, standardized tests can be:**

    A. Given out with the same predetermined questions as what is administered to students without special needs

    B. Exempted for certain children whose special-needs conditions would prevent them performing with any reliability or validity

    C. Administered over a lengthier test period (i.e., four hours instead of three or two)

    D. All of the above

Answer: D. All of the above

The intent of testing modifications is to minimize the effect of a student's disability or learning challenge. This provides an equal opportunity for students with disabilities to participate in assessments to demonstrate and express their knowledge and ability. However, if the student's special-needs conditions would prevent them performing with any reliability or validity, they should be exempted from taking the assessment.

(Average) (Skill 8.1)

66. **Which of following is NOT the role of the teacher in the instructional process?**

    A. Instructor

    B. Coach

    C. Facilitator

    D. Follower

Answer: D. Follower

The teacher demonstrates a variety of roles within the classroom. Teachers, however, should not be followers. They must balance all of their roles in an efficient way to ensure that instruction is delivered to meet the needs of their students.

(Rigorous) (Skill 8.2)

67. **Discovery learning is to inquiry as direct instruction is to:**

    A. Scripted lessons

    B. Well-developed instructions

    C. Clear instructions that eliminate all misinterpretations

    D. Creativity of teaching

Answer: C. Clear instructions that eliminate all misinterpretations

Direct instruction is a technique that relies on carefully, well-developed instructions and lessons that eliminate misinterpretations. In this manner, all students have the opportunity to acquire and learn the skills presented to them. This approach limits teacher creativity to some extent, but has a good solid research-based following with much ability to replicate its results.

(Rigorous) (Skill 8.6)

68. When developing lessons it is imperative teachers provide equity in pedagogy so:

    A. Unfair labeling of students will not occur

    B. Student experiences will be positive

    C. Students will achieve academic success

    D. All of the above

    Answer: D. All of the above

    Providing equity of pedagogy allows for students to have positive learning experiences, achieve academic success, and helps to prevent the labeling of students in an unfair manner.

(Average) (Skill 8.6)

69. Which of the following is a good reason to collaborate with a peer?

    A. To increase your knowledge in areas where you feel you are weak, but the peer is strong

    B. To increase your planning time and that of your peer by combining the classes and taking more breaks

    C. To have fewer lesson plans to write

    D. To teach fewer subjects

    Answer: A. To increase your knowledge in areas where you feel you are weak, but the peer is strong

    Collaboration with a peer allows teachers to share ideas and information. In this way, the teacher is able to improve his skills and share additional information.

(Rigorous) (Skill 8.6)

70. Which of the following are ways a professional can assess her teaching strengths and weaknesses?

    A. Examining how many students were unable to understand a concept

    B. Asking peers for suggestions or ideas

    C. Self-evaluation/reflection on lessons taught

    D. All of the above

    Answer: D. All of the above

    It is important for teachers to involve themselves in constant periods of reflection and self-reflection to ensure they are meeting the needs of the students.

(Rigorous) (Skill 8.6)

71. Mr. German is a math coach. He is the only math coach in his building and within his district. Mr. German believes it is imperative to seek out the support of colleagues to work in a more collaborative manner. Which of the following would be an appropriate step for him to take?

    A. Collaborating with other teachers in his building regardless of their skill level knowledge in his area

    B. Asking the administration to find colleagues with whom he can collaborate

    C. Joining a professional organization such as the National Council of Teachers of Mathematics (NCTM)

    D. Searching the Internet for possible collaboration opportunities

Answer: C. Joining a professional organization such as the National Council of Teachers of Mathematics (NCTM)

Joining a professional organization, such as NCTM, would provide Mr. German with the ability to learn and update his own knowledge specifically in his field of study and also open up the opportunity for him to interact with colleagues in his field from across the country.

(Average) (Skill 9.1)

72. **Why is it important for a teacher to pose a question before calling on students to answer?**

   A. It helps manage student conduct

   B. It keeps the students as a group focused on the class work

   C. It allows students time to collaborate

   D. It gives the teacher time to walk among the students

Answer: B. It keeps the students as a group focused on the class work

It doesn't take much distraction for a class's attention to become diffused. Once this happens, effectively teaching a principle or a skill is very difficult. The teacher should plan presentations that will keep students focused on the lesson. A very useful tool is to use effective, well-thought-out, pointed questions.

(Rigorous) (Skill 9.1)

73. **What would be espoused by Jerome Bruner?**

   A. Thought depends on the acquisition of operations

   B. Memory plays a significant role in cognitive growth

   C. Genetics is the most important factor for cognitive growth

   D. Enriched environments have significant effects on cognitive growth

Answer: D. Enriched environments have significant effects on cognitive growth

In "Selecting and Applying Learning Theory to Classroom Teaching Strategies," by Donald R. Coker and Jane White in *Education* (1993), they write: "Jerome Bruner poses the ultimate question for teachers when he asked, 'How do you teach something to a child, arrange a child's environment if you will, in such a way that he can learn something with some assurance that he will use the material that he has learned appropriately in a variety of situations?' When presented with this query, most teachers have difficulty responding even though their days are spent trying to accomplish this very purpose. Why do those of us who teach have such an apparent inability to define the nature of our instructional activities in terms of lasting benefit to the learner? Perhaps this dilemma results from confusion regarding basic concepts of how children learn.

When we honestly examine our own learning, the information we crammed into our heads for Friday's spelling test or Wednesday's history quiz is long gone. What remains with us is typically learning we personally wanted or learning that actively involved us in the process, i.e., typing, sewing, woodworking, drama, acting, drafting, computers, writing, etc. A reflection on our own learning allows us to see what made the process work:

- Being taught by a teacher who knew more than we

- Being interested and active in the learning process

- Learning to focus on ideas, concepts, and being encouraged to generalize

- Being teased into new areas of insight by teachers who encouraged risks, making mistakes, and learning from them

- Seeing connections between the new information and what we already knew

- Being taught by a mentor who expected us to succeed

- Being taught in an atmosphere of support, not anxiety and fear

- Seeing, talking, and doing made the task easier, while sitting quietly and listening was difficult

- Being allowed to choose from a variety of appropriate classroom activities

- Being responsible for our own learning

As teachers, we should examine our own teaching strategies and check them against criteria such as these in an effort to answer the question, 'Does my classroom allow for all of these conditions?'"

(Easy) (Skill 9.1)

74. **When asking questions of students it is important to:**

   A. Ask questions the students can answer

   B. Provide numerous questions

   C. Provide questions at various levels

   D. Provide only a limited number of questions

   Answer: C. Provide questions at various levels

   Providing questions at various levels is essential to encourage deeper thinking and reflective thought processes.

(Rigorous) (Skill 9.3)

75. **Mr. Smith is introducing the concept of photosynthesis to his class next week. In preparing for this lesson, he considers that this concept will be new to many of his students. Mr. Smith understands that his students' brains are like filing cabinets and that there is currently no file for photosynthesis in those cabinets. What does Mr. Smith need to do to ensure his students acquire the necessary knowledge?**

   A. Help them create a new file

   B. Teach the students the information; they will organize it themselves in their own way

   C. Find a way to connect the new learning to other information they already know

   D. Provide many repetitions and social situations during the learning process

Answer: C. Find a way to connect the new learning to other information they already know

While behavioral theories indicate that it is through socialization and multiple repetitions that students acquire new information, new research into the brain and how it works indicates that students learn best by making connections Therefore, it is imperative when teaching new concepts that teachers find a way to connect new information to previously learned material.

(Rigorous) (Skill 9.3)

76. Curriculum mapping is an effective strategy because it:

A. Provides an orderly sequence to instruction

B. Provides lesson plans for teachers to use and follow

C. Ties the curriculum into instruction

D. Provides a clear map so all students receive the same instruction across all classes

Answer: A. Provides an orderly sequence to instruction

Curriculum mapping is a strategy used to tie the actual curriculum with the support materials (textbooks) being utilized to support the teaching of said curriculum. Mapping is usually done to the month or quarter and provides a logical sequence to instruction so that all necessary skills and topics are covered in an appropriate fashion.

(Rigorous) (Skill 9.5)

77. The teacher states that the lesson the students will be engaged in will consist of a review of the material from the previous day, demonstration of the scientific of an electronic circuit, and small group work on setting up an electronic circuit. What has the teacher demonstrated?

A. The importance of reviewing

B. Giving the general framework for the lesson to facilitate learning

C. Giving students the opportunity to leave if they are not interested in the lesson

D. Providing momentum for the lesson

Answer: B. Giving the general framework for the lesson to facilitate learning

If children know where they're going, they're more likely to be engaged in getting there. It's important to give them a road map whenever possible for what is coming in their classes.

(Average) (Skill 9.5)

78. What is an effective way to prepare students for testing?

A. Minimize the importance of the test

B. Orient the students to the test by telling them of the purpose, how the results will be used, and how it is relevant to them

C. Use the same format for every test are given

D. Have them construct an outline to study from

Answer: B. Orient the students to the test by telling them of the purpose, how the results will be used, and how it is relevant to them

If a test is to be an accurate measure of achievement, it must test the information, not the format of the test itself. If students know ahead of time what the test will be like, why they are taking it, what the teacher will do with the results, and what it has to do with them, the exercise is more likely to result in a true measure of what they've learned.

(Rigorous) (Skill 9.8)

79. **What are wikis?**

    A. Electronic communication boards

    B. Speech recognition devices that type text as it is spoken by the student

    C. Collaborative definitions posted to computers

    D. Readers that read aloud alerts on screens

Answer: C. Collaborative definitions posted to computers

Teachers are using wikis more and more each day. Wikis are collaborative definitions posted to computers, and often to the Web. After a unit, for example, a teacher might ask students in groups to post a wiki on a particular topic.

Professional Roles and Responsibilities (Skills 10.1 – 12.4)

(Average) (Skill 10.1)

80. **Which of the following should NOT be a purpose of a parent-teacher conference?**

    A. To involve the parent in their child's education

    B. To establish a friendship with the child's parents

    C. To resolve a concern about the child's performance

    D. To inform parents of positive behaviors by the child

Answer: B. To establish a friendship with the child's parents

The purpose of a parent teacher conference is to involve parents in their child's education, address concerns about the child's performance, and share positive aspects of the student's learning with the parents. It would be unprofessional to allow the conference to degenerate into a social visit to establish friendships.

(Easy) (Skill 10.1)

81. **Mr. Brown wishes to improve his parent communication skills. Which of the following is a strategy he can utilize to accomplish this goal?**

    A. Hold parent-teacher conferences

    B. Send home positive notes

    C. Have parent nights where the parents are invited into his classroom

    D. All of the above

Answer: D. All of the above

Increasing parent communication skills is important for teachers. All of the listed strategies are methods a teacher can utilize to increase his skills.

(Easy) (Skill 10.1)

82. **Tommy is a student in your class, and his parents are deaf. Tommy is struggling with math and you want to contact the parents to discuss the issue. How should you proceed?**

    A. Limit contact because of the parents' inability to hear

    B. Use a TTY phone to communicate with the parents

    C. Talk to your administrator to find an appropriate interpreter to help you communicate with the parents personally

    D. Both B and C

Answer: D. Both B and C

You should never avoid communicating with parents for any reason; instead you should find an effective way to communicate in various methods, just as you would with any other student in your classroom.

(Easy) (Skill 10.1)

83. **When communicating with parents for whom English is not the primary language you should:**

    A. Provide materials whenever possible in their native language

    B. Use an interpreter

    C. Provide the same communication as you would to native English speaking parents

    D. All of the above

Answer: D. All of the above

When communicating with non-English speaking parents, it is important to treat them as you would any other parents and utilize any means necessary to ensure they have the ability to participate in their child's educational process.

(Average) (Skill 11.1)

84. **What is a benefit of frequent self-assessment?**

    A. Opens new venues for professional development

    B. Saves teachers the pressure of being observed by others

    C. Reduces time spent on areas not needing attention

    D. Offers a model for students to adopt in self-improvement

Answer: A. Opens new venues for professional development

When a teacher is involved in the process of self-reflection and self-assessment, one of the common outcomes is that the teacher comes to identify areas of skill or knowledge that require more research or improvement on her part. She may become interested in overcoming a particular weakness in her performance or may decide to attend a workshop or consult with a mentor to learn more about a particular area of concern.

(Average) (Skill 11.1)

85. **Which of the following could be used to improve teaching skills?**

    A. Developing a professional development plan

    B. Using self-evaluation and reflection

    C. Building professional learning communities

    D. All of the above

Answer: D. All of the above

Creating a personalized plan for increasing your professional development, using self reflection, and working with other teachers in a professional learning community are all excellent strategies for improving one's teaching skills.

(Average) (Skill 11.3)

86. **Which of the following is NOT a sound educational practice for expanding the professional development opportunities for teachers?**

    A. Looking at multiple methods of classroom management strategies

    B. Training teachers in understanding and applying multiple assessment formats and implementations in curriculum and instruction

    C. Having the students complete professional development assessments on a regular basis

    D. Teaching teachers how to disaggregate student data in improving instruction and curriculum implementation for student academic equity and access

Answer: C. Having the students complete professional development assessments on a regular basis

Giving teachers tests on a regular basis, while providing information on what knowledge they may have, does not expand the professional development opportunities for teachers.

(Average) (Skill 11.4)

87. **What would happen if a school utilized an integrated approach to professional development?**

    A. All stakeholders' needs are addressed

    B. Teachers and administrators are on the same page

    C. High-quality programs for students are developed

    D. Parents drive the curriculum and instruction

Answer: C. High-quality programs for students are developed

The implementation of an integrated approach to professional development is a critical component to ensuring success of programs for students. It involves teachers, parents, and other community members working together to develop appropriate programs to ensure students are receiving the necessary instruction to be successful in the future workforce.

(Average) (Skill 12.2)

88. **Which of the following statements is true about computers in the classroom?**

    A. Computers are simply a glorified game machine and just allow students to play games

    B. The computer should replace traditional research and writing skills taught to school-age children

    C. Computers stifle the creativity of children

    D. Computers allow students to access information they may otherwise be unable to

Answer: D. Computers allow students to access information they may otherwise be unable to

Computers, particularly those connected to the Internet, provide students with the ability to research information school libraries might otherwise be unable to provide because of funding issues. It opens the doors and pathways for students to increase the amount of information they acquire in school.

(Average) (Skill 12.2)

89. **While an asset to students, technology is also important for teachers. Which of the following can be taught using technology to students?**

    A. Cooperation skills

    B. Decision-making skills

    C. Problem-solving skills

    D. All of the above

Answer: D. All of the above

Having students work together on a project using the technology available to you within your school not only teaches the content you wish them to learn but can also provide them with skills in cooperation, decision-making, and problem-solving.

(Easy) (Skill 12.2)

90. **As a classroom teacher, you have data on all of your students that you must track over the remainder of the school year. You will need to keep copies of the scores students receive and then graph their results to share progress with the parents and administrators. Which of the following software programs will be most useful for this?**

    A. Word processing program

    B. Spreadsheet

    C. Database

    D. Teacher utility and classroom management tools

Answer: B. Spreadsheet

Spreadsheets help a teacher to organize numeric information and can easily take that data and transfer it into a graph for a visual representation for administrators or parents.

(Average) (Skill 12.2)

91. **Which of the following statements is NOT true?**

   A. Printing and distributing material off of the Internet breaks the copyright law

   B. Articles are only copyrighted when there is a © in the article

   C. E-mail messages that are posted online are considered copyrighted

   D. It is not legal to scan magazine articles and place on your district Web site

Answer: B. Articles are only copyrighted when there is a © in the article

Articles, even without the symbol, are considered copyrighted material. This includes articles from newspapers, magazines, or even posted online.

(Average) (Skill 12.2)

92. **Which is true of child protective services?**

   A. They have been forced to become more punitive in their attempts to treat and prevent child abuse and neglect

   B. They have become more a means for identifying cases of abuse and less an agent for rehabilitation because of the large volume of cases

   C. They have become advocates for structured discipline within the school

   D. They have become a strong advocate in the court system

Answer: B. They have become more a means for identifying cases of abuse and less an agent for rehabilitation because of the large volume of cases

Nina Bernstein, who wrote *The Lost Children of Wilder*, told of a long-running lawsuit in New York City that attempted to hold the city and its child-care services responsible for meeting the needs of abused children. Unfortunately, while it is an extreme case, it is not atypical of the plight of children all across the country. The only thing a teacher can do is attempt to provide a refuge of concern and stability during the time such children are in her care, hoping that they will, somehow, survive.

(Average) (Skill 12.4)

93. Which of the following increases appropriate behavior more than 80 percent?

    A. Monitoring the halls

    B. Having class rules

    C. Having class rules, giving feedback, and having individual consequences

    D. Having class rules and giving feedback

Answer: C. Having class rules, giving feedback, and having individual consequences

Clear, consistent class rules go a long way to preventing inappropriate behavior. Effective teachers give immediate feedback to students regarding their behavior or misbehavior. If there are consequences, they should be as close as possible to those they would receive in the outside world, especially for adolescents. Consistency, especially with adolescents, reduces the occurrence of power struggles and teaches them that predictable consequences follow their actions.

(Average) (Skill 12.4)

94. A 16-year-old girl who has been looking sad writes an essay in which the main protagonist commits suicide. You overhear her talking about suicide. What do you do?

    A. Report this immediately to school administration and talk to the girl, letting her know you will talk to her parents about it

    B. Report this immediately to authorities

    C. Report this immediately to school administration, make your own report to authorities if required by protocol in your school, and do nothing else

    D. Just give the child some extra attention, as it may be that's all she's looking for

Answer: C. Report this immediately to school administration, make your own report to authorities if required by protocol in your school, and do nothing else

A child who is suicidal is beyond any help that can be offered in a classroom. The first step is to report the situation to administration. If your school protocol calls for it, the situation should also be reported to authorities.

(Rigorous) (Skill 12.4)

95. Jeanne, a bright, attentive student, is in her first hour English class. She is quiet, but very alert, often visually scanning the room in random patterns. Her pupils are dilated, and she has a slight but noticeable tremor in her hands. She fails to note a cue given from her teacher. At odd moments, she will act as if responding to stimuli that aren't there by suddenly changing her gaze. When spoken to directly, she has a limited response, but her teacher has a sense she is not herself. What should the teacher do?

   A. Ask the student if she is all right, then let it go, as there are not enough signals to be alarmed

   B. Meet with the student after class to get more information before making a referral

   C. Send the student to the office to see the nurse

   D. Quietly call for administration, remain calm, and be careful not to alarm the class

Answer: D. Quietly call for administration, remain calm, and be careful not to alarm the class

These behaviors are indicative of drug use. The best thing a teacher can do in this case is call for help from administration.

(Average) (Skill 12.4)

96. In successful inclusion of students with disabilities:

   A. A variety of instructional arrangements are available

   B. School personnel shift the responsibility for learning outcomes to the student s

   C. The physical facilities are used as they are

   D. Regular classroom teachers have sole responsibility for evaluating student progress

Answer: A. A variety of instructional arrangements are available

Here are some support systems and activities that are in evidence where successful inclusion has occurred:

Attitudes and beliefs

- The regular teacher believes the student can succeed

- School personnel are committed to accepting responsibility for the learning outcomes of students with disabilities

- School personnel and the students in the class have been prepared to receive a student with disabilities

Services and physical accommodations

- Services needed by the student are available (e.g., health, physical, occupational, or speech therapy)

- Accommodations to the physical plant and equipment are adequate to meet the students' needs (e.g., toys, building and playground facilities, learning materials, or assistive devices)

School support

- The principal understands the needs of students with disabilities

- Adequate numbers of personnel, including aides and support personnel, are available

- Adequate staff development and technical assistance, based on the needs of the school personnel, are being provided (e.g., information on disabilities, instructional methods, awareness and acceptance activities for students, and team-building skills)

- Appropriate policies and procedures for monitoring individual student progress, including grading and testing, are in place

Collaboration

- Special educators are part of the instructional or planning team

- Teaming approaches are used for program implementation and problem solving

- Regular teachers, special education teachers, and other specialists collaborate (e.g., co-teach, team teach, or work together on teacher assistance teams)

Instructional methods

- Teachers have the knowledge and skills needed to select and adapt curricular and instructional methods according to individual student needs

- A variety of instructional arrangements is available (e.g., team teaching, cross-grade grouping, peer tutoring, or teacher assistance teams)

- Teachers foster a cooperative learning environment and promote socialization

(Average) (Skill 12.4)

97. **How may a teacher use a student's permanent record?**

A. To develop a better understanding of the needs of the student

B. To record all instances of student disruptive behavior

C. To brainstorm ideas for discussing with parents at parent-teacher conferences

D. To develop realistic expectations of the student's performance early in the year

Answer: A. To develop a better understanding of the needs of the student

The purpose of a student's permanent record is to give the teacher a better understanding of the student's educational history and provide him with relevant information to support the student's learning. Permanent records may not be used to arrive at preconceived judgments or to build a case against the student. Above all, the contents of a student's permanent record are confidential.

(Rigorous) (Skill 12.4)

98. You receive a phone call from a person who indicates she is now tutoring a student in your class. She would like you to provide an overview of the academic areas in which the student is having difficulties. What is the first thing you should do?

    A. Find a time and talk with the tutor about issues you see within the classroom

    B. Call the parents

    C. Put together a packet of information to share with the tutor

    D. Offer to invite the tutor in to have a discussion and observe the child

Answer: B. Call the parents

Before you share any information with anyone about a student, you should always secure parental permission in writing.

(Rigorous) (Skill 12.4)

99. Marcus is a first-grade boy of good developmental attainment. His learning progress is good the first half of the year. He shows no indicators of emotional distress. After the holiday break, he returns much changed. He is quieter, sullen even, tending to play alone. He has moments of tearfulness, sometimes almost without cause. He avoids contact with adults as often as he can. Even play with his friends has become limited. He has episodes of wetting not seen before and often wants to sleep in school. What approach is appropriate for this sudden change in behavior?

    A. Give him some time to adjust; the holiday break was probably too much fun to come back to school from

    B. Report this change immediately to administration; do not call the parents until administration decides a course of action

    C. Document his daily behavior carefully as soon as you notice such a change, and report to administration the next month or so in a meeting

    D. Make a courtesy call to the parents to let them know he is not acting like himself, being sure to tell them he is not making trouble for others

Answer: B. Report this change immediately to administration; do not call the parents until administration decides a course of action

Any time a child's disposition, attitude, or habits change significantly, teachers and parents need to seriously consider the existence of emotional difficulties. Emotional disturbances in childhood are not uncommon and take a variety of forms. Usually these problems show up in the form of uncharacteristic behaviors. Most of the time, children respond favorably to brief treatment programs of psychotherapy. At other times, disturbances may need more intensive therapy and are harder to resolve. All stressful behaviors need to be addressed, and any type of chronic antisocial behavior needs to be examined as a possible symptom of deep-seated emotional upset. In a case where the change is sudden and dramatic, administration needs to become involved.

(Rigorous) (Skill 12.4)

100. **Andy shows up to class abusive and irritable. He is often late, sleeps in class, sometimes slurs his speech, and has an odor of alcohol. What is the first intervention to take?**

   A. Confront him, relying on a trusting relationship you think you have

   B. Do a lesson on alcohol abuse, making an example of him

   C. Do nothing; it is better to err on the side of failing to identify substance abuse

   D. Call administration, avoid conflict, and supervise others carefully

Answer: D. Call administration, avoid conflict, and supervise others carefully

Educators are not only likely to, but often do, face students who are high on something. Of course, they are not only a hazard to their own safety and those of others, but their ability to be productive learners is greatly diminished, if not nonexistent. They show up instead of skip, because it's not always easy or practical for them to spend the day away from home but not in school. Unless they can stay inside, they are at risk of being picked up for truancy. Some enjoy being high in school, getting a sense of satisfaction by putting something over on the system. Some just don't take drug use seriously enough to think usage at school might be inappropriate. The first responsibility of the teacher is to assure the safety of all of the children. Avoiding conflict with the student who is high and obtaining help from administration is the best course of action.